DUNDEE LEGENDS

Published by:
Yore Publications
12 The Furrows, Harefield,
Middx. UB9 6AT.

© Kenny Ross 2010

....

All rights reserved.
No part of this publication may be reproduced
or copied in any manner without the prior permission
in writing of the copyright holders.

British Library Cataloguing-in-Publication Data.
A catalogue record for this book
is available from the British Library.

ISBN 978 0 9564103 6 8

Managed and Manufactured by
Jellyfish Solutions Ltd.

Introduction

*'You can sing of the glories of teams you have seen,
Of the Saints or the Dons up in Old Aberdeen,
But in all this wide world there's but one team for me,
It's the bold boys who wear the dark blue o' Dundee.'*

The Dundee Song: Hector Nicol (1962)
(Traditional Scots tune *Bonnie Dundee*)

I have supported Dundee Football Club all my life and went to my first game when I was three years old in 1976, poetically at the scene of Dundee's only League Championship triumph at Muirton Park in Perth. It took me ten years to see my first victory over Dundee United and I remember November 5th 1983 like it was yesterday. It was a 1-0 win over The Arabs at Tannadice, thanks to a Peter Mackie goal in front of the Dundee support at the Arklay Street end and the left winger became my first hero, my first legend.

Everyone's criteria is different for their own legends and heroes and in compiling this book, I had no rigid rules or regulations about who should make the final list. Dundee F.C. has such a rich history of wonderful players, managers and personalities, that for me it was not just about how many times someone has played for the Club and not every cup winner or internationalist made the cut. Instead I have tried to include players who have in some way made their own telling contribution to the Dark Blues, whether or not they left Dens Park with a medal or a cap and I am sure there is not one Dundee fan who will say that the player in this book with the least number of appearances for The Dee – twenty-five to be exact – should not be in there.

I have enjoyed the many conversations with my fellow Dees about who they think is a Dundee legend and I am sure I will have missed players that some will believe should be in there. If I have, I apologise but it is not slight on those not included. As F.I.F.A. said at their annual conference this year, *'football is often debate'* and I look forward to debating about who I missed out and who should be in the sequel.

I have enjoyed immensely, the researching and writing of this book and I hope it brings back many happy memories of some great players who have graced the dark blue jersey.

At the end of biographies I have listed players' honours, appearances and goals and the games that are listed as 'other' are the Summer Cup, the 1962 New York Tourney, the Texaco Cup, the Anglo-Scottish Cup, the Drybrough Cup, the North-East Supplementary Cup, the Scottish War Emergency Cup, the Scottish Victory Cup and the Supplementary Cup. Regional wartime league matches, I have listed with Scottish League peace time matches.

In the honours' lists, I have noted local cup competitions before the First World War when they were still considered to be prestigious and still commanded good attendances and these include the Forfarshire Cup and the Dewar Shield. I have also listed entry into the Dundee F.C. Hall of Fame which was first awarded in 2009 and the current Dundee Supporters' Association Player of the Year trophy which was set up in 1994 in memory of a good friend Andy De Vries who was tragically killed while worked abroad in America early that year.

I have followed Dundee through the good times and the bad and there have been plenty of great times watching Dundee. It is the hard and hurtful moments that make the brilliant ones so sweet and memorable and I can't imagine life without Dundee F.C. It was an honour to write this book.

There are a great many Dundee supporters who feel the same as I do and I have been lucky enough to get to know a few of them. I have been even luckier enough to call some of them my friends and I have been privileged to share the watching of the team I love with some great people.

I wish therefore to dedicate this book to anyone I have ever sat next to at a Dundee match namely, in no particular order, Alistair Strachan, Bob Donald, Ron Hill, Robbie Hill, Lindsay Hill, David Young, Tommy Young, Alasdair Leslie, Hector Macdonald, Grant Dixon, Alex Chacko, Douglas Keir, Norrie Price, Harry Jenkins, Joe T-A (The Wild Rover), Paresh Patel, Andy Fenwick, Millar Liddle, Bob Slessor, Ray Whyte (my room mate in Albania), Shiela Whyte, Paul McMaster, Gregor Wake, the lesser spotted Stuart Matheson, Arthur McGuiness, Jean McGuiness, Andy Lynn, Gary Joiner, Derek Burgess, Grant Anderson, John Roy, Leigh Kingston, John Wade, John Knight, Scott Reid, Willie Reid, Martin Reid, Chic Haggert, Scott Glenday, Gary Milne (the Villain), Andy De Vries, Andy 'Sippy' Dunlop, Richard Hendry, Jim Hendry, Alan Hendry, Graeme Guild, Peter Garmany, David Mair, Roddy Black, Graham Smith, Dave Forbes, Rob Whelan, Alan Pattulo, Rebecca Robbins, Jacqui Robertson, Peter Caproni, Kenny MacPherson, Lewis MacPherson, Peter McDougall, Andrew Gibson, Malcolm Soutar, Alistair Soutar, Ian Smith, Mark Small, Niall Joss, Keith Joss, my sister, who my old man only took once to a Berwick Rangers game but never again because she looked bored, my Mum who I once persuaded to come to a derby in the Bonetti era but whom I'm not sure really enjoyed it and of course my Dad who introduced me to it all way back when flares were all the rage.

This list should also include various girlfriends who I have dragged to Dens now and again especially my ex fiancé PJ who once got Chic Charnley's sock at a derby. After we knocked United out of the League Cup on penalties at Tannadice in 1996, some of the Dundee players chucked their shirts into the Dundee crowd and fans' favourite Chic Charnley also chucked his shorts, boots and socks, one of whom my Paula-Jane caught when I launched her into the air. Upon returning to the Centenary Bar post match, she was boasting to all and sundry that she had Chico's sock and suddenly she was lifted shoulder high around the bar as she waived the sweaty sock above her head.

That alone should have made Chic Charnley a legend for me but he didn't make the cut but then again, neither did Peter Mackie. I tried not to be too selfish in my selection and I hope you enjoy reading about the ones who did and continue to support Dundee as new legends are born. Memories are made of such things and as Bobby Brady once sang:

'Eh'm a Dee, Eh'm a Dee, Eh'm a Dee till Eh Deh, If Eh didnae see ma Dees, then Eh wid surely cry, If Eh said Eh liked United, then that'd be a lie,Eh'm a Dee, Eh'm a Dee, Eh'm a Dee till Eh Deh!'
Dee Till Eh Deh: Jump The Q (2003)

Kenny Ross
August 2010

Acknowledgements

The author would like to acknowledge the help, support and advice from Norrie Price, David Young, Ron Hill, Jim Hendry, Scott Glenday, Mark Robertson, Alan Patullo, Dave Webster, Kris Scrimgeour, Bob Donald, Alistair Strachan, Paul McMaster, Paul Wear and Peter Caproni. The author would also like to particularly thank official Dundee F.C. website editor David Young, Dundee F.C. historian Norrie Price, Stephen Borland and Paul Wear for their help, sourcing and permission with the photographs. The author acknowledges the use of illustrations and photographs from past and current newspapers plus Dundee Football Club and while every effort has been made to trace the ownership of illustrations, apologies are given should copyright have inadvertently been infringed.

The author would like to acknowledge the information in Norrie Price's *Up Wi' The Bonnets* and *They Wore The Dark Blue* and Jim Hendry's *Dundee Greats.* These superb books have been a valuable source of information as have the autobiographies of Charlie Cooke, Alan Gilzean and Brian Irvine the biographies of Billy Steel and Alec Troup, and the websites Dundee Fitba Shrine, The Dundee Programme Collector, Boab's Little Piece of Scotland and the official Dundee F.C. website.

Thanks are also due to the support of Dundee Football Club and in particular Chief Executive Harry McLean. The author would like to thanks all the Legends who gave up their time to reminisce and support the book, especially Barry Smith who kindly agreed to write the foreword. Thanks must also go to the Legends for all the great memories they have produced on the park and without whom this book wouldn't be possible.

Foreword

Dundee F.C. is a wonderful club and I am proud to have played for them for eleven years and captain them through some terrific times. I was proud to lift the First Division trophy in 1998, captain The Dark Blues into premier European competition for the first time in twenty-nine years and I was honoured to lead Dundee out at Hampden in the Scottish Cup Final in 2003. If only my shot in the early stages of the match had been a couple of inches to the left, I might have had the chance to lift a major trophy for The Dee that the Dundee fans deserve.

Having played for Dundee for over a decade, I was lucky enough to turn out enough times to put me high on the all-time appearance list which surrounds me with such Dundee legends as Doug Cowie, Bobby Cox and Jocky Scott.

I played the same number of times for the Club as Jocky Scott, whom I played under and Bobby Cox, who was a wonderful man who was always there if I needed some advice and knowing these guys helped me realise the rich history and truly legendary players that Dundee has.

It is fascinating to look at the list of legends that the author Kenny has compiled for this book and of the eighty or so featured, I was lucky enough to play alongside fifteen of them and under two of the managers.

There are some great players, managers and characters in this book and I am delighted to have been listed amongst all these legends.

I enjoyed some terrific times with Dundee, including nine derby wins over United but endured some hard times too during the dark days of administration and its aftermath. The way in which everyone, from the fans to the staff at Dens alike rallied around the Club in order to save it, is something to be proud of and the scenes of joy at Partick when I scored in the last minute just after we went into administration showed what Dundee meant to everyone who was there.

It means an awful lot to me and it was a wrench to leave Dens Park in 2006 but when I got the offer to return in a coaching capacity a couple of years later I jumped at the chance. As I try to play my part in shaping the future of the club by coaching the Under 19s, I'm sure you will enjoy reading about the legends of the past as we all hope to see Dundee return to the top tier of Scottish football where it rightly belongs.

Barry Smith
August 2010

~ The 82 Legends ~

1. Dariusz Adamczuk
2. Thomson Allan
3. George Anderson
4. Jimmy Bellamy
5. Alfie Boyd
6. Bill Brown
7. John Brown
8. Fabian Cabellero
9. Kenny Cameron
10. Andy Campbell
11. Claudio Caniggia
12. Gordon Chisholm
13. Archie Coats
14. Robert Connor
15. Charlie Cooke
16. Alan Cousin
17. Jack Cowan
18. Doug Cowie
19. Bobby Cox
20. Tommy Coyne
21. Herbert Dainty
22. Billy Dodds
23. Ally Donaldson
24. Robert Douglas
25. Jim Duffy
26. John Duncan
27. Iain Ferguson
28. Bobby Flavell
29. Gerry Follon
30. Cammy Fraser
31. Jimmy Gabriel
32. Tommy Gallacher
33. Bobby Geddes
34. Alan Gilzean
35. Bobby Glennie
36. James Grady
37. Davie Halliday
38. Alex Hamilton
39. George Hill
40. Doug Houston
41. John 'Sailor' Hunter
42. Brian Irvine
43. Albert Juliussen
44. Temuri Ketsbaia
45. Pat Liney
46. William Longair
47. Sandy MacFarlane
48. Bill Marsh
49. Neil McCann
50. Tosh McKinlay
51. George McLean
52. George Merchant
53. Giorgi Nemsadze
54. Nacho Novo
55. Andy Penman
56. Iain Phillip
57. Billy Pirie
58. Gavin Rae
59. Hugh Robertson
60. Bobby Robinson
61. Juan Sara
62. Jocky Scott
63. Bobby Seith
64. Bob Shankly
65. Eric Sinclair
66. Bert Slater
67. Barry Smith
68. Gordon Smith
69. Billy Steel
70. Jim Steele
71. Ray Stephen
72. George Stewart
73. Gordon Strachan
74. Alex Stuart
75. Alec Troup
76. Ian Ure
77. Gordon Wallace
78. William Wallace
79. Morten Wieghorst
80. Bobby Wilson
81. Bobby Wishart
82. Keith Wright

Dundee F.C. Supporters' Association Player of the Year
The Andy De Vries Memorial Trophy
1994 - 2010

In 1994, Dundee supporter Andy De Vries was tragically killed while working abroad in America and his friends and family decided to set up a Dundee F.C player of the year trophy to be presented annually in his memory to which the then Chairman Ron Dixon also made a personal contribution.

In 2004 it was donated to the Dundee F.C. Supporters' Association to be presented at their annual dinner and is now recognised as the Club's official player of the year trophy.

The following is a list of the recipients:

1994	Neil McCann	2000	Willie Falconer	2005	Steve Lovell
1995	George Shaw	2001	Claudio Caniggia	2006	Bobby Mann
1996	George Shaw	2002	Temuri Ketsbia	2007	Scott Robertson
1997	Barry Smith	2003	Lee Wilkie	2008	Kevin McDonald
1998	Robert Douglas	2004	Nacho Novo	2009	Robert Douglas
1999	Darius Adamczuk			2010	Jim Lauchlan

Dariusz Adamczuk

Dariusz Adamczuk was a cult hero to the Dundee support during the nineties when he arrived for a Club record transfer fee, left eleven games later for another Club record fee, returned to Dens three years later to help Dundee win promotion and then was part of the side which secured The Dark Blues' highest ever Premier League finish.

Born on October 20th 1969 in Szczecin, Poland, Dariusz started his football career with local club Pogon Szczecin in 1987 and in 1992 was part of the Polish Olympic Football squad which won the silver medal at the Barcelona Olympic football tournament.

Dariusz played in five matches in the tournament and as a result earned himself a move to Bundesliga side Eintracht Frankfurt but after failing to win a regular place in the starting line up, was more than happy to move to the Scottish Premier Division to sign for Dundee after just a year in Germany.

Dundee manager Simon Stainrod had been building a cosmopolitan side after winning promotion in 1992 and Adamczuk was signed for a Club record fee of £250,000 on the same day that fellow Polish internationalist Pietr Czachowski was also signed for the same money from Legia Warsaw.

Czachowski had played forty-five internationals for Poland but as a non-E.E.C. player he still required Home Office clearance and a Scottish League work permit before he could play but Adamczuk also held a German passport and was able to make his debut on August 21st 1993 in a 1-1 draw with Aberdeen at Dens.

The fair-haired Pole, who had not played for two months after a dispute with his club, looked fast and skilful and played with great commitment and as the weeks passed he regained his fitness and looked every inch an international player, particularly in the holding midfield role.

After just eight starts however, the Dundee support were stunned when the hard tackling midfielder was transferred to Serie A club Udinese for a record transfer fee received of £500,000, double what Dundee had paid for him just two months before. His eleven appearances had yielded one goal in a 1-0 win over Kilmarnock in October and his departure came just days after he was red carded for a retaliatory tackle on Darren Jackson in a 3-2 win over second placed Hibs but there was no doubt that his sale was a blow.

It was not the end of the Darius Adamczuk / Dundee F.C. story however as his new club Udinese had failed to pay his fee in full and he was loaned out to Portuguese side Belenenses. The Italian side refused to complete the payments due to the Dark Blues and eventually F.I.F.A. deemed him to still be a Dundee player and insisted that in turn, Dundee should complete the remainder of their debt to Eintracht Frankfurt while waiving the balance due by Udinese.

Initially Adamczuk stated that he did not want to resume his career with Dundee and played a handful of games again for his hometown team Pogon Szczecin but then completely out of the blue, he turned up at the door of Dens Park at the end of 1995 and offered his services to Dundee manager Jim Duffy.

Duffy was only too happy to welcome the player back to Dens and he returned to the side in January when he came off the bench to replace Paul Tosh in a 2-1 home defeat to St. Mirren.

Dundee were by now in the Scottish First Division and Adamczuk would make thirteen appearances before the end of the season but in 1997/98 Dariusz would become a key figure as Dundee attempted to return to the Premier Division at the fourth attempt.

Dariusz would be used both at full back and in midfield and he would make forty-one appearances as Dundee won promotion by mid April and eventually won the League Flag by five points from Falkirk.

Dundee's first season back in the top tier would be as part of the newly created Scottish Premier League and it would be a terrific season for the Pole as he scored six goals to help Dundee finish fifth and above Dundee United for the first time in twenty-five years.

On the day in which Dundee were assured to finish above The Arabs with a 2-0 win at Tannadice, Dariusz was named as the Dundee Supporters' Player of the Year and he accepted the trophy himself after the match by coming straight from the victory 'across the road' to the Dundee Social Club, much to the delight of the assembled Dees.

It was Dundee's best ever finish in the Premier League and in fact equalled Dundee's highest league placing since they had won the League Championship in 1962. Adamczuk had been an integral part of the success and Dundee supporters will remember the remarkable goal he scored against St. Johnstone in Perth in December when he picked the ball up in his own box and ran almost the length of the pitch to slip the ball under Alan Main and send the Dundee fans behind the goal wild.

Dariusz had also scored a terrific goal against Rangers at Ibrox and by the end of the season was being courted by both halves of the Old Firm. Initially Dundee agreed to let Adamczuk join Celtic for £40,000 in April but the Parkhead side backed out after they saw the Pole's wages demands but the Rangers weren't put off and he joined the Ibrox side at the end of the season.

While at Dens, Dariusz was capped by Poland four times and just after joining Dundee, he was part of the famous Poland v England World Cup qualifier in Chorzow (as was Czachowski) when the Channel Four documentary team captured England boss Graham Taylor shouting, *'Do I not like that'*, for which he became synonymous.

Taylor's bizarre exclamation came when Adamczuk put Poland's ahead by lobbing Chris Woods in the England goal and pubs all across Dundee let out a huge cheer when the caption came up on the television screen of *'Dariusz Adamczuk (Dundee F.C.)'* to acknowledge the scorer.

Adamczuk was an extremely popular player in his two spells at Dens and it was sad to see Dariusz fail to break into the Rangers side and echo his failures in Germany and Italy, making his time at Dundee, his most successful and enjoyable for player and fans alike.

Honours at Dundee:
Scottish League First Division winner: 1997/98
D.S.A. Player of the Year: 1999
Poland International caps: 4
Appearances, Goals
League: 102 + 10 subs, 9 goals
Scottish Cup: 8 + 1 sub
League Cup: 8
S.F.L. Challenge Cup: 3
Totals: 132, 9 goals

Thomson Allan

Dundee have had a fine traditional of good goalkeepers over the years and Thomson Allan certainly fits into that category winning the League Cup while at Dens and going to the World Cup in West Germany in 1974. He was confidence personified and inspired his team mates with his immaculate handling and wonderful ability to cut out crossed balls and is one of the best keepers to have worn the number one shirt for The Dee.

Thomson Sandlands Allan was born on October 5th 1946 in Longridge, West Lothian and after enjoying his youth career at Edina Hibs, was signed by Hibernian in 1963. At Easter Road Allan would go on to become a League Cup runner-up in 1968/69 after being part of the Hibs side which defeated Dundee in the semis but with just seventy league appearances under his belt for the Edinburgh side, he was disappointed to be freed in the summer of 1971.

Fortunately for Allan, Dundee were on the look out for a keeper as regular number one Ally Donaldson was in dispute with the Club and manager John Prentice signed Allan on a free transfer as a more experienced option to youngster Mike Hewitt.

Being surplus to requirements in the Capital only made Thomson's resolve to succeed all the greater and he went on to enjoy the best spell of his career with the Dark Blues.

He made his debut in the first game of the 1972/73 season in an 8-2 League Cup win away to East Stirlingshire and in all played 226 games for Dundee and kept a clean sheet on fifty-two occasions.

His finest moment in a Dundee shirt came on December 15th 1973 when Thomson was part of the Dark Blue side which won the League Cup at Hampden with a 1-0 win over Celtic and it was sweet revenge for Allan who had been on the losing side to Celtic in the Final five years previously.

In the twelve match League Cup run, Allan kept a clean sheet in seven of them including clean sheets in the quarters, semis and Final. He also played in the two Scottish Cup semi-finals in consecutive years against Celtic and in two European campaigns but the League Cup win was the highlight of his eight years at Dens.

At this time Thomson was turning in brilliant performances on a weekly basis and he was rewarded with a place in the 1974 Scotland World Cup squad. He was one of three custodians in the twenty-two, alongside goalkeepers David Harvey of Leeds and Jim Stewart of Kilmarnock and he was given the number twelve squad number. Despite not playing in any of Scotland's three matches in West Germany, Thomson was rewarded with two caps in the build up matches and played the full ninety minutes in a 2-1 defeat in Frankfurt against the World Cup hosts and in Oslo against Norway where the Scots won 2-1.

In 1977, Allan's team mate Tommy Gemmell took over the hot seat at Dens and when the team's form took a dip, the former Lisbon Lion brought Ally Donaldson back from Falkirk to replace Allan.

Allan decided to continue part-time at Dens and started working at British Leyland's plant in Bathgate and turned down the chance to sign for Hearts and St Mirren. After almost a year in the reserves, Thomson was recalled to the first team in September when Donaldson sustained broken ribs and stayed in the side until Christmas but Donaldson's return spelt the beginning of the end for Allan.

At the end of the season Thomson walked out on Dundee and went on loan to Meadowbank Thistle before former international boss Willie Ormond took him to Tynecastle in February 1979 for £10,000. At Hearts he made twenty-four appearances before moving to Falkirk and then East Stirlingshire before retiring in 1982.

These days Allan is a season ticket holder at Falkirk but he was welcomed back to Dundee in 2003 for the thirtieth anniversary dinner to celebrate Dundee's League Cup win at the city's Invercarse Hotel. The consistent, reliable and agile keeper is remembered fondly by Dundee supporters who were lucky enough to see him and he came out with the most number of votes in fan's favourite goalkeeper online poll on Dundee's official site in 2009.

Honours at Dundee:
Scottish League Cup winner: 1973/74
Scotland full caps: 2
Appearances:
League: 159
Scottish Cup: 16
League Cup: 41
Europe: 4
Other: 6
Total: 226

George Anderson

'If you want to be big, think big', was Dundee's managing / director George Anderson's philosophy during his ten years in charge at Dens and he certainly practiced what he preached as he brought Dundee their first silverware in forty-one years, broke the world record transfer fee and brought Dundee to within a whisker of being Champions of Scotland. His post-war time in charge from 1944 to 1954 was the most successful era in The Dee's history and George Anderson deserves his place amongst the Dundee greats.

Anderson's first encounter with Dundee actually came as a player during World War One when he was a guest from his parent club Aberdeen and played in goal in the 1917/18 season. At the end of the previous year Dundee had been asked to drop out of the Scottish League Division One until the end of the War to reduce travelling costs and so instead went into the Scottish League Eastern Division and Anderson was part of the successful side which won the league on goal average and won two of the league's cup competitions.

When he returned to Aberdeen at the end of the War, Anderson was awarded with a benefit match from The Dons once again Dundee featured in his playing career when they provided the opposition.

By the start of second global conflict in 1939, Anderson was director of his hometown team Aberdeen and was placed in charge of team affairs when the Dons manager Davie Halliday went off to war. Anderson revelled in the position of caretaker manager but as it was being held for the return of Halliday, Anderson made a move for the position at Dens which had been left vacant when Dundee closed for the War in 1940.

Dundee had been relegated on the eve of the conflict and two months after the D-day landings, The Dark Blues resumed their league campaign in the Scottish League North-East Division. Dundee won the North-East Division in 1944/45 and the Scottish 'B' Division the season after that but had to wait until it had won a third championship in a row in 1946/47 before promotion was granted. Due to the large number of guest players used by clubs and the number of players still being demobbed, the Scottish League decided not to re-insert promotion or relegation until 1947. After ten years out of the top flight, the Dark Blues were back in the big time for the start of the 1947/48 campaign and Anderson was the toast of the city.

Known affectionately by the players as 'Toffee Dod' because of the confectionary business he owned in Aberdeen, Anderson showed himself to be a forward planner and a progressive football thinker. He had constantly been gearing Dundee for life in the top flight and had been signing players with the 'A' Division in mind and amongst those signings were future captain Alfie Boyd, Doug Cowie (who holds the record number of appearances for the club), Tommy Gallagher and goal scoring machine Albert Juliussen.

Anderson was a master of man-management and popular with the players with his emphasis on ball-work in training. He excelled in public relations and attempted to raise the profile of the Club. He also had an eye for talent and had constructed a skilful, attractive side in a relatively short space of time; so much so that they were ready for an assault on Scotland's elite.

Anderson still lived in Aberdeen where he was a town councillor and from where he ran his confectionary business.

He travelled down to Dundee twice a week and the day-to-day training was left to assistants Willie Cameron and Andy McCall but the bowler-hatted, bow-tied, larger-than-life Anderson had the full support and respect of the players, despite his infrequent appearances at the Club.

Anderson would tell the players to *'go out and enjoy themselves'* and he liked to encourage attractive football and Dundee's first season back in the top flight was rewarded with a fourth place finish, their highest placing for twenty-six years.

Season 1948/49 saw Dundee reach the semi-finals of both the League and Scottish Cups and in the League Championship finished second after a heart breaking last day defeat. Dundee were one point ahead going into the final match at Falkirk and a win would guarantee the League Flag, regardless of what Rangers did at Albion Rovers but it wasn't to be.

The Dundee players were flooded with nerves and the effervescent and chirpy Anderson was unable to dispel them. When confronted with the usual pre-match opposition banter, Anderson locked his troops in the dressing room an hour before kick off and tried to protect his players from unnecessary distractions. It back fired however as Dundee first missed a penalty while at 0-0 and then fell apart in the second half and went down 4-1 as Rangers snatched the title with a similar score line at Coatbridge.

In just five short years however, Anderson had taken Dundee from Division Two also-rans to Championship contenders but the fact was that there was no major trophies in the Dens Park cabinet and he had to work out how he was going to change that.

To begin with, he started to transform Dundee in a cosmopolitan crew signing various Englishmen, two South Africans (Gordon Frew and Ken Ziesing), a Canadian (Jack Cowan) and several Scandinavians as well as promising Scottish youngsters Bobby Flavell and Bill Brown.

However it was the signing Anderson made in September 1950 which was the final piece in the jigsaw, when pulled off one of the transfer coups of the century when he signed Scottish superstar Billy Steel for a world record fee of £23,500. Anderson had fought off competition from Rangers to land Steel and the inside forward brought power, skill and imagination to the Dundee forward line. It was extraordinary for a provincial club like Dundee to pay such an extraordinary fee and Anderson's philosophy of *'think big'* was repaid when silverware was soon on its way to Dens.

With the strong back-line of Cowie, Gallacher and Boyd added to the goals of Flavell and the skill of Steel, Dundee lifted their first trophy since 1910 when on October 27th 1951, Dundee won the League Cup in an exciting 3-2 win over Rangers at Hampden.

Twelve months later Dundee became the first club to retain the League Cup when the defeated Kilmarnock 2-0 in the Final and with a Scottish Cup Final defeat to Motherwell squeezed in between the two League Cup wins, Anderson had finally turned Dundee in a trophy winning, Scottish footballing force.

Anderson himself was not at the Final against Kilmarnock as he had taken ill with pleurisy and listened to the game on the radio in a nursing home in Aberdeen and just two years later had to resign his post of manager due to ill health though retained his seat on the board.

He left as Dundee's oldest serving manager at the age of sixty-seven after being dogged by ill health for a couple of years.

His departure marked the end of Dundee's post-war golden age but Anderson had done much to lay the foundations of Dundee Football Club as a prominent force in Scottish football. He has won more trophies than any other manager since Dundee's formation in 1893 and saw his dream of a successful Club come true. In 2003, he was listed in the top fifty Scottish managers of all time by *The Sunday Herald* and he raised the profile and stature of the Club. Anderson's legacy was set and the foundations were in place for Dundee to move to the next level within the next decade.

Honours at Dundee:
(As Player)
Scottish League Eastern Division winners: 1917/18
Penman Cup winners 1917/18
Loftus Cup: 1917/18
Eastern Cup joint winners
(with Dundee Hibs): 1917/18
(As Manager)
Scottish League Cup winners:
  1951/52, 1952/53
Scottish League Championship
runners-up: 1948/49
Scottish Cup runners-up: 1952
Scottish League B Division winners:
  1945/46. 1946/47
Scottish League North-East Division
(first series) winners: 1944/45
Appearances:
League: 17
Loftus Cup: 3
Penman Cup: 3
Eastern Cup: 1
Total: 24

Managerial Record with Dundee:
(1944-1954)

	P	W	D	L	F	A	Pts.
League:	298	161	53	84	684	435	379
Scottish Cup:	26	13	5	8	55	36	
League Cup:	63	34	10	19	140	97	
Other:	10	5	2	3	20	17	
Total:	397	213	70	114	834	585	

Jimmy Bellamy

Anyone who scores a goal in a Scottish Cup Final in which The Dark Blues win, rightly deserves a place in any list of Dundee F.C. legends and Jimmy Bellamy did just that in 1910. Bellamy scored the equalising goal in the second replay of the 1910 Scottish Cup Final as The Dee went on to win 2-1 and helped Dundee to win the only major trophy they secured in the first fifty-eight years of their existence.

James Francis Bellamy was born in Bethnal Green in London on September 11th 1881 and started his football career with Barking, Grays United and Reading before moving to Woolwich Arsenal in 1904. After four goals in twenty-nine league appearances for the south-east London club, Bellamy moved to Portsmouth and then Norwich City before joining Dundee in the summer of 1908.

Bellamy was brought to the Club by scout Peter Allan who in earlier years had been guilty of poaching local players for clubs down south but now in the employ of Dundee, he helped Dundee develop something of a partiality towards English players. Indeed at least six of Dundee's successful 1910 Scottish Cup winning team were brought to Dens by Peter Allan from English clubs including Herbert Dainty from New Brighton, skipper Bert Lee from Southampton, John Hunter from Portsmouth, Jack Fraser and Sandy McFarlane from Newcastle United and Jimmy Bellamy from Norwich.

Bellamy made his debut for Dundee on the first game of the 1908/09 season in a 2-1 home win against Hearts and scored his first goal for the Club a fortnight later when he scored the winner for Dundee as they defeated defending champions Celtic in a famous 2-1 win at Dens.

Playing at either outside-right or right-half, Bellamy scored fourteen goals in is debut season as Dundee would finish league runners-up to Celtic who piped them by just one point.

In the Scottish Cup, Jimmy scored his first hat-trick for Dundee when he netted a treble, of which two were penalties, in a 9-0 first round victory over Ayr Parkhouse at home and in the second round played in front of a new Dens Park record crowd of 28,000 against Rangers. The tie finished 0-0 and The Dee went out 1-0 in the replay but Ibrox was to be the scene of Dundee's greatest Cup triumph fourteen months later when Dundee would go all the way in the 1909/10 competition.

The first round paired Dundee with non-league Beith and with the Ayrshire side agreeing to 'sell' home advantage, the tie was played at Dens Park. On a frosty surface, Bellamy missed an early penalty but despite going ahead through George Comrie, Beith fought back for a 1-1 draw. The game attracted 9000 fans but 3000 fewer turned up for the replay seven days later at Dens to witness George Langlands give Dundee the narrowest of margins.

At the next stage the Dark Blues entertained Falkirk who were challenging at the top of the league and 20,000 fans turned up as Cup fever started to take a grip. This time Bellamy was a goal hero on a Dens Park mud bath when he scored the second goal in a 3-0 win.

Quarter and semi-final wins over Motherwell and Hibernian saw Dundee reach their first ever Scottish Cup Final against Clyde in April, with Ibrox being the venue after damage done to Hampden in the previous year's abandoned Old Firm Final had not yet been repaired.

Bellamy lined up in the Dundee side on April 9th and after being 2-0 down at half time, fought back with two late goals to earn a replay. Seven days later, Bellamy retained his place as the sides met again in Govan but a lack of goals meant that the following midweek would see the clubs try to break the stalemate for a third time.

~ 12 ~

So on Wednesday 20th April, Dundee would create history when in, according to *The Courier*, *'The best final seen in years'*, they would defeat Clyde 2-1 thanks to goals from Jimmy Bellamy and John 'Sailor' Hunter.

Clyde had shocked Dundee by taking the lead in three minutes through Chalmers but after fifteen minutes, Bellamy brought The Dee level when he headed home from a corner. It was Jimmy's fifteen goal of the season which was enough to see him finish as the Club's top scorer but more importantly, it gave Dundee hope that they could push on for a winner. They did just that in the second half when they got one from John Hunter when he broke through the Clyde defence and sent the ball into the net from a narrow angle.

The team were cheered off by several thousand at Glasgow's Buchanan Street train station, were cheered again by large numbers in Perth and when they arrived on foot in Dundee's West Station having alighted at Magdalen Green to avoid the crowds, exploding detonators told the 20,000 strong crowd that their heroes had returned. Dundee partied long into to the night and *'was drunk for a week'* according to modern day author Jim Crumley, whose grandfather had played in goal on that famous day.

At the start of the following season, the Scottish Cup was displayed before Dundee's first home game against Hibs and in defence of their trophy, The Dee reached the Scottish Cup semi-final where they lost out to Hamilton Academical at Douglas Park in the days before semis were played on neutral grounds.

The quarter-final against Rangers had attracted another record crowd at Dens, this time 30,000 and a 2-1 win for The Dark Blues had sent them through to the penultimate stage to meet The Accies.

Early in the second half two goals from Jimmy Bellamy had given The Dee a 2-0 lead but as Dundee became complacent, Hamilton fought back and won 3-2 to deny Dundee back to back Cup Final appearances.

Season 1911/12 was Jimmy's last in a Dundee shirt and it would see him win his second Forfarshire Cup winners' medal, having also collected one in his first season. Jimmy signed off from Dundee with twelve goals to bring his Dark Blue total to fifty and in the summer left Dundee to sign for Motherwell, before heading back down south and playing for Burnley, Fulham, Southend United, Ebbw Vale and his first club Barking.

His time at Dens however was his most prolific in goal scoring terms and he scored more goals for Dundee, than all his other clubs put together. After finishing playing, Jimmy embarked on a successful coaching career in Europe working in Germany, Italy and Spain. In Italy, he took charge of Brecia where he took them up into Serie A for the first time ever and then in 1929, he became manager of Barcelona, where he led them to victory in the first ever La Liga Championship.

At Dens Park, Jimmy Bellamy will always be remembered for his Cup Final exploits and having played in all ten matches on the way to winning the Cup and scoring Dundee's first goal in the Final, he is rightly remembered as an all-time Dundee great.

Honours at Dundee:
Scottish Cup winner: 1910
Scottish League Championship runner-up: 1908/09
Forfarshire Cup winner: 1908/09, 1911/12
Appearances, Goals:
League: 119, 43 goals
Scottish Cup: 20, 7 goals
Totals: 139, 50 goals

Alfie Boyd

From ball boy to net boy, to the captain with the most winners' medals in Dundee's history, Alfie Boyd can truly lay claim to the worthy mantle of Dundee legend having played for Dundee for six successful years in the late forties and early fifties.

Born in the city on October 22nd 1920, Alfred Boyd started his connection with the Club as a ball boy in the Roaring Twenties before being promoted to the prestigious position of net boy. With football coursing through his veins however, he was destined to become a player and the first signs of his exceptional talent came when he played in a 1-0 victory for the Scottish Schoolboys over their English counterparts in Newcastle in 1935.

Within three years of that cap, Alfie started his senior career not in his home town but up the river in Perth when he signed for St. Johnstone but like so many players of his era, his career was curtailed by the Second World War, when he joined the R.A.F. and was posted to South Africa.

At the end of the War, Boyd was stationed at Leuchars before he was demobbed, allowing him to rekindle his football career with the Saints but in February 1947, he was tempted to join Dundee by the Dark Blues managing/director George Anderson who parted with a Dens Park club record fee of £4000 to secure his services.

Within weeks of Alfie joining, Dundee chalked up back to back club record 10-0 wins over Alloa and Dunfermline and by the end of the season were 'B' Division Champions for the second year in a row. This time Dundee were allowed back into the top tier with promotion being resumed after the War for the first time and The Dark Blues were back in the big time.

In his six years at Dens, Alfie would miss only six games which is a remarkable record and is a testimony to his peak physical fitness. As a centre half or wing half, he formed part of the famous half-back line of Gallagher, Cowie and Boyd and played no fewer than 235 games for the Dee, scoring twenty-seven times.

Season 1948/49 was the nearly season in so many ways as Dundee reached the semi-final of both the League Cup and Scottish Cup and finished runners-up in the League Championship after a last day 4-1 collapse at Falkirk, where a win would have guaranteed the League Flag.

Those defeats hurt Alfie and in a newspaper interview in 1950 he stated, *'We had to win our last four games to be Champions but we were inclined to be too much on edge. In our last match with Falkirk at Brockville, a win would have made us Champions, but everything went wrong. We were all over them in the first half, but when Alec Stott failed with a penalty close on half time, we felt that the fates were against us.*

We got into the semi final of both the League Cup and Scottish Cup and I think our defeat by Clyde in the replay of the Scottish was as hard a blow as any. We had gone to Tynecastle in the round before the semi and won handsomely. I had visions of a Cup medal, the one thing we all dream of winning, but Clyde put an end to that dream."

It was during this time that Alfie won his only international honour playing for the Scottish League against the English League in 1949 and at the start of the following season took both the Scottish and English Trainers and Players coaching course, becoming the first player to complete both in Britain. While undertaking the Scottish certificate, he studied on the course with such luminaries as Jock Stein, Willie Ormond and Reggie Smith and Sammy Kean who would both be part of Dundee's backroom staff when they won the League in 1962.

In an effort to win their first honour since 1910, Dundee splashed out a world record transfer fee for Billy Steel in September 1950. Dundee then finished in third place, behind Rangers on goal average and Alfie surprisingly finished Dundee's top goal scorer that season with eight goals before also becoming the Dundee F.C. Cricket team's top batsman in the summer scoring forty runs in match against Forfarshire Cricket Club.

It wasn't long however before Alfie achieved his dream of a winners' medal when in October 1951, Dundee ended a forty-one year wait for silverware with a 3-2 League Cup Final win over Rangers at Hampden.

In front of 92, 325 at the national stadium, Dundee were leading 2-1 with only minutes left on the clock but unfortunately for The Dee, Rangers equalised in controversial fashion when Dundee keeper Bill Brown looked to have been fouled by future manager Willie Thornton.

From the restart however, Dundee won a free kick deep inside the Rangers half and with only thirty seconds remaining, Billy Steel is reputed to have said to his skipper, *'I'll place it on your head Alfie'*, and did just that as Boyd headed home the winner.

It was one of the most dramatic finishes ever seen at Hampden and Boyd held aloft the glittering League Cup before 30,000 ecstatic Dundonians in the crowd.

Later that season Alfie led Dundee back to Hampden for the Scottish Cup Final in April but were to be disappointed as Motherwell ran out 4-0 winners but in October 1952, Dundee made it three trips to Hampden in a year to defend their League Cup trophy.

This time they faced 'B' Division Kilmarnock, and two goals from Bobby Flavell was enough to let Alfie get the chance to lift the trophy for a second time as Dundee became the first side to retain the League Cup.

At the end of the following season, Dundee went on a marathon two month tour of South Africa as part of the Club's sixtieth anniversary celebrations and at the end of the tour,

Dundee granted Boyd permission to remain in South Africa. Alfie had enjoyed his time in South Africa during the War where he met his wife and now wished to return to her homeland where his daughter was born and signed for the Marist Brothers Club as player/coach.

Aflie turned down the chance to rejoin Dundee in 1957 as by then he was involved in the in the South African gold mining industry. He would go on to manage Durban City and manage a Sir Stanley Matthews Invitation XI during one of the Englishman's many visits to the continent and he also became a selector for the South African F.A.

Alfie however kept in touch with many of his team mates from Dens and in 1993 returned to the city to take part in Dundee's centenary celebrations and catch up with many old friends and colleagues.

Alfie sadly passed away in South Africa in July 1998 aged 78 and did so just a few weeks after sending Dundee a congratulatory message on winning promotion back to the Scottish Premier League. From having been a ball boy at Dens at a young age, Dundee was in his heart until the end and he will forever be remembered as the legendary double cup winning captain who lead by example and scored that famous last minute winner.

Honours at Dundee:
Scottish League Cup winner:
    1951/52, 1952/53
Scottish League Championship runners-up:
    1948/49
Scottish Cup runners-up: 1952
Scottish League B Division champions:
    1946/47
Scottish League cap: 1
Appearances, Goals:
League: 169, 18 goals
Scottish Cup: 21, 3 goals
League Cup: 44, 6 goals
Totals: 235, 27 goals

Bill Brown

Bill Brown was one of the greatest Scottish goalkeepers of the post-war period and is a legendary figure at both Dundee F.C. and Tottenham Hotspur. At Dundee he was a member of the 1951 League Cup winning side and represented Scotland in the 1958 World Cup while at Spurs he was a member of the 1962 double winning side and part of the first British side to win a European trophy.

William Dallas Fyfe Brown was born in Arbroath on October 8th 1931 and played at outside-left as a youngster, only switching to goalkeeper when his Arbroath High School team's regular keeper had to go off injured and Bill was asked to go in goal. It was obvious from that day on that Bill was 'a natural' in goal and but for that quirk of fate, Scotland may have been denied one of its greatest ever keepers as Bill had even had a trial for Scotland schoolboys as a winger.

After leaving school he began an apprenticeship as an electrician, whilst on the pitch he progressed from juvenile side Cliffburn to junior club Carnoustie Panmure, before joining Dundee shortly before his 18th birthday. It was something of a coup for Dundee manager George Anderson to secure the services of Brown as he had been courted by various clubs including Manchester City, Sheffield Wednesday, Dundee United, Blackpool, Brechin City and hometown team Arbroath. Anderson however persuaded the seventeen year old to turn out for Dundee in a trial match against league champions Hibs to reopen Dundee Violet's Glenesk Park and playing against the Hibs 'famous five' forward line was enough to persuade the impressionable Brown to sign for The Dee.

Bill made his debut for the Dens Park club against Clyde at Shawfield in January 1950, but it took him several seasons to become the club's first choice keeper, sharing the goalkeeping duties for a few seasons with Johnny Lynch and Bobby Henderson.

Tall and slim, Bill was a safe, unflappable keeper who rarely needed to be spectacular. Quick and agile he had good positional sense and great concentration, and playing behind Dundee's famous half back line of Gallagher, Cowie and Boyd he won his first honour when he was part of the Dundee side to win the League Cup in his third season.

Coming into the side in the final sectional tie against Raith Rovers, Brown kept his place in the side for the two legged quarter-final against Falkirk and for the semi-final against holders Motherwell at Ibrox where The Dee won 5-1 to book their place in the Final.

In front of 92, 325, Dundee clinched the trophy with a 3-2 win over Rangers and the side became instant local heroes having brought the first major trophy back to 'Juteopolis' for forty-one years.

Bill missed both the 1952 Scottish and League Cup Finals due to being away on National Service but by 1954, Bill had made the yellow jersey his own. It wasn't just for Dundee however that he excelled as in 1956 he was honoured for his consistent performances with a Scotland 'B' cap against England. The following year he made three appearances for the Scottish League against the English League, Irish league and the League of Ireland and as the World Cup in Sweden approached in 1958, Brown got two more league caps again against the English League and the League of Ireland.

His performances for the Scottish League were impressive enough for the Scottish selectors to name Brown in the World Cup squad for Sweden and he got to make his full international debut in the tournament when he took over from Tommy Younger for the final group match against France.

Brown would go on to become the most capped custodian for Scotland with twenty-eight appearances, a record which stood until overtaken by Alan Rough in 1979. Of those caps he earned another three of them as a Dundee player when he played in all three matches of the 1959 British Home International Championships and it was in the match against England at Wembley in April that he caught the eye of Spurs manager Bill Nicholson who was in the process of strengthening his side.

Brown would make another three Scottish League appearances while at Dens Park before Nicholson put in an offer of £16,500 for him in June and the popular keeper was on his way to London after Nicholson took the night train to Dundee to secure the deal.

Characteristically calm and unfussy, yet breathtakingly acrobatic at need, Bill Brown was the last line of defence when Tottenham Hotspur became the first club in the twentieth century to lift the English League and FA Cup double in 1961, and two years later was a member of the team that thrashed Atletico Madrid 5-1 in the European Cup Winners' Cup Final, thus becoming the first British club to win a major European trophy.

Brown did not conform to the popular notion of what a goalkeeper should look like at the time for although he stood half an inch over six feet, his frame was spare, stringy and seemingly insubstantial, in vivid contrast to the imposingly muscular individuals employed by most clubs to mind their nets. Every line of the Brown figure was angular, an impression emphasised by his aquiline features, although if some contemporary observers referred to him half-slightingly as willowy, there was no doubting his wiry resilience when it came to physical challenges with hulking centre-forwards.

Bill eventually left White Hart Lane in October 1966, spending a season with Northampton Town before emigrating to Canada where he played for Toronto Falcons. After retiring from the game he worked for a Toronto property developer and then spent many years in the employment of the Ontario Government Land Department and sadly passed away in Simcoe, Ontario at the end of November 2004 following a lengthy illness.

Brown's legacy at Dens was 274 appearances where he made sixty-two shut-outs, winning one major trophy and gaining thirteen Scottish caps at various levels and left a host of memories as a keeper who was elastically agile, endowed with remarkably sharp reflexes and was never less than impeccable for Dundee.

Honours at Dundee:
Scottish League Cup winner: 1951/52
Scotland full caps: 4
Scotland B caps: 1
Scottish League caps: 8
Appearances:
League: 215
Scottish Cup: 14
League Cup: 45
Total: 274

John Brown

John Brown was a wonderful player for Dundee who turned in a number of memorable performances for The Dee in his four years at the Club. He played primarily a midfielder and contributed thirty-nine goals in a 135 appearances, giving the Dundee support some terrific memories.

Born midway through Dundee's Championship season in Stirling, Brown started his footballing education at St. Mirren Boys' Club and signed for Hamilton Academical in 1979 with Rangers, St. Mirren, Newcastle and Carlisle all watching his progress.

He spent five years playing at Douglas Park under five different mangers and as a part time player he worked at the same time as a fitter. He put in a number of fine performances for The Accies, including a hat-trick against Berwick Rangers while playing at left back and this alerted a posse of clubs to his potential.

Amongst those watching was Dundee manager Archie Knox who in his first pre season with the Club was giving cause for optimism to the Dundee support with a clutch of summer signings. Knox was the first person to put a concrete offer for Brown and he was on his way to Dens for his first crack at full time football when the Dark Blues shelled out £40,000 for his signature.

Brown was signed as a defender but he was soon turning in tenacious attacking displays for the Club from midfield. He made his debut at home to Hibs on August 18th 1984 and scored his first Dundee goal eleven days later against Kilmarnock in the Skol Cup but it was his next goal in Dundee colours that would turn him into an instant hero.

Without a league win to their name so far that season, Dundee went into the derby at Tannadice on September 8th more in hope than in expectation but in a remarkable match Dundee emerged as 4-3 victors with Brown netting the winner. Three times Dundee took the lead through McWilliams, McKinlay and Harris, only for United to level but with fourteen minutes remaining Brown bulleted a header past Billy Thomson for the winner.

The key to success had been in midfield as Knox's new boys worked a treat where the speedy Rafferty complimented Connor's craft and the tackling and surging runs of Brown, with his powerful shooting and heading ability made him a constant threat.

Nicknamed 'Bomber', Brown settled in Carnoustie and his never-say-die attitude and no mean skill made him a firm favourite. In derbies, Brown would be on the winning side on five further occasions, including in the Forfarshire Cup Final in 1985 where he got the first in a 2-0 win as Dundee lifted the trophy for the first time in fourteen years.

In 1987, Brown put in a tremendous performance in the Scottish Cup semi-final against Dundee United at Tynecastle but it was to no avail as 'the Arabs' progressed to the Final. United won the match 3-2 but it came after Billy Thomson broke Dundee hearts when he saved two magnificent late John Brown free kicks which could have forced a replay or even a victory.

His best performances however usually came against the club he had supported as a boy, Rangers and he was instrumental in Dundee victories over the Light Blues on no fewer than six times, hitting the winner on three occasions.

In February 1985, Brown hit the only goal of the game to memorably knock Rangers out of the Scottish Cup fourth Round at Ibrox and then nine months later went one better (or is that three?) when he hit a hat-trick against Rangers in the league.

On November 23rd 1985, Dundee recorded a sensational 3-2 win at Dens to give them their fourth successive win in a six game unbeaten sequence against the Light Blues. Dundee's win was all the more remarkable considering that they were down to ten men after seventeen minutes when McKinlay was red carded for a trip on McMinn but a brilliant individual performance from John Brown made sure the points stayed at Dens. His second goal had come direct from a free kick while his third came from the spot but the first, which he netted after leaving a trail of Rangers defenders in his wake, would be long remembered by the fans.

His departure came as a huge disappointment to the Dundee support and not just because he had filled in so well as centre-half since the injury to Jim Duffy.

At Ibrox, he would go on to win six league titles, three Scottish Cups and three League Cups but his eighteen goals for the Glasgow club in eleven years would be less than half of what he managed for Dundee in four.

He would go on to become coach of the Rangers Under-17 squad and then their reserve side, then in 2008 took on his first managerial job when he became boss of First Division Clyde.

Brown scored the winner again in a 1-0 league win over Rangers at Dens in September 1986 and the Govan giants don't forget such things and signed him for £350,000 in early 1988.

At Dundee, he left the fans with some many great memories of a player who gave his all in a Dundee shirt and there are few who would begrudge him the chance to play for his boyhood heroes.

Appearances, Goals:
League: 111 + 3 subs, 31 goals
Scottish Cup: 11 + 1 sub, 6 goals
League Cup: 9, 2 goals
Totals: 135, 39 goals

Fabian Caballero

'He came down from Heaven, he wears number seven, he's Fabian Caballero', was the song sung by the Dundee support to cult hero Fabian Caballero who made 142 appearances for Dundee during two spells between 2000 and 2005 after he was signed for a Club record transfer fee, which still stands today.

Fabian Orlando Caballero was born on January 31st 1978 in Misiones, Argentina, which is surrounded by Paraguay to the north-east. It was in Paraguay that Caballero started his football career with Cerro Porteno in 1997, and it was with 'Le Ciclon' that he was spotted by Arsene Wenger who then took him on loan to Arsenal for twelve months.

Caballero made just three appearances from the bench for 'The Gunners' and his time at Highbury is more remembered for the bizarre incident when Ron Atkinson sat next to him in the wrong dug out in his first home game in charge at Nottingham Forest.

Upon returning to Paraguay, Caballero signed for rivals Club Sol De America but at the end of his first season at the Asuncion club, he was loaned out again to another U.K. club when he joined Dundee F.C. in the summer of 2000 as part of the 'Bonetti Revolution'.

Nicknamed 'Tyson' at his clubs in Paraguay, he quickly became known as simply 'Fab Cab' at Dens when the striker turned in some scintillating displays in his first few games. He made his competitive debut in the first game of the season at Motherwell but it was the following week at home to Dunfermline when Cab really caught the eye. Playing up front with fellow Argentinean Juan Sara who was signed on the same day from another Paraguayan club, the pair looked to have struck up an immediate understanding and both opened their Dark Blue goal scoring account from the spot in a 3-0 win which sent Dundee to the top of the S.P.L. for the first time in their history.

In his next home game, Caballero scored two stunning strikes against Montrose in the C.I.S. Insurance League Cup and the powerfully built forward was emerging as a deadly striker, with good technique and a powerful shot.

Unfortunately, this immediately made Cab a target for the hatchet men and at Easter Road was the victim of a shocking challenge from Mathias Jack after he had opened the scoring for Dundee. While the Hibs man received just a yellow for his two-footed tackle, Caballero got his marching orders when he had finally reacted to a number of disgraceful challenges and then received another red card post match a few weeks later when he was accused of throwing a teapot at the referee's door at Love Street.

Worse was to follow a few weeks later however in the first derby of the season when a horrendous double challenge from Dundee United's De Vos and McDonald resulted in Caballero going off with a serious knee injury.

The Dees went on to record a memorable 3-0 victory over their neighbours but it was a victory at a price as Caballero had sustained a ruptured ligament in one knee and a partial tear in the other. He would have to undergo surgery at the Isokinetic Fitness Institute in Bologna and would remain there for a lengthy programme of recuperation.

Within weeks, Caballero had received over two hundred well wishing letters from the Dundee support and on a visit back in November to watch the derby at Tannadice, he was overwhelmed when the fans chanted his name as they watched Dundee beat United 2-0.

Expected to be out for the remainder of the season, it was a major boost when he returned to the side in April for a vital match against Aberdeen. With his replacement Claudio Caniggia out injured, Caballero was returned to the starting line-up and although looking sluggish and over-weight, still managed to score Dundee's second to secure a top six finish in the S.P.L.'s first split.

Cabellero got to partner the Argentinean superstar Caniggia just once before he departed for Ibrox and in Dundee's last game of the season at Parkhead, Dundee completed a memorable season with a 2-0 victory over League Champions Celtic in which 'Fab Cab' scored both.

With Caballero due to return to Paraguay at the end of his loan period, Dundee had decided that they had seen enough on his return from injury to want to keep him and shelled out a Club record transfer of £600,000 to his club, Sol De America.

Almost immediately, Caballero was straight back into action when Dundee's season kicked off on the ridiculously early on June 16th. Dundee entered European competition for the first time since 1974, when they took part in the U.E.F.A. Intertoto Cup and drawn against Yugoslav side F.K. Sartid in the first round, Caballero came off the bench in a turgid 0-0 first leg match at Dens.

In the second leg in Serbia, Caballero was back in the starting line up and put Dundee ahead in the fourth minute when he cleverly chested home a head flick from Gavin Rae. However it was a case of déjà vu when he was targeted for some rough treatment and with the referee awarding Sartid two first half penalties, they were helped even further when Caballero was sent off for retaliation with the Sartid players going unpunished for their continual assaults on Cab.

It was a costly red card for Cab as he was given a three match suspension for future U.E.F.A. competitions and with Dundee going down 5-2 in the end, he would have to wait until Dundee were in the U.E.F.A. Cup two years later to serve it.

Throughout his second season, Caballero struggled with weight and fitness but that was to all change in the summer of 2002, when new manager Jim Duffy put Caballero on a strict fitness regime and the side started to see the best of the Argentinean.

The man from Misiones now seemed like a 'man on a mission' and scored in the first game of the season and went on to repeatedly put in man of the match performances throughout the season. In November, he supplanted his legendary status in the minds of the Dundee support with a brace against United in a 3-2 win at Dens and in the New Year was a key figure in the side which had embarked on 'The Road to Hampden'.

Having knocked out Premier League sides Partick Thistle and Aberdeen in the early rounds, Dundee were then taken to a replay by First Division leaders Falkirk in which Caballero scored the vital equaliser to take the tie into extra time before a 4-1 win.

Dundee progressed to the Final where their opponents were to be league champions Rangers, but before that, the sides were due to meet in the S.P.L. at Dens. Two beautiful long range strikes from Caballero earned The Dee a 2-2 draw in which Rangers were awarded three penalties and missed two and they showed Rangers that they would have a game on their hands the following month.

Cab's second strike was voted goal of the season at the D.S.A Player of the Year Dinner the week before the big day but there was no fairytale ending at Hampden as Rangers lifted the Scottish Cup with a 1-0 win as Caballero had to postpone his wedding for a week which had been due to take place on Cup Final day.

There was some consolation for Dundee as the runners-up were to be entered into the U.E.F.A. Cup the following season with Rangers in the Champions' League and for Caballero, consolation in being named as Dundee's Player of the Year.

Caballero missed Dundee's trip to Albania in the U.E.F.A. Cup Preliminary Round as he served his Intertoto suspension and missed the first leg of the First Round tie against Perugia before returning for the second leg in Italy.

Dundee however went down 3-1 on aggregate to the Serie A side and less than a month later more disappointment was to follow for Caballero when he was one of twenty-five Dens Park employees axed when the Club fell into administration. In wasn't the end for Dundee and Caballero however, when he returned to Dens in November 2004 after a deal was struck for the Dee4Life Fans' Trust to pay £10,000 towards his wages to sign him until the end of the season.

Caballero's appearance gave the administration weary fans a huge lift and his second game saw him involved in another victory over United.

However, Dundee were toiling under the weight of all the cutbacks and at the end of the season were relegated to the First Division and Caballero was once again the victim of D.F.C. cost cutting when was released.

His time at Dens will always be fondly remembered by the Dundee's support whose only regret with 'Fab Cab' would have been to see how brilliant a player he would have become without his injury, when he would have undoubtedly become a player worth a seven figure fee.

Honours at Dundee:
Tennents' Scottish Cup runner-up: 2003
D.S.A. Player of the Year: 2003
Appearances, Goals:
League: 104 + 20 sub, 20 goals
Scottish Cup: 8 + 2 sub, 1 goal
League Cup: 5, 4 goals
Europe: 2 + 1 sub, 1 goal
Totals: 142, 26 goals

Kenny Cameron

When picking out the greatest goals scored in the history of Dundee Football Club, there can be few better than the goal scored by Kenny Cameron in the Scottish Cup Final at Hampden in 1964. Within a minute of Rangers taking the lead in front of 120,982 spectators, Dundee went straight up the park and scored a terrific goal when Cameron volleyed past Billy Ritchie in the Ibrox men's net.

Cameron had actually kicked off the 1964 Final but it was his strike in the seventy first minute that has gone down in the annals of history as one of the best goals the National Stadium has ever seen.

When Jimmy Millar put Rangers ahead in the seventieth minute, it took Dundee only sixty seconds to resume parity when they equalised straight from kick off. Cameron himself took the restart and played it forward to Alan Cousin who passed it back to Alec Stuart who took two touches before launching it forward into the Rangers half.

Rangers captain John Greig went forward to meet the long ball about thirty-five yards out but he completely misjudged it and headed it backwards, high into the air into his own box where Dundee's number nine Kenny Cameron was lurking.

As the ball dropped over his shoulder, Kenny took a touch with his right foot and before the ball could hit the deck, he spun and hit a superb volley with his left which flew high over the Rangers keeper and into the top right hand corner of the net.

It was simply a stunning goal which was too quick for the British Pathe News cameras which missed it but it was caught by Scottish Television's coverage and almost made their commentator Arthur Montford speechless. Not known for his emotion, Montford stops in mid sentence and says, *'and it's a goal! Cameron scores for Dundee! What a goal, what a final, what a match! Two goals in forty-five seconds!'*

Ultimately it wasn't enough as two goals in the last ninety seconds from Millar and Willie Henderson were enough to take the Cup back to Govan but Kenny's goal lives long in the memory. In an online millennium poll in 2000, it was voted the third best goal ever scored at Hampden behind Davie Cooper's free kick against Aberdeen in the Skol Cup Final of 1987 and Kenny Dalgleish's goal against Spain in a World Cup qualifier in 1984 which equalled Dennis Law's scoring record for Scotland.

But there was so much more to Kenny Cameron's Dundee's career than his Cup Final goal as he scored seventy-one goals in 118 appearances over five years.

Born in the city on July 2nd 1943, Cameron joined the Dark Blues from Blairgowrie and made his debut for the current Scottish League Champions in a League Cup sectional tie against Dundee United in August 1962. It was the best of matches to pull on a dark blue shirt for the first time as Dundee ran out 2-1 winners but with a team full of the stars who would reach the European Cup semi-final that season, the nineteen year old was restricted to just five more appearances that campaign.

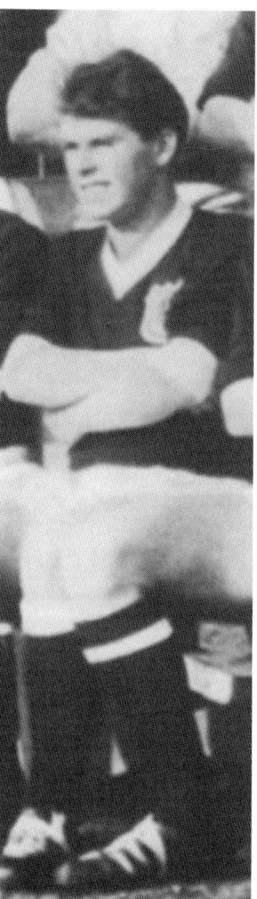

His chances of ousting the likes of Gilzean, Cousin and Penman from the striking berths were slim but Kenny showed his potential with three goals in three league starts, getting his first goal for the Club when he netted the winner in a 2-1 victory over Partick Thistle at Dens, three days after his team mates had beaten Anderlecht 2-1 in the European Cup quarter-final second leg.

Season 1963/64 saw Cameron establish himself in the side, scoring twenty-two goals in twenty-eight starts but he was third in the top goal scoring stakes behind Andy Penman who scored thirty and Alan Gilzean who netted a Club record fifty-two goals.

That season culminated in Kenny scoring in the Scottish Cup Final but despite that defeat, Dundee had qualified for the European Cup Winners' Cup with Rangers also winning the Scottish League title and entering the Champions Cup. After a bye in the First Round, Dundee met Real Zaragoza in the second and Kenny played in the second leg in Spain where the Dee lost 2-1 to go out 4-3 on aggregate.

Throughout his career at Dens Park, Cameron had faced stiff competition for a starting berth and after another two seasons which produced twenty-eight goals in sixty-two appearances, he decided to try his luck elsewhere and signed for Kilmarnock for £10,000 in the summer of 1967.

Before he left, Kenny scored some memorable goals including a brace in a 2-0 win over Celtic, a double in a 9-2 win over St. Mirren and a single in a 9-1 win over East Fife and he became Dundee's first ever substitute when he replaced Alex Bryce on the first day of the season after thirty minutes in a League Cup derby at Tannadice on August 16th 1966.

More notably against Dundee United however he got a double in a 3-1 League Cup win at

Tannadice in September 1965, the winner in a 1-0 victory in October and the first in a 4-1 win at Dens twelve months later and in total scored six goals against The Arabs.

It is slightly ironic therefore that Kenny would go on and make a name for himself further down Sandeman Street when he signed for Dundee United after only a year in Ayrshire and he holds the distinction of being the first United player to be the leading League scorer in the top division as well as scoring sixty-three times in his six years at Tannadice.

Cameron left United in 1974 to join Montrose whom he later managed but returned to Tannadice in 1981 and gave fifteen years service as first coach and then chief scout before leaving to take charge of Junior side Dundee St. Joseph's.

In 1997, St Joseph's' owners Peter and Jimmy Marr took over at Dens Park and one of their first acts was to bring their successful manager with them and appoint Cameron, who had been highly regarded as an S.F.A. staff coach at Largs as Head of Youth Development.

Kenny remained at Dens until the Club went in administration in November 2004 when he was the victim of the cost cutting guillotine and was among twenty-five Dundee employees who sadly lost their job.

Kenny's son Dougie also spent three years at Dundee between 2002 until 2005 but it was his Dad's strike in the Scottish Cup Final forty years before that Kenny would be forever remembered for at Dens Park and considering the enormity of the occasion and the special nature of the goal, it is without doubt one of the greatest goals ever scored by Dundee F.C., if not the greatest.

Honours at Dundee:
Scottish Cup runner-up: 1964
Appearances, Goals:
League   75 + 4 subs, 48 goals
Scottish Cup: 11, 8 goals
League Cup: 15 + 1 sub, 9 goals
Europe: 1
Other: 11, 6 goals
Totals: 118, 71 goals

Andy Campbell

Once in a generation Dundee fans are fortunate to witness that elusive achievement that catapults a player to legendary status and ensures his name will forever echo through the ages when they score a hat-trick against the enemy from across the road. It doesn't happen very often and if you have witnessed the feat, consider yourself lucky. If you have witnessed twice consider yourself blessed and if you witnessed the first time it happened you must be a right 'old foggie', having been fortunate enough to see Andy Campbell do it in 1926.

Already a prolific scorer by the time he scored his hat-trick against Dundee United at Dens on August 28th 1926, Campbell became not just the first player to score a hat-trick for The Dee in a derby but the first player to do it from any side. Andy however actually went one better by scoring four in the 5-0 win which is a feat never equalled by a Dundee player in either league or cup against The Arabs.

Campbell's derby heroics came in only the third league match between the city clubs as United had only gained promotion to Division One for the first time in April 1925. Founded in 1909 as Dundee Hibernian to cater for the city's catholic Irish population, Hibs had languished in the second tier for its first sixteen years and by the time they won promotion, they had changed their name to Dundee United in 1923 in an effort to gain wider appeal.

Dundee had taken three out of four points off the newly promoted side in 1925/26 then at the start of United's second season, Dundee put their neighbours firmly in their place with the 5-0 win in front of a terrific crowd of 20,000. Campbell's four was added to by a strike from Jim Meagher and that 5-0 win remains Dundee's highest winning margin against the Tannadice men who were relegated in bottom place at the end of that season.

There was so much more to Campbell's dark blue career than his derby double brace as in his eight years at Dens he scored 107 goals in 199 appearances, making him eighth in Dundee's all time leading goal scorer list. He finished top scorer on four separate occasions and is one of only ten players to have scored over 100 goals for the Club.

Campbell's debut for The Dee was an inauspicious start as it came in a 5-0 defeat to Cowdenbeath at Central Park on September 19th 1925. Andy was brought into the side to replace record breaking striker Davie Halliday who left to play for Sunderland in the aftermath of the Scottish Cup Final against Celtic in April and he scored his first goal for the Club the following week on his home debut in a 3-1 win over Clydebank.

By the end of the season he was starting the fill the big boots left by Halliday by finishing as Dundee's top scorer with eleven goals but then more than matched them in his second season, when Andy notched thirty-five goals in just thirty-six appearances.

Campbell's first hat-trick for The Dee was that four against United at the start of his second season and he would complete a further three hat-tricks before the end of the campaign against Hibernian, Morton and Motherwell, all at Dens.

Campbell, with his slicked-back hair was a big, bustling centre forward but injury saw him in and out of the team for the next couple of seasons. When he got back into the side on a regular basis in the 1929/30 season, Andy once again finished as top goal scorer with twenty goals and his return to form coincided with Dundee United's return to the top flight. Dundee beat United in both matches that season and Andy was again a thorn in the Terror's side when he scored the only goal of the game in a derby at Tannadice in January to help United go straight back down to Division Two.

A fourth season as top scorer for Dundee came in season 1930/31 and in the first round of the Scottish Cup, Andy was on the score sheet as Dundee notched up their record victory to that point with a 10-1 win over Fraserburgh from the Highland League.

Andy was an ever present the following year, playing in all thirty-nine league and cup games but made only nine appearances the season after and the writing was on the wall for Campbell when in May 1933, manager Jimmy Bissett resigned and was replaced by ex-Rangers Billy McCandless who decided to overhaul the squad.

Andy was therefore released that summer and in a typical football quirk of fate joined the side he had tormented in the past when he made the shortest walk in the game to join Dundee United on a free transfer.

Andy Campbell set the stall for Dark Blue derby heroics in a game which means so much to Dundee fans everywhere, in a fixture which all Dees look for first when the list comes out in June. His hat-trick heroics have been matched by only a few and it would be thirty years before another Dundee player would score a derby treble when Jimmy Chalmers achieved this in a 7-3 League Cup win in 1956 inspiring the famous Johnny Scobie song to boot.

Only Keith Wright and Juan Sara have followed since but with only three goals each in their moments of glory, Campbell stands out as unique with his four, for which most fans can only dream that they'll ever see its like again.

Appearances, Goals:
League: 178, 90 goals
Scottish Cup: 21, 17 goals
Totals: 199, 107 goals

Claudio Caniggia

Ask any Dundee fan and they will be able to tell you exactly where they were on October 3rd 2000 when the news broke that Argentinean World Cup legend Claudio Caniggia had signed for the Dark Blues.

The arrival of 'El Pajaro' (The Bird) in the City of Discovery stunned the footballing world and for Dundee it mirrored the signing of Billy Steel fifty years before as they both brought immediate mass media attention, both came with controversial reputations but were both quickly taken to the hearts of the Dark Blue support after they both showed their undoubted ability on their respective debuts against Aberdeen.

Claudio Paul Caniggia was born on January 9th 1967 in the Buenos Aires suburb of Henderson and in a club career that flitted between his native Argentina, Portugal and Italy, it was at international level were he made his name scoring in both the 1990 and 1994 World Cups where he partnered his friend Diego Maradona up front.

At the start of 2000, Caniggia was named as the 83rd best player in the history of the game in a F.I.F.A. millennium poll but his career was in decline. He hadn't played football for months as he was in dispute with his current club Atalanta and so the offer to join Dundee came at exactly the right time not just for Caniggia but also for Dundee.

At the start of the 2000/01 season, Dundee were under new management with Italian brothers Ivano and Dario Bonetti and they had brought in a number of exciting players from overseas who started to give Dundee fans the best football they had arguably seen in forty years.

Having worked with Caniggia before in Italy, the Bonettis approached him to join Dundee after they lost striker Fabian Caballero to a long term injury and incredibly, the fifty times capped Argentinean, who could cover a hundred metres in 11.2 seconds said 'yes'.

For days, Tayside buzzed with rumour and anticipation and finally on Tuesday 3rd October player manager Ivano Bonetti breezed into a packed Dens Park press room and announced, *'I have dreamed of bringing Claudio to this club and today it has come true. When Caniggia plays, everyone wants to watch for he is one of the biggest names in world football. He has come to help his friends and he hopes to play his way into Argentina's team for the 2002 World Cup.'*

The cynics scoffed at the suggestion that a move to Dundee could lead to Caniggia's recall to the Argentine national squad and suggested he was just there to pick up a hefty pay cheque, but 'El Pajaro' was immediately to dispel these thoughts, with a debut that was pure theatre.

The date of this momentous occasion was October 14th 2000; the venue Pittodrie Stadium, Aberdeen and the Dark Blue faithful quickly snapped up their all ticket allocation to turn up en mass in long, blond wigs in deference to their new idol.

Somewhat sort of match practice, Caniggia started on the bench but from the moment he took to the field to near hysteria there was no doubt that he was still the real deal.

Dundee were already ahead through a sublime chip from Bonetti (*'The best goal that no one will ever remember'*, said Bonetti post match) but Gavin Rae had been sent off to reduce The Dee to ten men by the time 'The Bird' came on.

Caniggia was globally recognized as one of the fastest footballers in the world, thus, he was also had the nickname of 'el hijo del viento' meaning 'the son of wind' and his pace was causing The Dons defence all sorts of problems before Aberdeen themselves were reduced to ten men when Phil McGuire scythed down the winger.

Then with only seconds left, Cannigia set the seal on a memorable afternoon when he raced

on a perfectly weighted Nemsadze pass and slid the ball inside the far post to send the Dark Blues into rapture and cement a win that lives long in the memory.

The following week on his home debut against Motherwell, the attendance was up over three thousand on the corresponding fixture the previous year and they were treated to a beautiful lobbed goal from outside the box in front of the B.B.C. Sportscene cameras.

Caniggia had chosen number 33 for his squad number to correspond with his age and in the weeks and months that followed, it was unusual to see a replica top with anything other than 'Caniggia 33' on the back.

Nicknamed, 'The Tayzurri' by the press, the team revelled in the Argentinean's presence and the darting runs of a man who still had phenomenal acceleration over short distances, lit up a season when entertainment seemed almost more important than results.

There was however some great results as Dundee squeezed into a top six finish in the first S.P.L. split after another 2-0 win against Aberdeen much to the delight of players and fans alike who displayed more Pittodrie hysteria.

On Remembrance Day in November, the players gave the fans a result to remember when they defeated Dundee United on their own patch at Tannadice and the first goal in a 2-0 win was scored by none other than Claudio Caniggia. It was the result that Dees everywhere had dreamed of, as their superstar scored a goal in a derby against their rivals and he would repeat that feat again in January in the return fixture at Dens.

The 'Caniggia season' also saw Dundee defeat both Rangers and Celtic away in Glasgow and they are to date the last team to achieve that feat. The 2-0 win at Parkhead over league champions Celtic in the penultimate game in May had been preceded by a win of a similar scoreline at Ibrox in March and that 2-0 win over Rangers probably did as much as anything to cement Caniggia's move to Govan. Caniggia turned in a virtuoso man of the match performance and scored the first goal in a performance described in *The Daily Mail* as: *'A Caniggia – inspired performance of verve and dynamism.'*

Initially signed on a six months deal, he penned a new three year contract in January 2001 but in hindsight it was obvious that he was unlikely to be at Dens for any length of time, although the signing of a new deal meant Dundee would get a substantial fee. That fee was to be in the region of £850,000 from Rangers and his dream of making the 2002 World Cup Argentina squad became a reality.

Caniggia's career had been revived and he caught the imagination of the footballing public and was nominated for the P.F.A. Players' Player of the Year Award which eventually went to Celtic's 53-goal Henrik Larsson. Of some consolation however, he won the Dundee Supporters Association Player of the Year trophy at the annual dinner at the Hilton Hotel in Dundee and in 2009 was inducted into the inaugural Dundee F.C. Hall of Fame, receiving the International Award.

In his short time on Tayside, he lit up every match he played and was popular amongst players and fans alike and on the evening of that famous win at Tannadice he was seen celebrating with fans and pulling pints behind the bar of a local pub just off the city's Hilltown.

From Henderson to the 'Hulltoon'; the life of a Dundee legend!

Honours at Dundee:
D.S.A. Player of the Year: 2001 winner
S.P.F.A. Player of the Year: 2001 nominee
Dundee F.C. Hall of Fame: 2009
International Award
Appearances, Goals:
League: 20 + 1 sub, 7 goals
Scottish Cup: 4, 1 goal
Totals: 25, 8 goals

Gordon Chisholm

Gordon Chisholm's five year playing career at Dens Park saw him become only the second captain in the Club's history to win two trophies with The Dee. After Alfie Boyd skippered Dundee to back to back League Cup wins in the early fifties, Gordon Chisholm became the only other captain to lead Dundee to two trophies wins when he had the honour of lifting the Scottish League Centenary Cup in November 1990 and then the Scottish League First Division trophy the following season in 1992.

Gordon Chisholm was born in Glasgow on April 8th 1960 and started his professional career with Sunderland where he made 235 appearances in seven years. In his final year with The Black Cats, Chisholm played in the League Cup Final against Norwich City at Wembley in March 1985 but unfortunately for Gordon, he deflected Asa Hartford's shot into the net to give The Canaries a 1-0 win.

Chisholm moved back to Scotland later that year, when he joined Hibernian for a £60,000 fee and he scored a goal on his Hibs debut in a Scottish League Cup semi-final win against Rangers. This meant that Chisholm achieved the unusual feat of playing in League Cup Finals in the same calendar year in both England and Scotland but unfortunately for Gordon, both finals were lost, as the Easter Road side went down 3–0 to Aberdeen.

In September 1987, Dundee captain Jim Duffy looked to have ended his playing career when he suffered cartilage and severe cruciate ligament damage and manager Jocky Scott turned to Hibs skipper Gordon Chisholm to replace the influential defender. The twenty-seven year old Chisholm was on freedom-of-contract and the clubs later agreed a fee of £72,500 which was party offset by The Dee with the sale of Ross Jack to Dunfermline for £15,000 and Derek McWilliams to Falkirk for £5,000.

Chisholm made his debut for The Dee on September 26th in a 2-0 away win at Motherwell and his introduction helped tighten a defence which had shipped eleven goals in the previous four games. By December, Dundee lay fifth with only three defeats in seventeen games since his arrival while at the other end of the park, the goals were flowing with back to back high scoring away wins against Falkirk (6-0) and Morton (7-1).

This run included a 3-1 win over Dundee United at Tannadice which gave Chisholm his first victory over The Arabs and he would feature in a further two derby wins and two draws, in one of which he scored, in a 1-1 draw at Dens on December 30th 1989.

Midway through his debut season however, Chisholm damaged a disc in his back, causing him to miss the rest of the season and could only watch in anguish as Dundee lost a Scottish Cup quarter-final to United and throw away a seven point lead over their neighbours to see them clinch the final European spot.

Chisholm was back in time for the start of the 1988/89 season and he started the season in goal scoring form with his first strike for Dundee in the opening game against Aberdeen at Dens which finished 1-1. Chisholm's goal scoring record for Dundee was very respectable for a centre-half and in total he scored sixteen goals in his 175 appearances.

Despite the composure he brought to the Dundee defence, The Dee were relegated in Chisholm's third season which had seen him pair up at the back with Jim Duffy, who had made a remarkable recovery from his injury. This formidable centre-half pairing played together for seven of the last eight games where Dundee lost just twice, but it wasn't enough to save Dundee from plummeting into the First Division.

Relegation into the second tier saw Dundee entered in a new cup competition for teams outside the Premier Division to celebrate the Scottish League centenary and Chisholm would play in three of the four ties on the way to winning the trophy. After receiving a bye in the first round, Chisholm missed the second round 5-3 win at Alloa but played from the quarter-final onwards.

Known as the B&Q Centenary Cup, Chisholm lead Dundee out for the Final against Ayr United at Fir Park in November and after a 3-2 extra-time win had the honour of lifting the one

off glassware trophy which resides in the Dens Park trophy cabinet today.

Installed as favourites to bounce straight back up, Dundee could only finish third but the following season, Chisholm captained Dundee to the First Division title which they won by a point from Partick Thistle. Chisholm scored five goals in thirty-seven appearances on the road to promotion and on the last day of the season, lifted his second piece of silverware as Dundee captain when he was presented with the First Division trophy.

Midway through the title winning year, Dundee replaced manager Iain Munro with Simon Stainrod and in pre season, Chisholm looked well-placed for the vacant post of assistant manager. However the job went to Jim Duffy who was enticed back from Partick Thistle and Chisholm instead went in the opposite direction where he was soon appointed to the coaching staff.

Chisholm hung up his boots after his first year at Firhill and embarked on a coaching career that would also take him to Clydebank, Ross County, Airdrie, Falkirk and Dundee United before he took on the top job at Tannadice in March 2005 following the sacking of Ian McCall.

After leaving United, Chisholm again joined up with Ian McCall, this time at Queen of the South and when McCall left to join Partick in the summer of 2007, Chisholm was appointed as manager at Palmerston.

He led The Doonhamers to the 2008 Scottish Cup Final and into Europe for the first time in

Queens' history but in March 2010, he returned to Dens Park to take over from Jocky Scott who was sacked while top of the league. In doing so he became the first man to have managed both city clubs and he brought with him Billy Dodds as his assistant manager, with whom he had played with at Dens in those Centenary Cup and First Division triumphs.

While promotion wasn't achieved in the last nine games, Chisholm will be hoping that it will be second time lucky once again as he looks to once again lead Dundee to the First Division title. In doing so he will pick up the third winners' medal of his Dundee career and will emulate Alfie Boyd who also won a hat-trick of medals with The Dee.

Honours at Dundee:
Scottish League First Division winner: 1991/92
B&Q Scottish League Centenary Cup winner: 1990
Appearances, Goals:
League: 153+2subs, 15 goals
Scottish Cup: 9
League Cup: 6 + 1 sub, 1 goal
S.F.L. Challenge Cup: 4
Totals: 175, 16 goals

Managerial Record with Dundee (2009-10 season)
	P	W	D	L	F	A	Pts
League:	9	3	3	3	11	7	12

Archie Coats

When the world was in the Great Depression of the 'Dirty Thirties', Dundee F.C. weren't much different as they were fighting much of it at the wrong end of the table, were repeatedly knocked out the Scottish Cup in the early rounds, were eventually relegated for the first time in their history in 1938 and failed to get promotion back to the top tier before football was suspended for the Second World War.

Amongst all this doom and gloom however was a player would repeatedly bang in the goals for The Dee and would eventually become the second highest scorer in the Club's history just eleven goals behind Alan Gilzean. He would score more league goals than the legendary Gillie and would finish top goal scorer on four occasions and with a goal average of one strike in every 1.48 games, his name was Archibald Coats.

Coats started his career at Wishaw Juniors before securing a lucrative move to Portsmouth but after a disappointing spell on the English south coast, he moved across the Irish Sea to Bangor and quickly became a prolific scorer in the Irish League.

In the summer of 1934, Dundee manager Billy McCandless was on the lookout for a replacement for departing striker Johnny Murdoch and when he raided his Northern Ireland homeland to bring Archie to Dens for a fee of £500, it would soon prove to be one of the bargains of the century.

The chunky twenty-three year old forward settled quickly and made his debut at home to Albion Rovers on August 11th 1934 where he immediately endeared himself to the Dens Park faithful with a brace in a 3-2 win.

By the end of the season, Archie was the only player to have played in all 39 competitive games and finished the season with thirty goals, all in the league. The following season he would be again an ever present and bettered his goal tally with thirty-one in all competitions and made it a hat-trick of seasons without missing a game in 1936/37 when he was again top scorer for the third year with twenty-seven goals in forty-two matches.

This remarkable scoring record could hardly go unnoticed by the international selectors and on September 1st 1937, Archie won a Scottish League cap against the Irish League in Belfast where the Scots won 3-2.

No more international honours were forthcoming however and perhaps that was more to do with Dundee's league position than to Archie's goal scoring ability as The Dees had finished eight, twelve and ninth since he had arrived.

Worse was to follow however the following year, when in 1937/38 Dundee were relegated for the first time in their history as they finished second bottom ahead of Morton and with thirty-two points, they were just a point behind six clubs immediately above them.

The 5ft 7in striker scored fourteen goals as The Dee went down but again Archie was an ever present and remarkably failed to miss a Dundee game for six seasons on the trot until the Club went into abeyance for the War.

The following year would therefore be spent in the Second Division and despite being firm favourites to bounce straight back to the top tier, Dundee finished a disappointing sixth with Archie netting another impressive tally of twenty-six. Dundee had scored ninety-nine goals but had conceded sixty-three and if the defence could be sorted, hopes were high that promotion could be achieved at the second time of asking.

Adolf Hitler however put paid to that when he invaded Poland and Britain responded with a declaration of war and when the Scottish League suspended its programme on September 3rd 1939 Dundee were top of the Second Division unbeaten, with Archie scoring four in the first four matches.

When Hitler signed a non-aggression pact with the Soviets on August 21st, Dundee had defeated Airdrie 4-2 at Broomfield in which Archie scored a double but the impending outlook of war restricted the attendance to just 2,000.

Dundee did give their fans something to cheer on August 30th when they defeated Dundee United 6-1 in the Forfarshire Cup First Round with Archie scoring twice but by the time of the next league match in Greenock, the 1-1 draw paled into insignificance as German troops had swarmed across the Polish border and unleashed the first Blitzkrieg the world had seen just twenty-fours hours before.

The Scottish League quickly reformed itself into regional competitions as it was thought that the continuance of football would help morale and Dundee entered the Eastern Division. Archie would score twenty-six goals in twenty-eight games to give him another thirty goal season in which he was top scorer but with so many players being called up or volunteering for military service, Dundee decided to close down for the duration of the War.

In their last game on May 18th 1940, Dundee won 4-2 at home against Falkirk in front of just 3,000 fans and that match saw Archie score his last goals for the Club when he netted a brace.

At the end of the War, Archie returned to Dens for the 1945/46 season after being demobbed in the autumn of 1945 but time had taken its toll on the thirty-four year old who would only make two more appearances. With new managing/director George Anderson looking to revolutionise the Club and with scorers of the calibre of Turnball and Juliussen now at Dens, Archie was allowed to leave at the end of the season after eleven years on the books and would later coach at Tannadice on a part-time basis under Jerry Kerr.

Archie Coats had managed to score 158 goals in 234 games for the Dark Blues, a Dens total unsurpassed until the sixties by Alan Gilzean, over whom he scored thirty-nine more goals in the league. Had it not been for the Second World War, there is every chance that Archie would have gone on to be Dundee's all-time top goal scorer and he rightly earns his place among the Dundee elite.

Honours at Dundee:	
Scottish League cap:	1
Appearances, Goals:	
League:	220, 152 goals
Scottish Cup:	12, 6 goals
Other:	2
Total:	234, 158 goals

Robert Connor

The early eighties were often a tough time to be a Dee with Dundee United dominating derbies and winning a few trophies but one man who went about trying to change that was classy midfielder Robert Connor, who would score the winning goal in a derby and go on to become Dundee's only full Scotland internationalist throughout the whole of the decade.

Born in Kilmarnock on August 4th 1960, Bobby would start his footballing career with Ayrshire neighbours Ayr United for whom made 223 league appearances and among his cup outings for The Honest Men, was the two-legged League Cup semi-final against Dundee in November 1980 in which The Dee progressed 4-3 on aggregate.

Four years after that semi, Robert found himself at Dens, when he was among a number of inspirational signings that new manager Archie Knox would bring to Dens. These included John Brown, John McCormack, Stuart Rafferty and later Jim Duffy and after seven years at Somerset Park, Robert signed for Dundee for a £50,000 fee and immediately brought skill and creativity to the Dark Blue midfield.

'Roger', as he was known to his friends made his debut for Dundee on the first day of the season at Pittodrie where The Dee lost out 3-2 to Alex Ferguson's Aberdeen and in the next few weeks the newcomers showed a lot of promise despite some disappointing results.

That promise however came to fruition in the best possible way on September 8th 1984, when The Dee went across the road to Tannadice and defeated their neighbours 4-3 in a never-to-be-forgotten derby. Dundee were ahead three times through McWilliams, McKinlay and Harris but when John Brown powered in a header with a quarter of an hour to go, there was no coming back for the Arab this time as The Dee held on for a famous win.

Despite scoring four goals, it wasn't the front men who were the revelation but the midfield of Rafferty, Brown and Connor who ran the show with Bobby often dictating the tempo.

Rab's first goal for the Club had come a fortnight earlier in a 3-0 League Cup win at Dens over Hamilton, while his first league goal came at home against Aberdeen in October but it was his ninth and final strike of the season which became his most celebrated, when it came as a solitary strike in a derby.

Dundee had failed to defeat United at home for almost six years but in front over 14,000 fans packed into Dens for the last match of the season, Dundee laid that hoodoo to rest when Bobby scored the only goal of the game after half an hour. It came after Stuart Rafferty had gone on a lung bursting fifty yard run out on the right and when he sent in a well-placed, low, hard cross into the box, Bobby was on hand to ram the ball home.

Dundee had been chasing a U.E.F.A. Cup spot going into the last game and when Bobby Geddes saved his fifth penalty of the season from an Eamon Bannon effort, the euphoria only subsided when it was heard that St.

Mirren had also been victorious to clinch that last European spot.

Dundee did have the consolation of the derby day win and a finish to a season which had seen Dundee defeat the Arabs twice in a campaign for the first time in a season since the inauguration of the Premier Division. For Bobby, his winner catapulted him instantly into Dens Park legend.

Hopes were high that the following season might see Dundee make that European breakthrough but while Dundee were pipped again on the last day, despite denying Hearts the Championship with Albert Kidd's two goals, Bobby did make a breakthrough of his own by getting called up to the full Scotland side in May 1986.

By then Alex Ferguson was in charge of Scotland for the build up to the World Cup in Mexico, running both the national side and his club team Aberdeen following the death of Jock Stein in the qualifier in Cardiff the previous September and he called Bobby up for a friendly against the Netherlands in Eindhoven.

Bobby started the match to become the first Dundee international since Bobby Robinson in 1975 and at the same time earn the first of his four caps for Scotland. It was however to be his only cap during his time at Dens and would turn out to be the only time a Dundee player would play for Scotland throughout the eighties.

Despite losing the match 1-0, Ferguson must have liked what he saw of Connor for although he didn't take him to the World Cup, he did sign him for the Dons in August, for a fee of £275,000 plus Ian Angus, who had been on the bench when Aberdeen won the European Cup Winners' Cup in Gothenburg, three years before.

At Pittodrie, Bobby would become part of the double cup winning side of 1989/90 which was co-managed by Jocky Scott who had been forced to watch Connor move north just two games into his Dens Park managerial career and he would also play against England at Hampden in the Rous Cup in 1989.

Connor returned to his native Ayrshire in 1994 to turn out first for his hometown team Kilmarnock and then Ayr United and he returned to Somerset Park for a third time in 2005, when he managed them for the next two years.

Since finishing his playing days, Bobby has also worked in the media, writing for *The Mirror* newspaper amongst others and in May 2010, he was warmly invited back to Dundee to take a seat at the legends table at the Player of the Year dinner. Connor was a popular guest who had a busy evening as he was bombarded with requests for photographs with the man who sunk the Arabs on a warm sunny afternoon almost twenty-five years to the day.

Honours at Dundee:	
Scotland full cap:	1
Appearances, Goals:	
League:	71, 9 goals
Scottish Cup:	9, 1 goal
League Cup:	4, 1 goal
Totals:	84, 11 goals

Charlie Cooke

For a club to lose a legend and find another one within weeks of their departure seems highly unlikely but Bob Shankly managed to do just that when he signed Charlie Cooke from Aberdeen for £40,000 in December 1964 within a fortnight of Alan Gilzean leaving for Spurs.

Of course comparisons between Gillie and Cooke were inevitable given their Dens Park paths almost crossed but their styles were poles apart. The signing of Cooke was a masterstroke by Shankly as the Dens Park hierarchy looked to appease the fans in the wake of Gillie's departure by splashing out with a Dens Park record fee and 'The Bonnie Prince' had the Dundee fans eating out of his hands in an instant with his magical concoction of ball skills and wizardry. The Dens Park choir were soon singing 'Charlie is my darling' as a new hero was born and despite his short tenure as in a dark blue shirt, the memories he left were indelible.

Born in St. Monans in the East Neuk of Fife on October 14th 1942, Cooke began his professional career at Aberdeen in 1960, having joined them from Renfrew Juniors and soon became the golden boy of Pittodrie where he would score twenty-six league goals in a four year career. Amongst those goals was a strike in a 2-2 draw against the newly crowned Champions of Scotland in the second game of Dundee's title defence and on their way to winning the league, Charlie had turned in a man of the match performance in a 3-1 win for The Dons in the Granite City.

Charlie's debut for The Dee couldn't have gone any better when he scored in a 4-0 win over Airdrie at Dens six days before Christmas and the papers were singing his praises with headlines such as *'Cooke turns on the Style for New Fans'* and *'Cheers for Charlie'*. In the Daily Record they reported, *'It took 175 days to bring the Alan Gilzean transfer saga to an end, yet in 90 minutes, Charlie Cooke erased the whole wearisome episode from the minds of the Dens Park fans'.*

Cooke himself didn't like the comparisons with Gilzean saying in his autobiography *'The Bonnie Prince', 'I thought it was all pretty stupid, comparing us. We were nothing like each other is style or skills. I was completely different in that all I wanted was the ball at my feet, opponents to beat and chances to create for my team mates and occasionally myself. I had more than respectable statistics from midfield then, but any attempts to make goal-scoring or stylistic comparisons between me and Gilly were just plain daft.'*

By the end of the season, the fans had all but forgotten about Gillie, with Charlie scoring seven goals in twenty-five games as an ever present since joining the Club.

Within that spell, Charlie turned on a virtuoso performance against the team who would become League Champions Kilmarnock as he scored a brace in a 4-1 win at Rugby Park and just a few weeks later dazzled the eventual runners-up up Hearts with his ball skills as The Dee won 7-1 at Tynecastle. Considering that Hearts lost the Championship on goal average, Dundee's 7-1 win would do the Edinburgh side some serious damage and Charlie had been in the middle of it.

It wasn't long before Charlie's performances were rewarded with an international call up and starred on his full international debut in a 4-1 win over Wales at Hampden in April 1965. Later that year, he got his second full cap in the ill fated World Cup decider against Italy in Naples where Jock Stein's side lost 3-0 and in the same year also turned out twice for the Scottish League against the English and Irish Leagues and for the Under-23 side against their English counterparts.

Charlie's second season at the Club saw Dundee record some indifferent results but while he switched between wing-half and forward, his own performances were regularly terrific and he was rewarded with the supporters Player of the Year trophy in April 1966.

~ 34 ~

Having commuted by train from Aberdeen in his first few months at the Club, Cooke had now settled in a new house in Broughty Ferry and his happiness in his new surroundings were quickly being relayed on the park.

'Dundee was a good time in my life', Charlie told author Jim Hendry in his *Dundee Greats* book. *'I felt awfully good about my soccer and I thought some of the best games I played were around that time and I liked the people around me – especially Bobby Cox and some of the people I got to know in Broughty Ferry'.*

There were times however when the mercurial Cooke could be anonymous too but on his day there were few better on show in Scottish Football. Fortunately for Dundee, 'his day' was displayed on regular occasion and season 1965/66 saw Charlie inspire Dundee to a 9-1 win over East Fife in the Scottish Cup, two victories over Dundee United and a win over eventual League Champions Celtic in a League Cup sectional tie.

Cooke revelled in the freedom new manager Bobby Ancell gave him in an attacking role having switched places in the team with Steve Murray and after a brilliant performance at Dens against Stirling Albion, where Charlie scored twice in a 6-2 win, Chelsea manager Tommy Docherty announced his interest. Shortly afterwards, Charlie handed in a transfer request and on April 26th, just twenty-four hours after receiving the Player of the Year trophy, Charlie signed for Chelsea in a £72,500 fee.

Charlie had signed for Dundee for a record fee between two Scottish clubs and then left for a fee which equalled the Club record received for Alan Gilzean but the Dundee fans were furious once again to have lost another star man to a London side, whatever the fee. There was a storm of protest over his sale as unlike Ian Ure and Alan Gilzean, Cooke had still been under contract but the directors claimed that they wanted to avoid another protracted transfer saga.

Charlie's time at Stamford Bridge saw him win another fourteen Scotland caps, lift the F.A. Cup in 1970 and the U.E.F.A. Cup Winners' Cup twelve months later and at Dens he still remains a hero where a supporters' club is named in his honour and where a hospitality lounge bears his name after former Chief Executive Peter Marr, named it after his own personal favourite player.

Like Claudio Caniggia almost forty years later, Cooke's time at Dens was short, lasting a mere sixteen months but like the Argentinean superstar, Dundee's original 'CC' left a lasting impression with some wonderful performances.

Charlie states in his biography how proud he was to receive the Player of the Year trophy in 1965 and almost forty years to the day, he was welcomed back to the Dundee Supporters Association Player of the Year Dinner in the City's Apex Hotel in 2005. Charlie returned from his home in America where he now runs a soccer coaching school, to sit at the legends table and for those in attendance who had been lucky enough to see him show off his silky skills, there was a long queue for autographs and photographs with the man who had once graced the Dark Blue jersey.

In August 2010, at the first day of the league season against Queen of the South, Charlie once again returned to Dens Park as a surprise guest for match sponsor Willie Reilly and the following day held a question and answer session in a packed hospitality lounge at the ground where he once again held his adoring Dark Blue public in the palm of his hand.

Honours at Dundee:	
Scotland full caps:	2
Scottish League caps:	2
Scotland Under-23 caps:	1
Appearances, Goals:	
League:	44, 11 goals
Scottish Cup:	3
League Cup:	6
Other:	6
Totals:	59, 11 goals

Alan Cousin

Alan Cousin was a vital cog not just in the side which brought the Scottish League Championship to Dens Park in 1962 but throughout his eleven years at the Club, finishing as top goal scorer on three occasions.

Sporting mainly the number nine shirt, the lanky striker proved the perfect foil for fellow front man Alan Gilzean and between them proved to be a very effective partnership that shot Dundee not only to the league title but also to the European Cup semis and Scottish Cup Final in the subsequent years.

Born at the start of the Second World War in Clackmannanshire, Alan's first choice sport was rugby and it wasn't until the age of sixteen that his football career began in earnest when he helped out Alloa Y.M.C.A. as a centre-forward when they were short of players. Having played rugby for the school in the morning, he managed to impress with the round ball in the afternoon scoring twice and within a year was in the Scottish Youth side which defeated England 8-1 at Ayr.

Senior scouts were soon alerted to this fast emerging talent and Dundee manager Willie Thornton persuaded him to sign for the Dark Blues at the age of sixteen in 1955 and so by the time of Dundee's Championship triumph, he was Dundee's longest serving player.

Less than a year had passed before Alan made his debut to replace the injured George Merchant on March 3rd 1956 in a 3-1 defeat at Falkirk and his first goal for the Club came a month later at Dens, in a friendly against newly crowned English Champions Manchester United. In a match in which Bobby Charlton made his debut for the Red Devils, Dundee trounced the Busby Babes 5-1 and by the end of the season, Alan had made half a dozen appearances, scoring once more against Motherwell at Fir Park.

Alan was delighted to get a chance in the side that included big names like Doug Cowie and Bill Brown but he chose to combine his early senior career with a St. Andrews' University degree course which was to stand him in good stead in the years ahead. There he studied Greek and Latin for an Arts degree and became a secondary school teacher in his home town of Alloa after completing a teacher training degree in Dundee and continued to do so after retiring from the game.

Throughout his playing career, Alan astonishingly in modern day terms, remained part-time and while at University, trained on his own with a regime prepared by Dundee trainer Archie McAuley on the St. Andrews beach that was later made famous in the introduction to the film *Chariots of Fire*.

When Alan graduated to the classroom, he trained three nights a week with Falkirk but there was no fear that all his brains were in his head for during his time at Dens, he gained international caps for the Scottish League and at Under-23 and youth level.

Alan was soon knocking the goals in on a regular basis and he became Dundee's top goal scorer three years in a row from 1958 to 1960. He became known as 'the king of the double shuffle' with a unique scissors movement which seemed to propel him away from opponents in an instant and he regularly mesmerised teams at both home and abroad.

By the end of the 1959/60 season Bob Shankly was now in charge at Dens and Cousin was playing up front with Alan Gilzean and the good times were just around the corner.

By the start of 1961/62 Shankly had brought in the experience of Bobby Wishart, Bobby Seith and Gordon Smith to compliment the talented youngsters and history now shows that Dundee really clicked into gear. With a brand of football arguably among the best since the War, Dundee surged to the Scottish League Championship and Alan more than played his part, playing in all forty-one competitive games, scoring nineteen goals.

And so it was to Europe for the first time and footballing giants Cologne, Sporting Lisbon, Anderlecht and A.C. Milan all came and were conquered at Dens and only a 5-1 reverse in the semi-final in Italy stopped Dundee reaching the European Cup Final at Wembley. It was so near and yet so far for The Dark Blues for at half time in Milan, Dundee went in level after Alan had headed in an Andy Penman cross to make it 1-1. In doing so Alan became the first British player to score in the San Siro, a feat that was not matched until Paul Scholes scored against Internazionale for Manchester United in 1999.

On these European trips Shankly would rely not only on Cousin's skill on the park but also his skill off it and would employ Alan as interpreter when travelling abroad to get him to tell their hosts *'what we're wantin' for oor tea'*.

But it was his skill on the pitch which was most valuable to Shankly and in the quarter-final against Real Madrid's conquerors Anderlecht, Alan scored in both legs with a goal in the remarkable 4-1 away win in Brussels and the equalising goal at Dens in which Dundee won 2-1. He played in all eight ties on the way to the semi, scoring four times with his other strike coming in a 4-1 second leg win over Sporting Lisbon at Dens.

Season 1963/64 saw Dundee reach the Scottish Cup Final only to lose 3-1 to Rangers. Picking up a runners-up medal in the last of his fifty-three first team appearances that season took Alan's tally to 142 outings in three seasons – enough to make the modern day player cry 'fatigue'. It is all the more remarkable that he played these games as a part time player and he played in all seven matches on the road to Hampden, scoring four times.

By then, Dundee's greatest side had begun to break up and as a result of the changes to the side, Alan started to play in a deeper role at wing-half wearing the number four shirt before following Bob Shankly to Hibernian for a fee of £15,000 in November 1965.

In over a decade at Dens, Alan played a whopping 384 games for the Club, putting him comfortably in the top ten of most appearances for The Dee and he sits fourth in Dundee's all time scorer list with a terrific 141 goals.

One of the gentlemen of the game, Cousin was never booked in his career despite being the victim of some horrendous treatment both at home and on the continent as defenders tried, often unsuccessfully to stop the long striding forward.

Truly Dundee's 'Renaissance Man', Alan still retains his affection for the Club with a picture of the Championship side sitting proudly on his mantelpiece and the next time you see Ronaldo & Co. trying a step over or two, remember that it was the scholar at Dens who was the original 'king of the double shuffle'.

Honours at Dundee:	
Scottish League Champions:	1961/62
European Cup semi-final:	1962/63
Scottish Cup runner-up:	1964
Scottish League appearances:	4
Scotland Under-23 caps:	3
Appearances, Goals:	
League:	288, 103 goals
Scottish Cup:	21, 9 goals
League Cup:	53, 23 goals
Europe:	10, 4 goals
Other:	12, 2 goals
Totals:	384, 141 goals

Jack Cowan

Jack Cowan was a Canadian left back who played for Dundee F.C. from 1949 until 1954 and was a member of George Anderson's successful trophy winning Dees in the early fifties.

Born in Vancouver on June 6th 1927, Cowan became the first Canadian to play professional soccer in Europe when he signed for Dundee from the University of British Columbia in 1949. He also became the first Canadian to win a major football honour when he was part of the Dundee side which lifted the League Cup in 1951.

Cowan entered U.B.C. in Vancouver in 1945 to study electrical engineering and as well as playing for the University soccer team, he also played for Pacific Coast League team Vancouver City between school terms.

At U.B.C., he was awarded with five Big Block Awards for excellence in varsity sports and in his first spell with Vancouver City, he was awarded with the prestigious Rookie of the Year Award.

Upon finishing his degree, Cowan decided that there might be an opportunity to make a career out of playing soccer and to do so, he realised he would have to move to Europe to have a chance.

His opportunity came in 1949, when he was selected to play for the British Columbia All Star Team who were to travel to England to play two exhibition matches against Newcastle United and it was in these matches that he was spotted by ex-Dunfermline manager and ex-referee Bobby Calder, who was a friend of fellow Aberdonian, George Anderson. Calder recommended Cowan to Dundee manager Anderson who then moved to bring him to Dens and he would turn out to be one of Anderson's most astute signings, making 149 appearances in the next five years.

Cowan joined Dundee at a time when things were just starting to tick and his team mates during his spell included such legendary figures as Alfie Boyd, Doug Cowie, Tommy Gallagher, 'Pud' Hill, Bobby Flavell and Billy Steel.

Cowan made his Dark Blue debut in the first league match of the 1949/50 season away to Stirling Albion in a 2-2 draw and it was against 'The Beanos' that Cowan scored his only goal for Dundee in a 4-1 home win on December 22nd 1951 in front of 17,000 fans.

His home debut came the following week against Queen of the South and in both matches he would wear the number three shirt that he wore in every single match he played for Dundee.

At the end his first season, Cowan picked up his first winner's medal when Dundee beat Brechin City 3-2 in the Final of the Forfarshire Cup but his greatest moment in a Dark Blue shirt came in an altogether bigger final eighteen months later.

On October 27th 1951, Dundee lined up to face Rangers in the final of the Scottish League Cup in front of 92,000 supporters and in a classic encounter, Dundee edged out the Light Blues 3-2 with a last minute winner from skipper Alfie Boyd.

It was Dundee's first trophy in forty-one years and for Jack Cowan the first professional medal won by a Canadian player and both Cowan and Dundee very nearly made it two six months later in the Scottish Cup.

In April 1952, Cowan lined up for Dundee against Motherwell at Hampden in front an astonishing crowd of 136, 990, a record crowd for a match not involving either of the Old Firm but although Dundee were the favourites, it wasn't to be as Motherwell scored four second half goals without reply to take the Scottish Cup back to Lanarkshire.

Before that Final however, Cowan was named as the North American Football Confederation (N.A.F.C.) Player of the Year for 1951 after his terrific displays for Dundee and his League Cup winning achievement. In 1961, the N.A.F.C merged with the Football Confederation of Central America and the Caribbean (C.C.C.F.) to form the Confederation of North, Central America and Caribbean Association Football (C.O.N.C.A.C.A.F.) and become the modern day governing body for football in the region. Cowan is now listed therefore as the C.O.N.C.A.C.A.F. Player of the Year for 1951 as the winners from both federations were absorbed into the list for the new Association. It was a tremendous accolade for Jack who became the first Dundee player to be awarded with any player of the year award outside of the Club.

There was to be more final disappointment for Cowan however in October 1952 when he was unfit to play to in Dundee's third appointment at the National Stadium within twelve months, when they successfully defended their League Cup trophy against B Division Kilmarnock.

Cowan had played in all nine matches on the road to Hampden and so was bitterly disappointed to get injured the week before the Final in a league match against Hearts at Dens. He was replaced in the side by South African Gordon Frew but there was some consolation for Jack as he watched his side retain the trophy with a 2-0 win.

Whilst at Dens, Cowan was selected to play for both the Scottish International team and the Irish International team but he was unable to qualify because he was not of direct Scottish or Irish descent.

In his final season at Dens, Cowan made the decision to return to his native Canada but The Dee were unwilling to let one of their stalwarts go and made him a very good offer to stay. When he turned down the offer, Dundee tried to prevent him from continuing his football career, but an appeal to F.I.F.A. allowed him to sign for Vancouver Halecos and return 'home' with his Dundonian wife.

In his first season back at the Halecos (they had changed their name from Vancouver City who Jack had played for before joining Dundee), he captained them to the 1955 Dominion Soccer Championships and would go on to represent the Canadian national side.

He also played many games for the British Columbian All Stars and played for a Canadian All Star team against Lokomotive Moscow in Toronto in 1956 but when selected to play for Canada away to Mexico in a World Cup qualifier later that year, he turned down the invitation and decided to retire from football at the age of twenty-nine to concentrate on his engineering career.

In 1974, Cowan was inducted into the British Columbia Sports Hall of Fame and in May 2000 he was honoured to be one of the first inductees in the Canadian Soccer Hall of Fame and was listed in their Canadian Team of the Century. It is surely only a matter of time before a similar honour is bestowed upon him at Dens and he is inducted into the Dundee Hall of Fame.

Honours at Dundee:	
Scottish League Cup winner:	1951/52
Scottish Cup runner-up:	1952
C.O.N.C.A.C.A.F. Player of the Year:	1951
Appearances, Goals:	
League:	115, 1 goal
Scottish Cup:	13
League Cup:	21
Totals:	149, 1 goal

Doug Cowie

There are those who would argue that Doug Cowie is the greatest Dee of all time and they certainly have a case. Cowie is the player with the most appearances in a Dundee shirt, is the only Dundee player to have played in two World Cups, won two League Cup winners' medals, played in front of almost 140,000 for Dundee at Hampden in the Scottish Cup Final, was runner-up in the League Championship, won twenty full caps for Scotland, five League caps and one B international cap and is the Club's longest serving player in which his sixteen seasons in Dark Blue were to prove to be among the most successful periods in the Club's history, playing alongside some of the greatest names Dundee has ever witnessed.

Cowie arrived at Dens in 1945 when the men of Dundee were returning from war with a craving for some return to normality centred on sport and the masses were returning to Dens Park in search of inspiration and solace to ease their hurt. Perhaps a form of escapism, they found new Dundee manager George Anderson was in the process of building a great team and he looked towards an apprentice riveter working in the John Lewis shipyard in Aberdeen to be one of his heroes.

Cowie was within hours of signing for his local side Aberdeen but the bowler-hatted Anderson was prepared to get his man and after a quick discussion with Doug's father who was working across the road, the young centre-half signed for Dundee from his junior club Aberdeen St. Clements.

Doug played 446 competitive games for Dundee, a club record but incredibly it could have been so much more. At the age of nineteen, he made his competitive debut on 23rd February 1946 in Dundee's first ever League Cup match in a 2-0 defeat at Stirling Albion but it was his only appearance of the season.

In the following year Doug played just three times despite featuring prominently in a pre season tour of West Germany, Austria and Italy and one wonders just how many appearances he could have chalked up!

The highlight of his career came when Dundee won back to back League Cups against Rangers in 1951 and Kilmarnock in 1952 but he missed out on a treble when Dundee lost the 1952 Scottish Cup Final which was sandwiched between the League Cup triumphs. Favourites Dundee lost 4-0 to Motherwell in front of an amazing crowd of 136 990 at the national stadium which is a record crowd for a Hampden final which did not feature either of the Old Firm but was a huge disappointment to all in Dark Blue who had not won the trophy for forty-two years.

That cup final disappointment was perhaps even greater than the last day disappointment of 1948/49 when Doug was part of the side that travelled to Brockville knowing a win would give them a first League title but a nervy Dundee capitulated 4-1 to Falkirk after missing a penalty at 0-0 leaving them one point behind Rangers in second place.

He started his career at centre-half but always preferred to play left-half and became part of the famous half-back line of Tommy Gallagher, Doug Cowie and Alfie Boyd. Playing in either position made no difference to Doug as his skill and elegance were always on show and many Dundee players of the forties and fifties often quoted Doug as the best player they played alongside.

Amongst those was the mercurial Billy Steel who signed for Dundee in September 1950 and who was known for putting his team mates on the sharp end of his tongue but for Cowie he reserved his greatest complement by stating that the Aberdonian could *'play a wee bit.'*

In 1953 Doug made his international debut alongside Steel against England at Wembley and the 2-2 draw was the first of twenty caps which make him the second most capped player in the Club's history.

In 1954 Doug became the first Dundee player to play at a World Cup when he played in two games in the Swiss finals against Austria (0-1) and Uruguay (0-7) and four years later in Sweden played in another two matches against Yugoslavia (1-1) and Paraguay (2-3) which turned out to be his last game for Scotland.

Cowie played under three managers at Dens, namely George Anderson, Willie Thornton and Bob Shankly and all three made Doug captain at one time or another.

However on the eve of Dundee's greatest triumph, in the summer of 1961, Shankly decided to free the thirty-four year old Cowie citing age as the reason why but just a few weeks later, Doug was disappointed to see Shankly sign Gordon Smith who was three years Doug's senior. When Dundee went on to lift the League Flag just twelve months later, it meant that Cowie was denied a league winners medal for a second time and despite that great triumph at Muirton, there were many that thought that Doug had been released just a little too early.

Near the end of his playing days in 1961 Doug still lived in a Dundee tenement which is changed days indeed from now. It should therefore be remembered that football then was a working man's sport and they were a different breed of player in those days. No agents, no fancy hair styles, no perms or after shave, no fancy cars or lucrative wages. Some came from the shipyards or coal mines to play for their professional sides and Doug Cowie was one of those gems. He was among a generation who played with a pride in their team that would put most modern players to shame when the elements rarely caused a match to be cancelled or anything other than a serious injury cause them to miss a game.

They played with boots that covered their ankles, kicking and heading a ball that grew heavy if it rained, with a lace that hurt the head if by chance it met the napper straight on.

Always a gentleman, Doug was honoured by the Club when they named one of their original hospitality lounges at Dens as the Doug Cowie lounge. In his book *Dundee Greats*, author Jim Hendry described Cowie as a player with *'the touch of an angel'* and this *angel* was deservedly inducted into the inaugural Dundee F.C. Hall of Fame with a legends award in 2009. There is no doubt he deserves his place amongst the first of the elite to be honoured by Dundee in this way.

Honours at Dundee:
Scottish League Cup winner: 1951/52, 1952/53
Scottish League Championship runners-up: 1948/49
Scottish Cup runner-up: 1952
Scottish League B Div. champions: 1946/47
Scotland full caps: 20
Scotland B caps: 1
Scottish League caps: 3
Dundee F.C. Hall of Fame:
2009 Legends Award
Appearances, Goals:
League: 341, 19 goals
Scottish Cup: 32, 1 goal
League Cup: 73, 4 goal
Totals: 446, 24 goals

Bobby Cox

Bobby Cox was a local boy who did well – very well indeed. To be born within earshot of the crowd noise from Dens Park, then to grow up to lead your beloved Dundee F.C. to the club's greatest glory, is the stuff of legends. From the school teams of S.S. Peter and Paul and then St. John's High School, his aim was to become a professional footballer and to achieve that aim, he had to overcome great adversity when he had his leg in plaster for four years following a serious injury.

The young Bobby Cox then continued his football education with local junior side Dundee Osborne where his talents attracted the attention of a scout from Dundee United. Cox's heart lay at the top rather than bottom of Tannadice Street, but he went along for his trial anyway only to be told afterwards that he was, in United's opinion, 'too wee'.

Back then to Osborne and off to National Service with the Royal Signals, for which he was stationed at Ripon in North Yorkshire. His displays for the regimental team earned him recognition with the Northern Command side, but more importantly, persuaded Dundee F.C. to listen to the entreaties of his army buddy, Dundee provisional signing Sandy Evans, and have a look at Cox.

This man Evans deserves a plaque inside Dens. There might be no Bobby Cox stand, possibly no solitary league title, without his intervention. Manager Willie Thornton liked what he saw and in 1955 Cox began what was to be a 14-year playing association with the club that he supported all his life. He made the first of what were to be more than 400 appearances for the The Dee in a 3-1 Dens Park win over Queen's Park, on 20th October, 1956 after only four matches for the reserve side. For the remainder of his career only injury and illness would prevent him from wearing the number three shirt. Doug Cowie was one of the mainstays of the team that Cox came into and when Cowie left, Cox succeeded him as captain.

Cox would eventually notch up the second highest number of appearances for Dundee and his 433 starts are only bettered by the man who he succeeded as captain. The Club had waned from the halcyon early 1950 days of Billy Steel and co., but at the start of the next decade, as manager Bob Shankly introduced youngsters Alex Hamilton, Ian Ure, Andy Penman, Alan Gilzean, and Hugh Robertson and brought in experience in the shape of Bobby Seith, Bobby Wishart and Gordon Smith, the Dark Blues became genuine contenders for the major prizes. In 1962 they surpassed anything accomplished by a previous Dundee side, winning the Scottish League title by three points from Rangers – who they had the audacity to thrash 5-1 at Ibrox en route to the big prize.

Saturday, 28th April, 1962 became a date to remember for Dundee fans as Cox led his troops to the League Flag following a 3-0 win over St Johnstone at Muirton Park. At the end of the match, the Dundee support steamed their way onto the pitch to acclaim their triumph and the pictures of the fans lifting their captain onto their shoulders as he held arms up in the air are synonymous with Dundee's greatest day. Cox and his side's place in Tayside legend were assured.

The following season, Dundee set off on a memorable European odyssey as Bobby Cox led the Club into its first foray into continental competition. As they took their European Cup challenge to a semi-final against AC Milan, they showed that the classic Scottish passing game which they played, could work as well in Europe as in Scotland. Their campaign began with an 8-1 thumping of second favourites Cologne, before a bruising rematch in Germany. Sporting Lisbon and Anderlecht were also despatched before, significantly, with Cox injured and unable to play, AC Milan ended the dream in the San Siro. That team then began to break up, but in 1964, whilst owner of the aptly named public house, 'The Sliding Tackle' in Broughty Ferry (he was renowned for his trademark sliding tackle with the outside of his right foot), he once again captained the team to another memorable occasion as Dundee played Rangers in the Scottish Cup Final. It was Dundee's first appearance in the Final for twelve years but there was to be no fairytale ending for 'Coxer' as two late goals from Rangers cruelly denied the Dark Blues a replay.

Cox was again involved in another classic Cup Final three years later when he was on the bench for the 1967 League Cup Final against Celtic but he to be again denied a cup winning medal when the newly crowned Lisbon Lions ran out winners by five goals to three.

That same season, Dundee reached a European semi for a second and Cox was part of the squad which faced Leeds United in the Inter-Cities Fair Cup, the forerunner of the U.E.F.A. Cup. Cox didn't play in either leg against the men from Elland Road but he did play in the first two rounds again Dutch side DWS Amsterdam and Royal Liege from Belgium.

To have been an established member and skipper of at one stage the best team in the country, it is disappointing to note that Bobby did not receive the full recognition of his country. His only representative honour was for a Scottish League XI against the Scotland national side in a 'trial' international at Parkhead in 1961 but it was a match in which no caps were awarded. He was named as reserve on no fewer than twelve occasions but was repeatedly overlooked for that elusive cap.

Many observers of these times will tell you that Cox was of genuine international class as a left back.

Unfortunately, his career spanned the same time period as that of Eric Caldow, arguably Scotland's finest full back. Caldow's international career-ending broken leg at Wembley in 1963 ought to have opened the door for Cox: a left back with a proven track record as a team captain, but the Scottish selectors and manager Ian McColl turned instead to Hearts' David Holt to succeed Caldow. There is no doubt that if Bobby Cox had been playing today, he would have been one the first names on the squad list for every single match.

When Cox eventually retired in 1969, Dundee were still the top team on Tayside but that was by no means the end of his Dark Blue association. He was always a welcome guest at Dens Park, to which he returned on a more regular basis after chairman Angus Cook brought him back in 1989 as a match day host alongside friend and full back partner Alex Hamilton. It was a role he fulfilled with honour, entertaining a new generation of fans until he sadly passed away in February 2010. His place in Dens Park folklore was further cemented when, thanks to the S.P.L.'s requirements regarding all-seater stadia, the Provost Road end became a grandstand and the fans voted that it be named 'The Bobby Cox Stand'.

At 5ft 7in, Cox was a small but mighty defender. A rugged Dundonian, born and bred a few hundred yards from Dens Park in Wedderburn Street on January 24th 1934, he was described by Shankly's right hand man, trainer Sammy Kean, as a *'a real tiger, a born winner who never gave up and whose influence was immesnse.'* Great teams do not necessarily need a great captain, but, in Cox Dundee had such a man.

He led from the front, set the standard and made sure his team mates maintained it.

He continued to be an inspiration to the players who followed in his footsteps and he regularly travelled to away matches on the team's coach. He also accompanied Jim Duffy's squad on their European trips to Shkoder and Perugia in 2003 and was as proud as any Dee of their return to Europe after twenty-nine years, having led Dundee into their first campaign just over forty years previously. The venerable captain of the club's greatest team played down the honour, but he was secretly chuffed to bits. Bobby Cox was a one club man, giving the Club over fifty years loyal service and to many he was 'Mr Dundee'. No football team could count themselves more fortunate.

The fans loved him, that's for certain, referring to him as 'Sir' Bobby Cox and he was inducted into the inaugural Dundee F.C. Hall of Fame in 2009 to arguably the loudest cheer of the night. For many, Cox had simply lived our dream and we loved him for it.

Honours at Dundee:	
Scottish League Champions:	1961/62
Scottish Cup runner-up:	1964
Scottish League Cup runner-up:	1967/68
Scottish League appearance:	1
Dundee F.C. Hall of Fame:	
2009 Legends Award	
Appearances, Goals:	
League:	327 + 1 sub, 2 goals
Scottish Cup:	22, 1 goal
League Cup:	62
Europe:	11
Other:	11
Totals:	434, 3 goals

Tommy Coyne

Tommy Coyne's first spell at Dens was short – barely lasting two years – but it was certainly most illustrious. When manager Jocky Scott asked him to cross 'The Great Divide' from Tannadice, there were a few eyebrows raised but he went on to form a lethal partnership with Keith Wright with a goals-to-game ratio barely matched in Dundee's history.

Born in Govan in Glasgow seven months after Dundee became Scottish League Champions, Tommy started his professional career with Clydebank where he made his debut in the 1981/82 season, scoring nine goals in thirty-one matches. Twenty-nine goals in the next season and a half persuaded Premier Division Champions Dundee United to part with £60,000 for his services but he never really hit form at Tannadice hitting the net only nine times in three years.

On the last day of the 1985/86 season, Coyne missed a penalty at Dens for The Arabs as The Dee won 1-0 but a few months later he made Dens Park his home when Jocky Scott parted with £75,000 for the twenty-four year old.

Jocky also splashed out £50,000 on Keith Wright from Raith Rovers a week earlier and immediately it looked like money well spent for both when the new strike force spearheaded Dundee to a 6-3 win over St. Mirren at home on Tommy's debut in December.

Tommy had to wait until the New Year for his first goal in a Dundee shirt and it came on a waterlogged pitch at Bayview where Dundee met East Fife in the third round of the Scottish Cup. It was a crucial strike from Coyne as it proved to be the late equaliser which earned Dundee a replay where Dundee had no problem dispatching the Fife side 4-1 with Tommy scoring the third.

In between these two matches Coyne scored his first league goal away to his old club Clydebank and a goal in the next league match at Hamilton made it four strikes in four games to signal the start of Super Tommy's remarkable goal scoring record for the Club.

Coyne and Wright were now terrorising Premier Division defenders on a weekly basis and earned themselves the nicknames of The Cobra and The Mongoose and in the Scottish Cup, Coyne lived up to his new nickname with deadly strikes which killed off the hopes of Meadowbank and Clydebank.

Those wins had sent Dundee through to the Scottish Cup semi-final against Dundee United at Tynecastle and despite scoring his first goal against his former employers, Dundee went out in a heart breaking 3-2 defeat.

By the end of Tommy's first season at the Club, Coyne had scored his first Dundee hat-trick against Clydebank and in the last game of the campaign Tommy scored a penalty in a 7-3 win over Hamilton with those seven goals meaning Dundee had scored a remarkable 100 goals in all competitions.

Super Tommy finished his debut season with fifteen goals to make him two goals behind top scorer Graham Harvey's seventeen but he had played fourteen games less and had a strike rate of one goal in less than every two games.

The Cobra would start his second season with the Dark Blues in the same way he finished his first in fine goal scoring form and at the end of August scored four against Dunfermline at home in a 5-0 win.

In Dundee's next match, Coyne and Dundee got a chance for revenge for that Scottish Cup semi-final defeat to United when they met the Terrors in the League Cup quarter-final at Dens in front of a capacity 19, 724 crowd. With only six minutes on the clock, United took the lead through former Dee Iain Ferguson but with just five left,

Dundee took the tie into extra time when Tommy slid home a Tosh McKinlay cross.

Roared on by exuberant fans, Dundee now put United under severe pressure and five minutes into extra time, Dens erupted when The Mongoose finished off a superb move by the Cobra and Graham Harvey who had only been on the park two minutes. Dundee held on for a famous 2-1 win and Coyne had written himself into folklore with that equalising goal.

In November, Coyne inflicted more misery on The Arabs when he scored a brace in a 3-1 Derby win at Tannadice as the Dundee fans taunted their rivals by thanking them for giving them Tommy Coyne. In his time at Dens, Coyne would be a thorn in United's side scoring five goals, playing in three wins and five draws.

Just after that win at Tannadice, the goal-hungry partnership of Coyne and Wright netted nine goals in four days as the Dark Blues raced to spectacular away wins to Falkirk (6-0) and Morton (7-1) with Coyne scoring a hat-trick against the Greenock side.

By then, Coyne had now scored twenty-eight goals and when Dundee's New Year fixture was brought forward twenty-four hours to the 1st January, Tommy had the chance to grab the Daily Record's Goalden Shot title ahead of Ally McCoist whose Rangers side were playing in the Old Firm Derby the following day.

The Goalden Shot title was awarded to the first player to score thirty goals in all competitions in any division and Super Tommy grabbed the prize ahead of Super Ally with a brace against

The Pars. To score thirty goals by New Year was a terrific achievement for Coyne and he now also in the running for the U.E.F.A. Golden Boot for Europe's top league scorer.

Ultimately however, Tommy would score thirty-three league goals to finish third and win the Bronze Boot, with the Golden Boot being won by Tanju Colak of Turkish club Galatasaray. Such was the interest in Turkey in how much of a threat Coyne was to Colak that Turkish reporters were often dispatched to Dens towards the end of the season to suss out their rival.

Coyne finished the season however as the Premier Division's leading scorer and with a Tennents' Sixes winners' medal also in his pocket, his total of thirty-seven goals was only bettered in Dundee's history by Dave Halliday's 39 (38 league) in 1923/24, Alec Stott's 39 (30 league) in 1948/49 and Alan Gilzean's 52 (33 league) in 1963/64.

The following season saw Tommy playing for a new manager when Dave Smith took over from Jocky Scott but by the end of January, Smith resigned after only five league wins.

One of the wins on Hogmanay saw Tommy score a double in a 2-0 win over Aberdeen to give Dundee their first home win over The Dons since the opening day of the inaugural Premier Division in 1975.

Coyne was again by then Dundee's top scorer and The Dee had already turned down a £750,000 bid from West Ham for The Cobra after Chairman Angus Cook had stated pre season that neither Coyne or Wright were for sale, *'even for a million pounds.'*

Dark Blue legend Gordon Wallace took over the reigns from Dundonian Smith in February 1989 and he felt there was already the basis of a reasonable side at Dens and wanted to build his side around Tommy Coyne. However within weeks of his arrival, Coyne was on his way to Celtic as a replacement for Frank McAvennie for a Dens record fee of £500,000 and he was leaving behind a legacy of sixty goals in 109 games, a ratio of one goal every 1.8 games. Tommy took a couple of seasons to find his feet at Parkhead but in his third season again finished the Premier Division top goal scorer with eighteen goals in twenty-six games.

Coyne scored fifty-two goals in his four years at Celtic and was called up by the Republic of Ireland through his family connections and he was surprisingly sold to Tranmere Rovers early in 1993. His time at Prenton Park ended in tragedy however with the passing away of his wife and he returned to Scotland in November when he joined Motherwell for £125,000.

Tommy scored fifty-nine goals in 132 games for the Steelmen and in 1994/95, he was again the Scottish Premier Division's top scorer to become the only player to achieve that with three different clubs.

Tommy also created his own piece of Motherwell history when he became the first 'Well player to play in a World Cup Finals in 1994 when he played in three of Ireland's four matches and in total he won twenty-two caps for the Republic, scoring six goals.

In the summer of 1998, Jocky Scott re-signed The Cobra for newly promoted Dundee and he was part of the side to achieve Dundee's highest ever Premier finish of fifth, equaling Dundee's highest league placing since they were Champions in 1962.

Tommy then returned to his first club, Clydebank, as player/manager in August 2000 and picked up the Scottish Second Division Manager of the Month award a month later but he was released after six months when the club entered administration despite the club being near the top of Division Two.

Soon after leaving Clydebank he joined Albion Rovers, where he ended his playing career turning out for the Coatbridge side at the age of thirty-nine.

Tommy Coyne will always be fondly remembered at Dens Park for his goal scoring exploits and at the Dundee F.C. Player of the Year

Dinner in 2010, he was welcomed onto the legends table to a standing ovation as the room sang 'Super Tommy'.

He had rightly earned his place on the legends table and as the song that was sung to The Arabs in his time at Dens says, *'Thank you very much for Tommy Coyne, thank you very much, thank you very, very, very much!'*

Honours at Dundee:
U.E.F.A. Bronze Boot: 1987/88
Tennents' Sixes winner: 1988
Appearances, Goals:
League: 96 + 9 subs, 50 goals
Scottish Cup: 14, 6 goals
League Cup: 7 + 1 sub, 4 goals
Totals: 127, 60 goals

Herbert Dainty

One hundred years ago, Dundee players plied their trade in front of large crowds that stood on the hallowed Dens Park terracing signing forgotten battle hymns of days long gone as they brought home the Scottish Cup for the only time in the Club's long history. One hundred years on there is a pride still felt by those who never saw them play but yet who know their names and feel an affinity that transcends time. Among those Dundee heroes is the goal scoring, centre half Herbert Dainty whose name itself evens conjures up images of a bygone age.

Herbert Charles Dainty was born in Geddington, Northamptonshire on February 6th 1879 and started his playing career with local club Kettering. In August 1899 he joined English Football League Second Division side Leicester Fosse but soon became a bit of a soccer nomad as he played for a different club in each of the next five seasons.

In May 1905, he joined Dundee F.C. and there must have been something to his liking in Jute City as he stayed at Dens Park for the next six seasons and became one of four Englishmen who helped Dundee win the Scottish Cup in 1910. He joined Dundee from Southern League side Southampton where he played alongside Dundee's 1910 Cup winning captain Bert Lee and when he decided to come to Dundee, it *'provoked an outcry in the town'*, according to authors Duncan Holley and Gary Chalk in their book, *'The Alphabet of the Saints.'*

Bert made his debut for Dundee on August 19th 1905 in a 2-1 home defeat to St. Mirren and he was an ever present in the side, making thirty-one appearances in his first year. Dainty would score his first goal from Dundee from the spot against Morton on September 2nd in a 3-1 win at home and he would score seven penalties during his Dark Blue career. Bert however wouldn't just score goals direct from twelve yards as in his time at Dens, he would score twenty-five goals, a terrific total for a centre-half.

In his second season, Bert would miss just one game, playing thirty-seven times as Dundee finished runners-up in the Scottish League Championship to Celtic and he would beat his debut season goal tally by one, scoring six times.

Bert was now a mainstay in the side and would miss just one game in the 1907/08 season and his goal tally would again increase to eight as Dundee finished in fourth but on the same points tally of forty-eight that they had had when they had finished in second place the previous year.

Dundee however would improve their points tally by two the following season but could again only finish as runners-up to Celtic in Division One with Dainty contributing four goals in thirty-three starts. Bert did however win his first medal with Dundee when they won the Forfarshire Cup with a 2-0 win over Brechin City in March but the real glory was just around the corner.

Just over twelve months later Dundee won the Scottish Cup in April 1910 with a 2-1 win over Clyde in a second replay and Dainty was one of the men of the moment as he was outstanding in all three games. As Clyde piled on the pressure towards the end of the third match to try and force another replay, Dainty marshalled the Dark Blue defence superbly as they resolutely held out to take the Cup back to Dens Park for the first and to date only time.

Dainty was now a local hero and in the same month as that cup success, a Dens testimonial for the popular defender attracted a crowd of 8,000 against Rangers. Six months later, the Englishman was given the honour of representing the Scottish League against the Southern League on October 24th but at the end of the season, he was off on his travels again when he joined Bradford Park Avenue in the summer.

After two year spell at Yorkshire, Bert was keen to come back to Dens as he still had business interests in the city but an argument with the Dundee board meant that he went instead to Ayr United. Within a year he was appointed player / manager with the 'Honest Men' but in 1915, he did return to the city, not however to Dundee F.C. but instead to the six year old Dundee Hibernian where he became their second ever manager in a similar capacity he had enjoyed at Ayr.

It was clear that his popularity in the city had endured, despite having 'crossed the road' to the club who would become Dundee United in 1923.

During the war, benefit and charity matches were held to fill the gap in the rather haphazard leagues which then existed, and Dainty became actively involved in organising teams, which he called 'Dainty's XI', from any footballers who happened to be stationed in the Tayside or Fife area.

Dainty relinquished managerial duties in at Dundee Hibs in 1917 and he retired from playing the following year when he was invited to become involved in running of the club. He was co-opted onto the club committee in 1920 and was made chairman in 1922 but towards the end of that year, with the club in serious financial difficulties, it was taken over and turned into a limited company and Bert's services were no longer required and thus ended his involvement with football.

It was our grandfathers or even great grandfathers who watched the legendary Herbert Dainty and his team mates achieve unequalled glory in Dundee's past and while we now sit where our forefathers once stood and sing a different tune, we can still love, cherish and idolise the heroes of a century ago.

Honours at Dundee:
Scottish Cup winner: 1910
Scottish League Championship runners-up: 1906/07, 1908/09
Forfarshire Cup winner: 1908/09
Scottish League cap: 1
Appearances, Goals:
League: 187, 24 goals
Scottish Cup: 25, 1 goal
Totals: 212, 25 goals

Billy Dodds

When Dundee manager Gordon Wallace paid Chelsea £75,000 to sign Billy Dodds in the summer of 1989, he could hardly expected that he had signed the player who would become Dundee's top goal scorer in each of the next four seasons and be the man who would score a hat-trick to win Dundee's first national cup competition in seventeen years. The task of replacing goal scoring phenomenon Tommy Coyne looked an arduous one, but Wallace came up with a gem of a striker in Billy Dodds, who would score seventeen more goals for The Dee than 'The Cobra' and strike up a partnership with Coyne's old mate Keith Wright that yielded sixty-eight goals in only two years.

Born in New Cumnock in Ayrshire on February 5th 1969, Billy signed for Dundee after a successful season in Chelsea's reserves where he scored over thirty goals. Three appearances in the first team at Stamford Bridge though restricted his chances but Billy showed his potential during a loan spell at Partick Thistle in 1987/88 where he scored nine goals in thirty league appearances.

Dodds made his debut for Dundee on the opening day of the 1989/90 season when he came off the bench at East End Park for Duncan Campbell and made an immediate impact when Dunfermline's Jimmy Nichol was sent off after bringing him down.

However, after turning up late, it took Billy a couple of months to make his second appearance and did so when he got a start away to St. Mirren on October 4th and marked his promotion to the starting line up with a goal in a 3-2 defeat.

He did enough to stake a claim for the number ten shirt and was an ever present for the rest of the season in which he finished as Dundee's top scorer with thirteen goals.

That season however finished a disaster in bottom place in a ten team Premier Division and so Billy's second season at the Club was going to be spent in the First Division. As favourites to go straight back up, Dundee started the season well and Billy scored three goals in the first four matches as the Dark Blues hit the top.

That season also marked the one hundredth anniversary of the Scottish League and to mark the occasion they introduced a new cup competition called the B&Q Centenary Cup, which was open to all clubs outside of the Premier Division. Dundee started the new competition with a bye in the First Round before dispatching Alloa Athletic away from home in the second in which Billy scored twice in a 5-3 win.

The quarter-finals took Dundee back to Fife where they had drawn 1-1 with Raith Rovers in the league ten days before and this time Billy was the hero when his extra time strike from outside the box was enough to knock the Kirkcaldy side out.

A 2-0 win in the semi away to Kilmarnock was enough to send Dundee through to the Final on Remembrance Sunday where they would meet Ayr United at Fir Park, Motherwell and Dundee carried a large support amongst the 11,506 crowd.

They were silenced however when Ian McAllister put Ayr ahead in thirteen minutes but gradually Dundee took control with Colin West causing havoc on the right and were awarded a penalty when the flying winger was downed soon after the break. Dodds, who had missed a penalty against Meadowbank the previous week, sent David Purdie the wrong way and twenty minutes later, the flaxen haired striker put Dundee ahead with a header from an inch perfect cross by West. Dundee continued to press but against the run of play, a long range shot by David Smith was deflected high past Tom Carson in the Dundee goal to put Ayr back on level terms. There was no further scoring so the game went to extra time and as Dundee continued to press, they looked the

~ 49 ~

most likely to avoid making the game go to penalties. As so it was when with only five minutes left Purdie made a brave save at the feet of Keith Wright and when the ball spun free, Dodds was on hand to complete his hat-trick from the edge of the box and win the Centenary Cup for The Dee.

Billy was the hero as Dundee won their first national cup competition since 1973 when manager Gordon Wallace scored the winner to lift the League Cup and as a one off competition, Dundee were allowed to keep the glass trophy which resides in the Dens Park boardroom today.

Billy finished the season with twenty-two goals in all competitions, piping his strike partner Keith Wright by one goal but the season ended again in disappointment as Dundee failed to win promotion by just one point.

There was joy however twelve months later when the First Division championship was won with Billy scoring nineteen goals on the way to the title and to finish top scorer again. He now wanted to prove himself in the Premier Division after thirty-three goals in the second tier and did so when he finished top scorer for the fourth time in a row with eighteen goals to help Dundee finish five points above the drop zone.

There were plenty of highlights in the first season back in the top flight as flamboyant manager Simon Stainrod led Dundee to famous victories over Dundee United and Rangers as well as keeping them up. Having failed to win any of their first three league games, Dundee took on league champions Rangers at Dens and against all the odds recorded a memorable 4-3 win with Billy scoring twice including the winner from the spot after one of the softest penalties ever awarded against either of the Old Firm.

Billy kept his nerve from the spot a month later at Tannadice when he netted the winner in a 1-0 win over Dundee United to give himself five goals in five games since that Rangers win.

Dodds was often a thorn in the Arabs' side in his time in Dens, playing in two derby wins and scoring three times and had a good record also against both sides of the Old Firm, scoring six times, proving himself to be a big game player for The Dee.

The following season would prove to be Billy's last at Dens as a player as he was surprisingly sold to relegation rivals St. Johnstone in January for a fee of £360,000 and when the fans and sponsors were upset that their star striker had been sold to a local rival, a number of them were invited to Dens to meet with manager Jim Duffy so that he could explain his decision.

On the day he made his debut for St. Johnstone, Billy still found time to attend the funeral of Dundee supporter Andy De Vries who had been tragically killed while working abroad in America and attended the service before making his debut at night. He left the Club as the season's top scorer to that point and while the money from his sale was used to sign Gerry Britton and George Shaw, it still a huge blow to the support to see their hero leave at such a crucial time.

Within twelve months of joining the Saints, Billy was on the move up the east coast to Aberdeen before returning down the A90 to the City of Discovery to join Dundee United after four years in the North East.

A subsequent move to Rangers in 1999 saw Billy win all three major honours in Scotland and by that time was well established in the Scotland team where he scored seven goals in twenty-six internationals.

A move back to Dundee United in 2003 saw Billy join Gordon Chisholm's coaching staff in 2005 and in March 2010 Billy returned to Dens Park as Chisholm's number two after working together at Queen of the South when they left Tannadice.

Billy is now charged with the task of helping lead Dundee back to the S.P.L. as assistant manager and when he does so, he will cement his reputation as a Dundee legend which he earned with his 100% commitment, vital goals and cup final hat-trick and strike rate of one goal in every 2.5 games which puts him in the top fifteen leading scorers in the Club's history.

Honours at Dundee:
Scottish League First Division winner: 1991/92
B&Q Scottish League Centenary Cup winner: 1990
Appearances, Goals:
League: 171+2 subs, 67 goals
Scottish Cup: 11, 3 goals
League Cup: 6, 1 goal
S.F.L. Challenge Cup: 5, 6 goals
Totals: 195, 77 goals

Ally Donaldson

Ally Donaldson was a fine Dundee goalkeeper for many, many years where he made 408 appearances for the Club, for seven different managers during two spells. He is sixth is Dundee's all time appearance list and is fondly remembered amongst the fine tradition of goalkeepers that Dundee has. His career at Dundee was colourful to say the least, with the big keeper involved in no fewer than three disputes in his times at Dens and without them, he could have gone on to make the most appearances in the Club's history.

Edinburgh born, Donaldson joined Dundee in 1961 from Tynecastle Athletic and made his first team debut in the final game of the 1963/64 season in a 5-1 Summer Cup win over St Johnstone, in a side that included such luminaries as Bobby Cox, Bobby Seith, Andy Penman, Alan Cousin, Alec Stuart and Alan Gilzean all of whom had won Championship medals.

He had replaced another legendary figure in the goal in Bert Slater, and Slater was back in the goal for the start of the following season. However after a poor start to the season and Dundee's interest in the League Cup already over, manager Bob Shankley decided to make sweeping changes for the final sectional tie at home to Motherwell, with morale at a low ebb.

Out went the experienced Slater, Cox, Seith, Cameron and Houston and in came youngsters Ally Donaldson, Alex Totten, John Phillips and Jocky Scott and the gamble paid off with an astonishing 6-0 win.

Ally's career at Dens was up and running and by the end of the season he had played forty games including both matches against Zarragoza in the European Cup Winners' Cup.

The number one shirt was now primarily Donaldson's for the next seven seasons although he did share the goalkeeping duties with John Arrol for a couple of years and it was the former Clyde man who was preferred between the sticks for the 1967 League Cup Final defeat against Celtic where the Lisbon Lions won 5-3.

Donaldson returned to the side for the Inter-Cities Fairs Cup first round, second leg match against D.W.S. Amsterdam and played in both legs in the quarter-final tie against F.C. Zurich and in both legs of the semi-final against Don Revie's Leeds United.

In his first spell at Dens, international recognition came Ally's ways when he won two Under 23 caps against England and Wales in 1965 and won a two Scottish League caps against the Irish League in 1966 and 1970 but that first spell came to an end in 1972 after a dispute with manager John Prentice.

The emergence of youngster Mike Hewitt and the signing of Thomson Allan from Hibs put pressure on Ally's position and he was prepared to give up the game, being at one point ready to join the police. However Falkirk manager Willie Cunningham came in with a £14,000 bid for Ally and he was on his way to The Bairns after making 256 appearances for Dundee.

He stayed at Brockville for four years before manager Tommy Gemmell brought him back to Dens in 1976 after the Club were relegated to the First Division and he got Donaldson for around half the fee Dundee had originally received for him.

Donaldson was an ever present in the 1978/79 First Division title winning side and although his first ever season in the Premier Division ended in relegation, it ended on a high for Ally as he was part of the side to famously defeat Celtic 5-1 at Dens in April 1980 and his testimonial three weeks later against Dundee United saw a 4874 crowd enjoy a thrilling 4-4 draw.

Gemmell left at the end of 1979/80 season but a dispute with new manager Donald McKay ended his second spell at Dens and after another 152 first team games, Ally left Dens Park to play for Hibs and Raith Rovers before a short spell as Steve Murray's assistant at Montrose.

During his sixteen years at Dens, Donaldson played for seven different managers from Bob Shankly to Donald McKay and in Shoot magazine in 1971, Ally quotes Bob Shankly as having a huge influence on his career.

Ally proved to be an outstanding custodian, whose height was invaluable at dealing with high centres, was a big favourite with the fans and when during some quieter moments in a match, the Dens Park terracing chanted, *'Ally, Ally, give us a wave'*, Donaldson always obliged to his adoring Dark Blue public.

Honours at Dundee:
Scottish League First Division winner: 1978/79
U.E.F.A. / Inter-Cities Fairs Cup s emi-final: 1967/68
Scottish League caps: 2
Scotland Under 23 caps: 2
Appearances:
League: 314
Scottish Cup: 23
League Cup: 49
Europe: 10
Other: 12
Total: 408

Robert Douglas

When Robert Douglas re-signed for Dundee in August 2008, it was a returning hero coming home after almost eight years away. Dundee's history is peppered with great goalkeeping, heroic last lines of defence and wonderful saves and Douglas had returned to the place where he had done all that and more and became Dundee's player of the year again, eleven years after he had first earned that honour.

Born in Lanark on April 24th 1972, Robert James Douglas started his professional football career later than most when he signed for Meadowbank Thistle in 1993. Loaned back out to Junior side Forth Wanderers from where he was signed, Rab became Meadowbank's first choice keeper upon his return and enjoyed a successful Third Division title winning season in 1995/96 after the club had relocated and renamed themselves Livingston.

After just missing out on back to back promotions the following season, Dundee boss John McCormark lured the 6ft 5in keeper to Dens Park in the summer of 1997 for a fee of £100,000 plus Kevin Magee. Douglas became an instant hit with the Dens Park support with his commanding performances and excellent shot stopping ability and made the best possible starts to his Dark Blue career by keeping a clean sheet against promotion rivals Falkirk in a 3-0 win on the opening day of the season.

That was the first of forty-four competitive appearances for Rab in his debut season and was also the first of twenty clean sheets while being ever present in the side. The most impressive of those clean sheets came at Ibrox in the quarter-final of the Scottish Cup when Dundee held the then Scottish Champions Rangers at bay with a 0-0 draw. Dundee also managed to keep thirty-goal Marco Negri quiet and a series of brilliant saves by Douglas helped Dundee rightly earn a reply in front of the BSKYB television cameras.

Rab's performance in Govan was one of a number of top drawer outings he enjoyed that season with a match against Raith Rovers in October being particularly memorable for number of breathtaking saves. By the end of the season, Dundee were Scottish First Division champions with Rab conceding just twenty-four league goals and his performances earned him a call up to the Scotland 'B' side where he won his first international cap at any level against Wales at Broadwood.

Dundee goal keeping coach Billy Thomson was full of praise for the ex-bricklayer, bouncer and part-time fireman stating that *'he has a great presence and I love the way he comes for crosses'* and with promotion being secured in no small thanks to Rab's contribution, he was awarded with the Club's Player of the Year trophy at the end of the season.

Dundee's return in the top flight after a four year absence saw them secure their highest placed finish since 1974 and was the first time Dundee had finished above Dundee United for twenty-five years with Rab making the most appearances of any player, missing just one.

It was another terrific season for Douglas which included two clean sheets at Tannadice in two derby wins as Dundee defeated United twice on their neighbours patch for the first time since 1944/45.

In the derby in November in front of a live television audience, Dundee secured their first win over their the Arabs since 1992 and while James Grady's wonder strike grabbed the headlines in the 1-0 win, it was the heroic saves of Douglas which did as much to win the day.

One save in particular with only seven minutes left is without doubt one of the greatest saves ever made by a Dundee goalkeeper. With United piling on the pressure, Swedish striker Kjell Olofsson fired the ball into the ground from about ten yards out and as it bounced high towards the top left hand corner of the net, Rab somehow managed to get a finger tip to the ball and touch it over the bar.

It is a save which lives long in the memory in a match which cemented Rab's place in Dundee folklore and it broke Arabs hearts so much, that one of them even invaded the pitch at the end to confront the big keeper, which he handled with the same skill that he had handled United's attacks all night.

Rab continued as Dundee's number one for his second full season under Jocky Scott and when Jocky's contract wasn't renewed at the end of the 1999/2000 season, Dundee turned to a more continental style under former Juventus man Ivano Bonetti.

Despite Bonetti bringing in a host of foreigners, Rab kept the goalkeeper's position but by October Celtic came in with an offer of £1.2 million which was too good to refuse and Rab was on his way for the highest fee ever received for a Dundee player. An emotional farewell in front of a packed away end at Pittodrie for a match that saw Claudio Caniggia make his debut was Rab's last action before the move to Parkhead which was to bring him three S.P.L. titles, three Scottish Cups, eighteen international caps, Champions League experience and an appearance in the U.E.F.A. Cup Final.

After five years in the East End of Glasgow, Rab moved down south to Leicester City (where he picked up cap number nineteen for Scotland) in a spell which also saw him turn out for Millwall, Wycombe Wanderers and Plymouth on loan. As his contract ran out in the summer of 2008, Rab was on the verge of giving up his playing days and moving to the United States to do some coaching but a last minute call from Dundee manager Alex Rae persuaded the popular former Dee to return to Dens Park.

It proved to be a great move for both Club and player, as Rab turned in some fantastic displays and won the Player of the Year trophy for the second time at The Dee's end of season dinner at the Hilton in May 2009. It was like he had never been away.

Midway through his first season back, Jocky Scott had replaced Alex Rae in the Dens Park hot seat and Rab's former boss made him club captain in the summer of 2009. In November, Dundee would win the ALBA Challenge Cup in a thrilling 3-2 win in Perth and Rab, along with team captain Eric Paton had the honour of lifting the trophy as he also collected his second winners' medal in his time at Dens.

By the end of season 2009/10, Rab had kept 68 clean sheets in just over five seasons with the Club and has turned out to be one of the best number ones Dundee has ever had. There is no doubt that the Dark Blues mean an awful lot to Douglas, regularly attending Dundee matches even after he left the Club and he even had his wedding reception on the Dens Park pitch when married the Chief Executive's daughter Debbie Marr in May 2000.

Rab would often return to the Player of the Year dinner on the legends table while playing elsewhere and now that he is back, he continues to be an inspirational keeper, as Dundee vie to return to the upper echelons of Scottish football.

Honours at Dundee:
Scottish League First Division winner: 1997/98
ALBA Scottish League Challenge Cup winner: 2009/10
Scotland 'B' cap: 1
D.S.A. Player of the Year: 1998, 2009
Appearances:
League: 168 + 1 sub
Scottish Cup: 10
League Cup: 9
S.F.L. Challenge Cup: 2
Total: 190

Jim Duffy

Jim Duffy has been a tremendous servant to Dundee Football Club in his various roles as player, coach, assistant manager and manager in his four spells with the Club.

When he returned to Dundee to start his second stint in the manager's seat in July 2002, he claimed that he felt like he was returning home and said, *'Sometimes you have a place that continuously draws you back and you don't know why. For me that seems to be Dens Park and I am delighted to return to what must be my spiritual home.'*

Jim first joined Dundee in 1985 when the then manager Archie Knox secured something of a coup by signing the Scottish Players' Player of the Year from Greenock Morton.

He was a tremendous centre-half for Dundee and a rock in a Dark Blue jersey and a solid albeit 'thin on top' inspiration not just to the fans but to all around him. Only the wealth of talent in the Scottish defence at the time prevented him from gaining any full international caps but he did earn one at under-21 level when he captained Scotland against Eire. Surely if he was still playing nowadays, he would be not only an automatic choice but also the captain and mainstay of the team.

Jim's playing career was, of course cruelly curtailed when a knee injury forced him to give up the game in 1987 and a testimonial match against a Premier League Select in December seemed to be a final farewell to a Dundee hero.

But in 1990 against all the odds, Jim returned to a Dark Blue jersey and immediately, it was like he had never been away! *'If only he had returned earlier, we would not'*, as the then manager Gordon Wallace lamented, *'have been relegated.'*

After returning to his native Maryhill at the end of the season, Jim again returned to Dens in 1992 as Simon Stainrod's playing / assistant before taking the big job himself as player / manager in 1993. In his first spell as manager, Jim led Dundee to the League Cup Final and then to the semi final the following season, which was a tremendous feat for a First Division side.

His second spell at the helm saw him lead Dundee to their first Scottish Cup Final since the days of Bob Shankly, capture a top six finish with a fourteen match unbeaten run and lead Dundee into Europe for the first time in twenty-nine years.

In both spells Jim fought against financial constraints to lead Dundee to Hampden and helped literally to keep them afloat. During his first tenure, Duff dipped into his own pocket at times to help pay the players wages and had the ridiculous situation of having a chairman who came back before the Coca-Cola Cup Final, demanding that one of his best players be sold before we went to the National Stadium. Jim persuaded Ron Dixon to keep hold of Weighorst until the day after the big game and got the Club double the money from Celtic and Dundee legend Barry Smith as part of the deal to boot!

Before the 1995 Airdrie semi final, Jim was told the Dundee simply had to reach the League Cup Final to survive and he must have been under tremendous pressure. Eight years later, Jim was again under severe pressure as Dundee were again in the financial mire, lurching into administration and he quickly became the heart and soul of the Club. He must have wondered exactly which spirit lured him to Dens Park for a fourth time.

He carried the flag superbly against impossible odds and in the media he portrayed and projected the Club immensely well and showed tremendous loyalty to The Dee as vultures circled to try and lure Duff away. He took it upon himself to personally inform the staff who were released and there is no doubt that administration would have been a lot, lot worse without Jim Duffy.

Jim Duffy was a tremendous player for Dundee, and played 238 times (plus one sub appearance) scoring two goals, both of which were penalties. He also scored the winning goal in a penalty shoot out away to Caledonian Thistle in the B&Q Cup in 1994, after which he shook the hand of every Dundee fan present, apologising for a poor display. He was also therefore a fantastic leader who is the only manager in the last thirty years to take Dundee to a cup final (and did it twice!)

Duffy also reared some great young players for the Club such as Neil McCann, Jim Hamilton, Ian Anderson and Gavin Rae and some of them have been sold simply to allow the Club to survive.

History therefore will be very, very kind to Jim Duffy and he deserves recognition as one of the all time great figures in the Club's history and was inducted into the 2010 Dundee F.C. Hall of Fame as a genuine Dark Blue legend.

Honours at Dundee:
Dundee F.C. Hall of Fame:
2010 Legends Award

(As Player)
Scotland Under-21 caps: 1

(As Player / Manager):
Coca-Cola League Cup runner-up: 1995/96
B&Q Challenge Cup runner-up: 1994/95

(As Manager):
Tennents' Scottish Cup runner-up: 2003
Appearances, Goals:
League: 199, 2 goals
Scottish Cup: 17
League Cup: 14 +1 sub
S.F.L. Challenge Cup: 8
Totals: 239, 2 goals

Managerial Record with Dundee: (1993 - 1996, 2002 - 2005)

	P	W	D	L	F	A	Pts
League:	214	69	61	84	275	293	260
Scottish Cup:	16	7	3	6	22	18	
League Cup:	19	10	2	7	41	17	
Europe:	4	2	0	2	7	3	
S.F.L. Challenge Cup:	12	8	1	3	28	16	
Total:	265	96	67	102	373	347	

John Duncan

Anyone who was allowed the honour of the nickname of 'Gillie' at Dens Park must have a pretty special player, and John Duncan was most certainly that. Local boy made good, John Duncan is one of the privileged few who grew up supporting Dundee before getting chance to play for the club that they loved and in a seven year Dens Park career scored 109 goals, including forty in season 1972/73, where he finished as Scotland's top scorer.

Born in Lochee on February 22nd 1949, the Morgan Academy pupil worshipped the Dundee Championship side when knee high to a crush barrier behind the Provost Road goal and got a chance to join his beloved Dees from Butterburn Youth Club in 1966. John joined the Dundee staff on part-time basis to begin with as he was studying to become a P.E. teacher at Jordanhill College in Glasgow and once he completed his degree, he joined the Dark Blues full time and soon starting knocking in the goals in the reserves on a regular basis.

Within four years of watching Dundee lift the League Flag, John was now sharing the dressing room with the likes of Bobby Cox and Andy Penman and when in his first practice match he rose unguarded at the back post to powerfully head home, he was given the nickname of 'Gillie' by George Stewart, which quickly stuck.

The fact John was allowed to proudly carry such an iconic nickname, showed the high regard he was held in by his team mates and his peers at Dens Park and soon he was following in his famous predecessor's footsteps.

Duncan made his debut for the first team on the first day of the 1968/69 season and it was a memorable occasion for John, as he scored in a 4-0 League cup home win over Kilmarnock.

By the end of his first season, John had scored eleven times in eighteen starts but with the Club well served in the striking department thanks to Jocky Scott and Gordon Wallace, his appearances were restricted to just three in his second year.

However, the 1971/72 season was to see John finally make his mark with a permanent berth in the starting line and he rewarded the manager's faith with fifteen goals in twenty starts and five appearances from the bench; an excellent ratio of a goal every 1.6 games.

But if that ratio was good, it was nothing compared to the following year when John finished Scotland's top scorer with forty goals in forty-six appearances. It was no surprise therefore that John was to receive international recognition that season and when selected to play in a Scotland v England inter-league international, he made his mark for the Scottish side with both goals in a 2-2 draw at Hampden in March 1973.

Nine months later, John was back at the National Stadium, this time in the dark blue of Dundee as The Dee met Celtic in the League Cup Final. In the lowest attended national cup final at Hampden, due mainly to the poor weather and the national energy crisis, Dundee overcame strong favourites Celtic with a 1-0 victory thanks to strike partner Gordon Wallace's second half winner.

Lifting the League Cup with The Dee was a major career highlight for Duncan and for John it was right up there with the U.E.F.A Cup adventure of two years previous when Dundee met European giants Cologne and A.C. Milan.

In the second round tie against the Germans, Dundee overcame a 2-1 first leg deficit but with just twenty minutes left on the clock in the second leg at Dens, it looked like Dundee were heading out as they were 2-1 behind and 4-2 down on aggregate.

Duncan had given Dundee the lead in the twelfth minute before drawing the sides level on the night in sixty-nine minutes and then roared on by the vociferous home support, the big striker completed his hat-trick to put Dundee 3-2 ahead, making it 4-4 on aggregate.

With away goals counting double however, Dundee had to score again and as the minutes ticked away, Jim Steele and Duncan had shots cleared off the line as it looked like Dundee might run out of time but with just sixty seconds remaining Bobby Wilson crashed home a memorable winner.

In the next round Dundee drew another of their 1962/63 European Cup foes in the guise of A.C. Milan and after a disappointing 3-0 first leg defeat in Italy, another difficult comeback would be required if The Dee were to reach the quarter-finals.

It wasn't to be however for despite besieging the Milan goal for the entire ninety minutes they could get more than the two goals scored by Gordon Wallace and John Duncan.

Duncan's goal scoring prowess soon put him on the radar of the big clubs down south and in October 1974, Terry Neil persuaded John to be his first signing at Tottenham for a fee of £140,000, then a Dens Park record, which saw him once again follow in the footsteps of 'Gillie' who had made the same move ten years before.

Duncan's goals for Dundee rightly earned him legendary status at Dens Park and he holds the Club's record for the most goals in a League Cup tie when he scored five against East Stirlingshire in an 8-2 League Cup sectional win at Firs Park. His hat-trick against Cologne came in a game described in the *People's Journal* as *'the greatest contest at Dens that century'*, while his final European goal for Dundee against R.W.D. Molenbeek came in the Club's last European tie for twenty-nine years.

John Duncan sits seventh on the Club's all time leading scorer list and he did what all Dundee fans dream of, by making the step up from fan on the terracing to fan on the park. His goals earned him the adulation of the supporters he used to stand next to on the Provie Road as they were proud to watch one of their own make it in dark blue.

Honours at Dundee:
Scottish League Cup winner: 1973/74
Scottish League cap: 1
Appearances, Goals:
League: 121 + 3 subs, 64 goals
Scottish Cup: 12 + 1 sub, 10 goals
League Cup: 37 + 3 subs, 26 goals
Europe: 5 + 1 sub, 6 goals
Other: 4 + 1 sub, 3 goals
Totals: 188, 109 goals

Iain Ferguson

Iain Ferguson is one of a hat-trick of players to have had three spells as a player at Dens Park, during one of which he finished as Dundee's top goal scorer every year from 1982 to 1984.

Born in Newarthill, North Lanarkshire, Ferguson joined Dundee as a sixteen year old when they signed him from Fir Park Boys Club in 1978 and just a year later he made his debut for The Dee when he scored in a 3-1 home win over Kilmarnock on December 15th 1979.

Deputising for the injured Ian Redford, the Scottish Youth Internationalist made an immediate impression in the Premier Division with his level of skill and powerful shooting. By the end of the season, he had made thirteen appearances, scoring five times and had endeared himself to the Dundee support when two of those goals came against title chasing Celtic in April 1980 in an astonishing 5-1 win.

Fighting against relegation, Dundee met league leaders Celtic at Dens with three games to go and within five minutes, the match went to form when Roy Aitken gave the Parkhead side the lead. However on sixteen minutes, Dundee were back on level terms thanks to Ferguson and ten minutes later he gave Dundee the lead with a penalty before Ian Fleming made it 3-1 just before the interval.

After the break, goals from Eric Sinclair and Peter Mackie made it 5-1 to Dundee, before a missed Celtic penalty set the seal on a famous Dark Blue win.

It wasn't enough however to save Dundee from going down to the First Division a fortnight later but twelve months on, Dundee recovered from a very poor start to the season, being bottom after the first eight games, to storm back into the promotion race and clinch the second spot on the last game of the season.

'Fergie' played his part in the promotion campaign as a squad player, making just a dozen appearances but once back in the Premier League, he established himself in the starting line up and finished as top scorer with fourteen goals. Dundee retained their top flight status on the last game of the season with a 1-0 win over Airdrie at Dens and 'Fergie' capped an excellent personal season with the winning goal to make Dundee safe.

Season 1982/83 saw Ferguson start in the same goal scoring form with a double in the first two League Cup games away to Aberdeen (3-3) and at home to Dumbarton (3-2) and he forced his way into the Scotland Under-21 side, being called up by Jock Stein to play against East Germany in an Under-21 Euro qualifier.

Up front Ferguson was partnered by the experienced Eric Sinclair or fellow youngster Ray Stephen and by the end of the season, he was top scorer again for the second year in a row, bettering his previous year's total by two.

He made it three years in a row as top marksman, netting twenty times in 1984/85 and in the Scottish Cup, he turned in two terrific displays against Rangers in the quarter-final. In the first match at Dens, Fergie cheekily lobbed Nicky Walker in the Rangers goal in a 2-2 draw and in the replay in Glasgow, Ferguson scored twice in a 3-2 win. With just three minutes to go, Ferguson got the winner when he crashed the ball high into the Ibrox net to send the travelling fans wild and give Dundee their fifth win over Rangers since promotion.

In that time, Ferguson had scored eight times against the Light Blues and it was perhaps no surprise when Rangers manager Jock Wallace tabled a bid of £400,000 for both Ferguson and Cammy Fraser. Dundee manager Archie Knox, who had only been in charge for six months was desperate to keep the pair and build his side around them but despite being offered Dundee's best ever terms, they both left for Govan, with a tribunal ordering Rangers to pay £200,000 for Ferguson.

At Ibrox, Fergie scored the winning goal in the 1984 League Cup Final win over Dundee United but when Graeme Souness took over as manger in 1986, his large use of the Rangers' chequebook, meant Ferguson became surplus to requirements.

Jocky Scott took over from Archie Knox in the Dark Blue hot seat in the summer of 1986 and in a surprise move, he secured Ferguson on loan from Rangers until the end of the season. Straight away he was the darling of the Dens Park fans again when he netted in each of Dundee's opening wins against St. Mirren and Hibs but it simply alerted others to his flair for scoring goals which was never in doubt at Dens.

Across the road, Dundee United cast envious glances in Ferguson's direction and in an unprecedented move, they approached Rangers for his transfer. Initially, the striker had no wish to go to Tannadice but with Souness keen to sell, he was recalled to Glasgow before Rangers accepted a £140,000 bid from the Arabs. Dundee themselves offered a six figure sum but they couldn't match their neighbour's offer and it was a serious disappointment to see their hero line up in tangerine in a league match at Dens a few weeks later.

After a career at United, Hearts, Motherwell, where he scored in the 1991 Scottish Cup Final win, Airdrie and Portadown, Ferguson returned to First Division Dundee for a third spell at the age of thirty-four when he was signed by manager Jim Duffy who himself had played for Dundee three times.

Upon returning Ferguson to Dens Park 1996, Ferguson told the press that, *'Ten years ago, I wanted to make my loan spell from Rangers permanent and I twice knocked United back. It wasn't to be then but I am pleased to be back now'.*

Although past his best, it was great to see 'Fergie' back in a Dundee shirt for another season and the undoubted highlight was the League Cup third round win over Premier Division Dundee United at Tannadice. With the scores tied at two each, Ferguson came off the bench in the last minute of extra time with a view to taking a penalty and he cooled slotted home Dundee's fourth spot kick, before Billy Thomson saved from Owen Coyle to win the shoot out 4-2.

It was a memorable evening for the Dundee support, which was celebrated long into the night and for many a Dee, it was pay back for the time in which they stole 'Fergie', whose goals will always be remembered at Dens with fondness.

Honours at Dundee:
Scottish League First Division runner-up: 1980/81
Scotland Under-21 caps: 3
Appearances, Goals:
League: 115 + 22 subs, 43 goals
Scottish Cup: 10, 6 goals
League Cup: 15 + 3 subs, 10 goals
S.F.L. Challenge Cup: 2 subs
Totals: 167, 59 goals

Bobby Flavell

To score a goal in a winning cup final for Dundee is pretty special but to do it twice is incredible and only one man has achieved this tremendous feat. When Dundee became the first side to win back to back League Cups in 1951 and 1952, Bobby Flavell wrote himself into the Dark Blue history books by scoring in both victorious Finals.

Robert Flavell was an exceptional forward who was born in Annathill in North Lanarkshire on September 1st 1921 and he joined the senior game by signing for Airdrieonians in 1940. He had to wait until the 1946/47 season to make a league appearance, due to the Second World War and during the conflict, Flavell had made guest appearances for both Arsenal and Spurs. When the Scottish Football League resumed in 1946, Flavell scored over a goal per game for Airdrie and won two full caps for Scotland, which convinced Hearts to pay £10,000 to acquire his services.

He again scored frequently at Tynecastle, but he became a football outcast in 1950 by signing for Millonarios of the breakaway Colombian league. Bank rolled by cattle barons, this league was unrecognised by F.I.F.A. and proved to be a controversial career advancement plan for a determined group of British players such as Stoke's centre-half Neil Franklin, Manchester United's Charlie Mitten and Bobby Flavell.

Money was the main draw for top European players and Flavell played alongside Alfredo Di Stefano for the Bogata based Millonarios and maintained a friendship with the great man meeting up again at the Champions League Final in Glasgow in 2000. The side became renowned for its artistry and were nicknamed the 'Ballet Azul' (Blue Ballet) and after eighteen months in South America, Bobby returned to Scotland where he signed for Dundee.

He officially joined the Dark Blues from Hearts as the Tynecastle side still held his registration and he made his debut on the first day of the 1951/52 season away to St. Mirren in the League Cup where he scored in a 2-2 draw.

That match in Paisley was the first on the 'Road to Hampden' as Dundee went all the way to the Final where they were to meet Rangers in front of 92, 325 fans. Flavell had quickly struck up a potent partnership with Billy Steel and in the semi-final against Motherwell at Ibrox, Bobby scored a hat-trick in an impressive 5-1 win to see The Dee through to the Hampden showpiece.

At half-time, Dundee went in 1-0 down but two minutes after the restart, Dundee were back on level terms when the ever alert Flavell fired home a cross from George Christie, despite the best efforts of Rangers keeper Bobby Brown.

In sixty-nine minutes, Johnny Patillo put Dundee ahead but Rangers equalised with just two minutes left thanks to future Dundee boss Willie Thornton. Straight from the restart however Dundee went right up the field and scored when Billy Steel floated a free kick up to skipper Alfie Boyd, whose header brought the League Cup back to Dens for the first time.

Twelve months later, Dundee were back at Hampden for a third time, having lost the Scottish Cup Final to Motherwell in April and this time they faced B Division Kilmarnock on October 25th 1953 as Dundee tried to successfully defend their League Cup.

Flavell had scored nine goals on route to Hampden, including a hat-trick against old club Airdrie in a sectional tie and Dundee's second in the semi-final win against league champions Hibs where Billy Steel got the first but now he would be the sole hero in the Final.

Dundee were overwhelming favourites to overcome their lower league, part-time opposition but Kilmarnock were not just there to make up the numbers and took the game to Dundee. Thanks largely to some inspired goalkeeping from The Dee's Bobby Henderson, the score remained 0-0 at the interval and the pattern continued into the second half.

With ten minutes left however, Dundee made the break through when Jimmy Toner sent the perfect pass to Flavell from the wing and the wee centre shot low past Niven into the Ayrshire side's goal.

Six minutes later, Dundee made certain when a Bobby Henderson long punt reached the Killie penalty area and as centre-half Thyne hesitated, Flavell raced in to thump the bouncing ball into the corner of the net.

'Hampden Smash-And-Grab by Flavell', proclaimed the headline in *The Courier* on the Monday but Dundee didn't care as they became the first side to retain the Scottish League Cup.

At the end of the season, Flavell finished as the Dark Blues' top scorer for the second season in a row with twenty-five goals, wearing the number nine shirt with which he became synonymous.

After enjoying a two month summer tour of South Africa, in which Bobby scored fifteen goals in Dundee's seventeen match unbeaten visit, Bobby started the new season in the same goal scoring form by grabbing four in a 6-1 League Cup win over Stirling Albion in the first game.

However after scoring seven goals in eighteen starts by Christmas, the ageing Flavell found himself out of the team as George Merchant moved from centre-half to centre-forward and started scoring goals. He therefore moved to Kilmarnock for two years before transferring to St. Mirren where he would later become manager and knock Dundee out of the Scottish Cup in the Championship season.

Flavell however will be remembered for more glorious cup exploits with Dundee and his sixteen goals in the two League Cup campaigns in the early fifties did as much as anything to help Dundee win back to back trophies for the only time in the Club's history.

Honours at Dundee:
Scottish League Cup winners: 1951/52, 1952/53
Scottish Cup runner-up: 1952
Appearances, Goals:
League: 68, 32 goals
Scottish Cup: 6
League Cup: 24, 21 goals
Totals: 98, 53 goals

Gerry Follon

Gerry Follon's career was temporarily halted before it really got underway when World War Two broke out in the year he was signed from Lochee Harp in 1939 and considering he went on to play 301 times for Dundee, it is remarkable to think how many times he could have played had Hilter not enforced a six year hiatus.

Follon's time at Dens coincided with an incredibly successful post war period and he would go on to collect four winner's medals and two runners-up medals while at Dens Park as well as a Scottish League cap.

In his inaugural season, Gerry played ten games for Dundee in the Scottish League

Eastern Division as a right winger and continued on the wing after the end of hostilities but it wasn't until the 1946/47 season when he moved to right back that he became a regular in the side and made the number two jersey his own.

Originally a G.P.O. engineer, Gerry went on to University to attain an honours degree in teaching and despite many tempting offers from Dundee manager George Anderson, he remained part-time during his spell at Dens. The flamboyant Dundee boss wouldn't usually accommodate part-timers in his first team but such were Gerry's skills that he bent his own rules to play the Geography teacher.

Gerry was part of the side that won back-to-back Scottish League B Division Championships and in 1948/49 made forty-two appearances as Dundee were pipped by one point to the Scottish League A Division Championship after a last day disaster at Falkirk.

Silverware was just around the corner however as he played no mean part in the back-to-back League Cup wins in 1951 and 1952 as Dundee became the first side to successfully defend the trophy.

Gerry played in all nine matches on the 'Road to Hampden' in the autumn of 1951 and in the tenth and ultimately successfully League Cup Final match, he was part of the side which beat Rangers 3-2 with a last minute goal in front of a estimated 30,000 Dundonians in the crowd.

He played in seven of the ten matches in the 1952/53 League Cup campaign and was one of seven players to pick up a second cup winning medal when Dundee defeated 'B' Division Kilmarnock 2-0 with two goals from Bobby Flavell.

In between these two successes, Follon suffered more Dark Blue heartache to add to the disappointment of 1949, when Dundee lost out to Motherwell in the 1952 Scottish Cup Final.

Dundee were at Hampden for the second time in the season after bagging the League Cup in October but the Final against Motherwell in front of a staggering 136, 990 couldn't see Dundee do a Cup double with Motherwell defeating the strong favourites 4-0.

'We just did not play at all that day', said Follon to the Dundee match programme in 1999, *'but all credit to Motherwell who were worthy winners. It was a huge disappointment not to lift the Cup and was my biggest disappointment of my time at Dens along which that 4-1 defeat at Falkirk in 1949.'*

The second League Cup in October more than made up for the Scottish Cup defeat and it was a remarkable for Dundee to reach three national cup finals in a row at Hampden which were played in front of over a quarter of a million fans.

Gerry also played in the match in which Dundee's record home attendance figure was set when 43, 024 watched a Scottish Cup second round tie against Rangers. It's a record that is unlikely to ever be broken with Dens Park's capacity currently sitting at 11, 850 but unfortunately for Gerry, he was at fault for the second goal as Rangers won 2-0.

In Gerry's eighteen years at Dens, he also picked up international honours when he played for the Scottish League against the Irish League in 1947 not long after Dundee had returned to the top tier.

On leaving Dundee, Gerry signed for St. Johnstone where he teamed up with former team mate Johnny Pattillo at Muirton Park and then finished his career with a two year stint in the Highland League with Keith.

In the 1960s, he returned to Dens Park in a coaching capacity to look after Bob Shankly's reserve side with Jimmy Toner, a post he left only on attaining promotion to deputy rector at Lawside Academy in Dundee.

Honours at Dundee:
Scottish League Cup winner: 1951/52, 1952/53
Scottish Cup runners-up: 1952
Scottish League Championship runners-up: 1948/49
Scottish League B Division champions: 1945/46, 1946/47
Scottish League cap: 1
Appearances, Goals:
League   215, 4 goals
Scottish Cup: 25
League Cup: 58, 1 goal
Other: 3
Totals: 301, 5 goals

Cammy Fraser

When Dundee supporters went to watch the Dark Blues play Clydebank on December 7th 1991, they could hardly believe their eyes when they watched their side warm up on the Kilbowie pitch. There had been no news in the press about Dundee signing any players pre match but there on the park was a new face who looked familiar to those who remembered The Dee's last successful promotion campaign just over ten years before.

No one was quite sure if it was really him but when the teams were announced over the loud speaker about 2.30pm, it was confirmed that it really was Cammy Fraser, Dundee's inspirational midfield captain from the early eighties who had returned to try and use his experience to once again help Dundee back to the Premier Division.

Born in the home of Jute, Jam and Journalism July 22nd 1957, Fraser started his career with Heart of Midlothian in 1974 and won the Scottish First Division title with the Tynecastle side in 1979/80. One of the clubs that Hearts replaced in Premier Division was Cammy's home town team of Dundee and when the Dark Blues had a dreadful start on their return to the second tier, new manager Donald McKay splashed out a club record fee of £61,000 to bring Fraser to Dens Park in an attempt to kick start Dundee's promotion campaign.

After failing to win any of their first eight league games, promotion favourites Dundee lay bottom of the First Division but soon the hard tackling midfielder became a key figure in the Dens Park revival.

Despite the poor league results, Dundee had been going well in the League Cup having defeated Arbroath 5-0 on aggregate in the first round and Premier League Kilmarnock on penalties after two stalemates and now in the quarter-final they met Alex Ferguson's Aberdeen who had been crowned Scottish champions five months before.

The Dons were overwhelming favourites to win but in the first leg, it was Dundee who were unlucky not to take a lead up north after a scoreless draw. In the second leg, Jimmy Murphy was at his trickiest on the Dundee wing but in the second half The Dee had to rely on the heroics of Bobby Geddes in the goal to keep to tie level. However with just five minutes remaining, Cammy Fraser beat Jim Leighton with a fifteen yard drive and Dundee held on for a 1-0 win to book a place in the last four.

The moustached Fraser was the hero of the hour and in the semi-final against fellow First Division side Ayr United, he was again on the score sheet in the 3-2 second leg win at Dens which sent Dundee into the Final 4-3 on aggregate.

~ 64 ~

In the Final, Dundee met neighbours Dundee United in an historic match at Dens but the disappointment of the 3-0 defeat didn't derail the Dark Blue promotion push that was now picking up momentum.

Dundonian Fraser had brought drive and attacking flair to the midfield and having been bottom of the league just after his arrival, Fraser now helped Dundee secure a return to the top flight with a second place finish as Dundee went on a twelve match unbeaten run at the end of the season.

Back in the Premier Division, the swashbuckling Fraser was an inspirational figure as Dundee retained their top flight status by four points and the following season was appointed captain as Dundee pushed on now towards competing for a European spot.

Although a Dundee United fan as a boy, Fraser had been delighted to sign for the Dark Blues and in the centenary history of Dundee, *Up Wi' The Bonnets,* he told author Norrie Price that *'I had always hoped to play for the one of the city clubs and it was a great honour when I was made skipper.'*

Despite his Arab tendencies as a youngster, it always rankled with Fraser that he was only on the winning side in a Derby once, in a 1-0 win at Tannadice in November 1983 but at a Dee4Life fundraising event in 2004, he recalled the pleasure he got when Dundee defeated the Terrors in the 1984 Tennents' Sixes semi-final.

Dundee and Dundee United had decided to share a bus to the indoor six-a-side tournament at the Coasters Arena in Falkirk and the United players were trying to wind the Dees up that they were just a pub team.

When the sides met in the last four the Dark Blues took great pleasure in beating The Arabs 4-2 and for the coach home both sides were given a crate of the sponsor's product.

United manager Jim McLean however told his squad they weren't allowed to drink it and so the Dundee players took great delight in taking their case after being told on the journey west that they were *'only a pub team'*. Needless to say however, Dundee lost the Final twenty-four hours later to Rangers.

However it was Fraser's performances in the eleven-a-side version of the game which caught the Ibrox men's eye and six months later in the summer of 1984, they offered £200,000 for the skipper to change his shade of blue.

New manager Archie Knox had wanted to keep Fraser and build his midfield around him and despite being offered Dundee's best ever terms, Cammy joined the Light Blues for only £150,000. The fee had been set by a tribunal and it was a huge disappointment for Dundee to not only lose their captain but also receive £50,000 less than had been originally offered.

Cammy won two League Cups and the Premier Division title while in Glasgow, meaning he had won league medals with three different clubs before he joined Raith Rovers in the 1987 closed season.

Four years later, he returned to Dundee to add some experience to another faltering promotion campaign and help cover for a spate of defensive injuries. It was something of a surprise that manger Iain Munro brought back the fans favourite to Dens but those fans at Kilbowie saw the first of fifteen appearances which helped Dundee win the First Division title and promotion back to the Premier League.

At that Dee4Life fundraiser in the wake of Dundee going into administration, Fraser donated his 1980 League Cup Final shirt for auction and was asked by Radio Scotland's Off The Ball presenter Tam Cowan what he thought made him a legend. He replied tongue in cheek that it was because he was from Fintry but Fraser couldn't be further from the truth as it was not coming from one of Dundee's northern housing schemes that made him a Dark Blue legend but rather the fact he was a terrific player and captain for the Club who played in a national cup final and two successful promotion campaigns and who gave his all ever time he pulled on a Dundee shirt.

Honours at Dundee:
Bells' Scottish League Cup runner-up: 1980/81
Scottish League First Division winner: 1991/92
Scottish League First Division runner-up: 1980/81
Appearances, Goals:
League: 143, 19 goals
Scottish Cup: 11
League Cup: 25, 4 goals
Totals: 179, 24 goals

Jimmy Gabriel

Dundonian Jimmy Gabriel first came to the attention of Dundee F.C. when he played right-half for Scotland Under 15s in a schoolboy international at Dens Park in 1956. His talent shown through and Dundee boss Willie Thornton snapped him up after that game, describing him as, *'the best player I have ever seen at that age.'*

There had been interest from several other teams but Jimmy's dad of the same name, who played for East Fife, Chelsea and Charlton was in no doubt his son should join his home town team.

In a period of change and team building after the trophy winning successes in the early fifties, Thornton was keen on introducing young players into the side when he took over in 1954 and with debuts given to young players such as Alex Hamilton, Bobby Cox, Andy Penman, Alex Stuart, Hugh Robertson, Ian Ure and Alan Gilzean in the later half of the decade, the team were given the nickname of the 'Thornton Babes'.

Farmed out initially to local Junior side Dundee North End, Gabriel was recalled to Dens after just one year and he became part of the 'Thornton Babes' on August 13th 1958 when he made his debut against Motherwell at Fir Park in a 2-1 League Cup sectional win.

Lining up with his idol, Dundee captain Doug Cowie, the seventeen year old put in an impressive display and he immediately went on to become a first team regular, making sixty-seven appearances for the Club.

In the summer of 1959, Gabriel was part of the Dundee squad which went on a ten game tour of the U.S.A and Canada, sailing out on the S.S. Mauretania on May 6th. The fixture list included matches against West Bromich Albion and Legia Warsaw as well as with various North American sides and it was a tremendous experience for the young Gabriel which had a big influence on him for his future career.

Upon returning from America, the Dens Parkers were in shock when popular goal keeper Bill Brown was sold to Tottenham but Gabriel continued to put in some stylish performances as Dundee finished a credible fourth and looked like they were ready to mount a serious challenge to the Championship.

In 1960, Gabriel's impressive displays were rewarded with being called up to play for the Scottish League against Scotland with team mate Alan Cousin and in November, he was given an Under 23 cap for Scotland against Wales.

By then however, Gabriel had a new boss at Dens after Bob Shankly had taken over from Thornton a month before and Gabriel's time in Dark Blue was soon to be cut short as interest in the fair-haired defender started to mount.

As well as the sale of Brown to Spurs, Dundee had also sold popular inside-left Davie Sneddon to Preston for £12,000 but the board gave new manager Shankly assurances that no more players would be sold.

They were unable however to resist a £30,000 bid for Gabriel from Everton after an initial bid had been turned down and Shankly decided to leave the decision to the player himself. Although happy at Dens, Gabriel elected the big-money Goodison outfit and Shankly was bitterly disappointed.

There were storms of protests from disgruntled Dundee fans but with up-and-coming youngster Ian Ure in the wings, the loss to the team was not as great as it could have been.

In an instant, Jimmy became the most expensive player ever to leave Scotland, beating the previous record of £26, 500 that Spurs paid to Hearts for Dave McKay. It also became the highest transfer fee received for a Dundee player to date and was a club record which not broken until Gabriel's replacement in the team Ian Ure also left for London to join Arsenal three years later.

By the end of the season, Dundee had erected a 10,000 capacity covered enclosure opposite the main stand an a new floodlighting system was also installed which was hanselled by a friendly with Shankly's brother Bill's Liverpool side in March and it was suspected that that they had been paid for by the Gabriel fee received from 'The Toffees'. Some fifty years later, the legacy of Jimmy sale is still seen at Dens today as both the covered enclosure and the floodlights still stand and are both in regular match day use.

It is a mystery that Gabriel only ever won two full international caps while at Everton but he enjoyed success with the Goodison club, playing 304 times and scoring 37 goals as they won the English League Championship in 1962/63 and the F.A. Cup in 1966.

After four years on Merseyside, he went on to play for Southampton, Bournemouth, Swindon, Brentford and Seattle Sounders in the U.S., before returning to Everton in a coaching capacity in 1990. It wasn't long before he had a short spell as caretaker manager in November 1990 after the departure of Colin Harvey and then another one three years later when Howard Kendall left after his second spell.

Gabriel left Goodison in 1997 to return to America to take up a coaching post with his old club Seattle Sounders and in 2009 was awarded with a prestigious Golden Scarf Award for services to the Seattle club.

In his time with Dundee, Gabriel is remembered as a player with elegance and style and was described by his hero and skipper Doug Cowie as *'a natural'*.

Honours at Dundee:
Scottish League appearance: 1
Scotland Under 23 cap: 1
Appearances:
League: 55
Scottish Cup: 2
League Cup: 10
Total: 67

Tommy Gallacher

When Tommy Gallacher signed full-time for Dundee in 1947, it had an impact on football in the City of Discovery that went way beyond the normal span of a player's career. To begin with he became part of the famous, trophy winning half-back line of Gallacher, Cowie and Boyd and then when he retired prematurely, he became Dundee's foremost football correspondent for local newspaper *The Courier and Advertiser* for whom he wrote for twenty-nine years.

Born in Renfrewshire as one of five sons of Scottish football legend, Celtic's 'Mighty Atom' Patsy Gallacher, it would perhaps seem only natural that he would follow in his father's footsteps and it was to Dundee's fortune that the cultured and classy wing half would spend eleven years at Dens Park.

To begin with, his father Patsy was keen that his son would take up the game on a strictly amateur basis and in 1942, with a number of clubs after Tommy, he signed for amateur side Queen's Park while working in his reserved occupation job in the labs at the Royal Ordnance establishment in Bishopton.

Towards the end of the War however, Tommy was keen to try something else and within weeks of leaving the labs, his call up papers were through his letterbox and he joined the Highland Light Infantry in January 1945. Stationed at the Bridge of Don Barracks in Aberdeen, Gallacher worked as a P.E. instructor with the Army and was commanded by Colonel Jock McGregor, who was a friend of Dundee's Granite City born manager, George Anderson.

As was the norm during both wars, players turned out as guests for clubs near where they were stationed and towards by the end of the season, Tommy found himself turning out for Aberdeen. At the start of the 1945/46 season however, Anderson used his influence with his friend to have Gallacher turn out sixteen times for The Dee as they won the Scottish League 'B' Division championship.

Dundee were denied promotion to the top tier due to the Scottish League declaring the season unofficial with so many players still in the armed forces and by the time Tommy signed full-time on his first professional contract in the summer of 1947, Dundee had won the 'B' Division for a second time so that Tommy's return to Dens coincided with the Club's return to the top flight.

Tommy started his first full season with Dundee as an inside-right but soon he was to stamp his class and quality at Dens Park by wearing the number four jersey at right-half due to the intervention of his old army commander Colonel McGregor. When wing-half Reggie Smith was set to miss a match at Parkhead due to a boil on his leg, Anderson was unsure who to replace the English international with and when he spoke to old buddy McGregor, he suggested that to Anderson that he should play Gallacher at wing-half, having seen him play there for the army.

Despite this being a bluff, Gallacher very soon settled into his new position and the rest, as they say is history as he struck up a partnership with Doug Cowie and Alfie Boyd to become part of perhaps the finest half-back line in Dundee's history.

In his second full season, Dundee really clicked into gear with Tommy playing in all forty-four league and cup matches as Dundee finished runners-up in the Scottish 'A' Division Championship. Needing just a point on the last day at Brockville to win the title, Dundee lost 4-1 to Falkirk and gifted Rangers the League Flag by a solitary point.

'We hit them with everything that day but we couldn't get the ball past their brilliant little goalkeeper George Nicol', Tommy told author

Jim Hendry in his superb *Dundee Greats* book. *'He was invincible that day and he even saved Alec Stott's penalty. It was a sad end to a tremendous season....... and in my opinion we were a far better side than the one a couple of years later when Billy Steel came.'*

However silverware didn't elude Dundee for long and that side with Billy Steel won Dundee's first major honour in forty-one years when they lifted the Scottish League Cup in October 1951. In front of 92,000 at Hampden, Dundee defeated Rangers 3-2 with goals from Flavell, Pattillo and Boyd but missed out on a cup double that season when they lost 4-0 to Motherwell in the Scottish Cup Final.

Dundee did however achieve a cup double when the following season they became the first side to retain the League Cup after defeating Kilmarnock 2-0 in the Final but Gallacher missed the game after being dropped when he fell out with George Anderson over bonus payments due from a close season tour of Turkey.

Tommy continued to play for Dundee until 1956 but the beginning of the end came for Gallacher when Willie Thornton took over from George Anderson in the Dens Park hot seat. Thornton wanted Tommy to play in his old position of inside forward but it didn't work out and he was keen to move on to pastures new. Falkirk and Dunfermline were interested but Dundee wanted a fee and wouldn't release him and at thirty-four he decided to hang up his boots and pursue a career with local publisher's D.C. Thomson for whom he had been writing a column in their *Courier* newspaper for the previous eighteen months.

Football's loss was journalism's gain as he would write about football in Dundee over the next three decades reporting on all of Dundee's major triumphs and European trips in the sixties and seventies.

It is however as a strong, forceful and creative wing-half that Tommy will be best remembered at Dens and it is a tragedy that he won only one Scottish League cap against the English League in 1949, often overlooked for the full side despite being in reserve eleven times. Tommy with his deft touch, was a key figure in team built on foundations of quality and finesse who brought glory in a golden age that is rightly revered in the Club's history.

Honours at Dundee:
Scottish League Cup winner: 1951/52
Scottish League Championship runner-up: 1948/49
Scottish Cup runner-up: 1952
Scottish League B Division winner: 1945/46
Scottish League cap: 1
Appearances, Goals:
League: 200, 9 goals
Scottish Cup: 24,
League Cup: 50, 2 goals
Other: 5, 1 goal
Totals: 279, 12 goals

Bobby Geddes

Born on the 'Glorious Twelfth' in 1960, Robert (Bobby) Geddes joined Dundee in 1979 and made his debut on September 11th 1979 in the Anglo-Scottish Cup second round tie against Sheffield United.

In goal for that first leg in Sheffield had in fact been Dundee's regular keeper Ally Donaldson, and when the popular thirty-six year old retired at the end of a season in which Dundee were relegated, it gave Geddes his big chance at start of the following season in the First Division.

Geddes soon established himself in the Dundee goal and by October, Rab had been an ever present in the team as he lined up at Dens against Aberdeen in the League Cup quarter-final.

Dundee faced a formidable Aberdeen side which had become Scottish League Champions for the first time under Alex Ferguson the previous season but undaunted, Geddes went on to complete a clean sheet double over the Champions, as Dundee recorded a memorable 1-0 win in the second leg after drawing the first 0-0.

Dundee then beat fellow First Division side Ayr United in the semis while Dundee United knocked out Celtic in the other tie and the Scottish League sensibly decided the Final should be played in the city with the venue being Dens on the toss of a coin.

The official match programme for the Final featured a caricature picture of the goalkeepers from both clubs on the cover and so Geddes appeared on the front holding the trophy with United keeper Hamish MacAlpine but there was to be no happy ending for Rab. The Dees went down 3-0 to their neighbours and Geddes collected the first medal of his career in the shape of a runners-up medal but he was considered to be one of Dundee's few successes on a disappointing day.

Two weeks after the Final, Geddes' season was over when a clash with Rae of Hibs resulted in severe knee ligament damage. A fifteenth second diving header from Eric Sinclair proved to be the winner against The Dees' promotion rivals but it the points were only collected thanks to a brave display from Geddes.

After the collision, Geddes played on with a heavily strapped knee and played the game of his life, culminating with a miraculous save from Craig Patterson just on full time. This came after Geddes had also taken a bad head knock yet continued to play on he earned a place in the hearts of Dundee's supporters after such a brave and heroic display.

It was to be his last game of the season in which Dundee clinched promotion back to the Premier Division on the last day of the season at East Stirlingshire but he recovered in time to regain his place between the sticks for Dundee's return to the top flight for the 1981/82 season.

Geddes was amongst a clutch of youngsters along with Stewart McKimmie, Ian Ferguson and Ray Stephen who impressed in the Premier League and Geddes made thirty-five league and cup appearances as Dundee retained the Premier League place by four points.

Geddes was by now a Scottish Under-21 internationalist having made his debut against Sweden in 1981 and earned a total of five caps at this level including a cap against England in 1988 as an overage player. Throughout his time at Dens, Rab was called up to several Scotland squads but was unfortunate not to actually gain any full caps or even get a place on the bench.

For the next couple of seasons Rab vied for the number one spot with Colin Kelly and then returned in goal in October 1983 in time to play in a memorable 1-0 win over Dundee United at Tannadice in November when a Peter Mackie goal gave Dundee their first win over United since October 1979.

The following December Archie Knox replaced Donald McKay as boss and he led Dundee to the Scottish Cup semi final later that season. Geddes was part of the side which went down 2-0 to Aberdeen and Tynecastle but in Knox's first pre season, he brought in another keeper in the shape of Tom Carson from Dumbarton and Rab spent the 1984/85 season battling with TC for the number one spot.

Rab's record against United was fairly good and many Dundee fans will remember him for a fantastic save from Eamon Bannon at Tannadice that featured on the opening credits of Sportscene for a considerable time. In total he played in seven victories over United which included the League Cup quarter-final 2-1 win at Dens in front of a capacity 19,724 crowd.

He was part of the team that reached two cup semi finals in 1987 and in January 1988 picked up the second medal of his Dundee career when he captained Dundee to victory in the prestigious Tennents' Sixes competition.

In February 1989, Geddes was awarded for his ten years with the club with a testimonial match against Liverpool and over 9000 fans turned up to honour Rab and watch a classy Liverpool side win 3-1.

Geddes' last regular appearance for Dundee came on December 9th 1989 in a 3-3 draw at home to St Mirren and at the end of the season, when Dundee were relegated, Rab put in a transfer request after the disappointment of losing his place to Tom Carson.

In an effort to cost cut after relegation twelve players were put up for transfer and the club were only too happy to accept a £70,000 bid for Geddes from Kilmarnock in August 1990 where in 1993 he was part of their promotion-winning side back to the Premier League.

In 2008, Geddes returned to Dens as goalkeeping coach and then in April injuries forced 47-year old Geddes to appear as substitute goalkeeper in the final match of the season against Hamilton.

Geddes would again be on the Dundee bench five times in the 2009/10 season and very nearly had to come on in the ALBA Cup quarter-final tie away to Stirling Albion when Tony Bullock picked up an injury but decided to play on.

Incredibly however, Rab did have to come off the bench in a league match away to Raith Rovers in April when Tony Bullock injured his hamstring. His appearance took place almost thirty years after he played for Dundee in the final of the League Cup and he is the not only the oldest player to ever play for Dundee, eclipsing Gordon Smith by ten years but he is also the oldest player to play in a competitive match in Scotland.

At forty-nine years and 256 days, Geddes beats Jim Calder's Scottish League record who turned out for Peterhead at the age of 46 in 2007 and he beats Davie Irons Scottish Football record who earlier the same season came off the bench in the last minute in the Scottish Cup for Threave Rovers against Whitehall Welfare aged 48 years and 98 days.

In his eleven years at Dens as a player, Geddes made a total of 312 appearances for The Dees, making the fifteenth highest number of appearances for the club to which he added his 313th game twenty years after he left. Rab made a total of ninety-seven clean sheets for The Dark Blues, which is an impressive average of one clean sheet every 3.2 games.

Bobby Geddes is a genuine hero of the Dundee support and has been welcomed back onto the legends table at the Player of the Year Dinner in recent years.

Honours at Dundee:	
Bells' Scottish League Cup runner-up: 1980/81	
Scottish League First Division runner-up: 1980/81	
Tennents' Sixes winner:	1988
Scotland Under-21 caps:	5
Appearances:	
League:	254 + 1 sub
Scottish Cup:	24
League Cup:	33
Other:	1
Total:	313

Alan Gilzean

Alan Gilzean is the 'King of Dens Park' and is without doubt one of the greatest players to ever grace a Dark Blue jersey. There have been some great forwards in Dundee's history but none had a strike rate to match 'Gillie' (as he was affectionately known) and his record speaks for itself.

Top Overall Scorer - 169 goals in 190 competitive games.
Top Scorer In One Season - 52 goals in 1963/64.
Top European Scorer - 9 goals.
Top Scorer In One Game - 7 goals against Queen of the South. in 1962. (Record shared with Bert Juliussen)
Top Successive Scorer - 7 goals in 7 consecutive games. (January 1st to February 1st 1964)
Top Hat-Trick Scorer - 17 hat-tricks.

Hailing from Coupar Angus in Perthshire, Alan John Gilzean was born in Perth on October 22nd 1938 and began his football career with his hometown team Coupar Angus Juveniles. He then joined Junior side Dundee Violet in 1955 before signing for Dundee in 1957 after his father persuaded the young Gilzean that Dundee were a better choice than boyhood heroes Hibernian who were also interested.

After banging in goals for the reserves, Gilzean made his first team debut on August 22nd 1959 in a 4-1 League Cup defeat at home to Motherwell and by the end of the season had scored eight goals in eight league games.

Gilzean was the last Dundee player to complete his National Service while at the Club and he would travel up by train on Thursday nights from his base in Aldershot. This may have contributed to the fact that his first goal for the The Dee didn't come until six months after his debut when he scored in a 3-1 home win against St. Mirren in February and the 11,000 present that day had little indication of what a goal phenomenon was to follow.

Standing 5ft 9in, with short, dark hair, Gilzean quickly became the answer to Dundee's goal scoring problem. Playing mostly at inside-left, wearing the number ten shirt, Gilzean had a tremendous shot and a great finishing prowess, plus heading ability for which he became famed. He was able to spring high above defenders and was described in Dundee's European Cup quarter-final Anderlecht match programme in 1963 as *'the best header in Scotland.'*

Gille's first hat-trick for The Dee came before the end of his debut season in the penultimate match at Dens against Stirling Albion and the following season saw Gilzean start in fine scoring form when he hammered home four hat-tricks in the first month of the campaign.

By the end of the season, he had scored thirty-two goals in forty-two appearances and with the emergence of young stars such as Gilzean, Ian Ure, Andy Penman and Hugh Robertson gave rise to optimism that something special was about to happen at Dens Park.

And special it did as Dundee brought home the Scottish League Flag for the first time in their history and the 1961/62 season was also the season in which Gillie really showed his class. Dundee's eighty goal league campaign saw them triumphantly finish as Champions with Gilzean scoring twenty-four goals in twenty-nine league games and included in those were two goals against St. Johnstone on the title winning day at Muirton.

For Dundee fans of a certain generation, whenever the Dark Blues tackle Rangers, thoughts go back to one of the great one man demolitions of the Ibrox giants.

That happened on November 11th 1961, when Alan Gilzean was part of the Dundee line-up which recorded an extraordinary 5-1 over their hosts and Gillie emerged as the star of the game when he notched four goals to really ram home Dundee's title credentials. It really was a Remembrance Day for Dundee fans to remember but with rumours circulating that the game had been postponed due to thick fog and the police turning back Dundee fans at Glasgow's Buchanan Street station, many Dundee fans missed Dundee's greatest ever league result.

Season 1962/63 would also be another momentous season for Dundee as their brilliant European Champions Cup campaign took them all the way to the semi-finals, spearheaded by Gilzean's brilliant run of scoring form of nine goals in eight games in the Continent's premier tournament.

He terrorised the back lines of some of Europe's best sides and hit hat-tricks against Cologne and Sporting Lisbon and a brace against Anderlecht in the Heysel Stadium in Brussels. In the semi-final against Serie A side A.C. Milan, Gilzean came in for some pretty rough treatment from the Italians and was sent off in the second half of the second leg at Dens for retaliation but not before he headed the only goal in a 1-0 win.

That season finished with forty-one goals from forty-three games and Gilzean set himself a personal milestone in December 1962, when he netted seven in a 10-2 massacre of Queen of the South. Equalling Bert Juliussen's club record of seven goals in one match set in 1947, it was just one short of Jimmy McGrory's record of eight goals in one game for Celtic in 1928.

Despite Gillie's fantastic goal scoring record, he was incredibly not yet a full internationalist although he had been capped three times at Under-23 level and had made two of his three appearances for the Scottish League side. That was to change in 1963/64 when Gilzean won the first of his twenty-two caps for Scotland when he made his debut for Scotland against Norway in November 1963.

He won five full caps for Scotland while at Dundee and in April 1964 would become a hero in the dark blue of Scotland as well as Dundee when he scored the winner against England at

Hampden in a 1-0 win with the first of his twelve international goals. Gilzean then scored twice for the national side against West Germany in Hanover in May and those goals would be the last scored for Scotland by a Dundee player for thirty-nine years.

Domestically, Dundee reached the Scottish Cup Final as Gilzean set a new club record of fifty-two goals in a season in forty-eight games. He scored nine goals on 'The Road to Hampden' including a hat-trick against Brechin City in the second round and he netted two in the semi-final win over Second Division Kilmarnock at Ibrox.

Two late goals from Rangers denied Gilzean a cup winners' medal as Rangers completed the Treble and he would score just five more times for Dundee as his high profile strikes had brought him to the attention of England's leading clubs who would come calling for his talent.

In December 1964, a new Scottish record fee of £72, 500 from Tottenham Hotspur was enough to prize Gillie away from Dens and his move to London brought him more success as he won the F.A. Cup, League Cup and U.E.F.A. Cup while forging potent partnerships up front with first Jimmy Greaves and then Martin Chivers.

The money from Tottenham was the highest transfer received by the Club at that point and it is frightening to think how much Gilzean would be worth in today's transfer market.

Gilzean is revered as much today by the Dundee support as he was in the glory years of the early Sixties with a fanzine named *'Eh Mind O' Gillie'* and in 2003 he was voted as the Club's most valuable player from the Championship winning side.

In April 2009, Gilzean was inducted into the inaugural Dundee F.C. Hall of Fame, when the award was accepted on his behalf by the son Ian who himself made twenty-five appearances for the Club in the 1992/93 season and also scored in a memorable win over Rangers and his father had done almost thirty years previous.

In 2010, Gilzean was nominated for Scottish Television's Scotland's Greatest Team and as top goal scorer in all competitions four years running from 1960/61 to 1963/64, it is probably safe to say that his 169 goal haul for Dundee will never be bettered.

A true Dundee legend in every sense of the word, we may never see his goal scoring like again. 'All Hail Gillie – the King of Dens Park.'

Honours at Dundee:	
Scottish League Champions:	1961/62
European Cup semi-final:	1962/63
Scottish Cup runner-up:	1964
Scotland full caps:	5
Scottish League caps:	3
Scotland Under-23 caps:	3
Dundee F.C. Hall of Fame:	
Legends Award 2009	
Appearances, Goals:	
League:	134, 113 goals
Scottish Cup:	15, 15 goals
League Cup:	24, 26 goals
Europe:	8, 9 goals
Other:	9, 6 goals
Totals:	190, 169 goals

Bobby Glennie

Bobby Glennie is a Dens Park stalwart who was lucky enough to play for the club he supported as a boy, for twelve enjoyable years. As a Dundee player, there is arguably no one who was more committed to the Dark Blue cause and he quickly became a fans favourite, who is still revered today.

Dundonian Bobby played his schools' football at St. Mary's and then St John's but it was when he started to turn out for local amateur side St. Columba's that he was spotted by Aberdeen scout Hugh Kean, who persuaded Bobby to sign for Jimmy Bonthrone's side in 1974.

Although he enjoyed his time in the Granite City, his first team chances were limited as The Dons had regulars Willie Miller, Doug Rougvie and Willie Garner holding down the central defensive positions.

Dundee boss Tommy Gemmell recognised this and with the promise of first team football, Bobby returned 'home' to sign for the Dark Blues in 1977.

His debut was a 2-0 home win over East Fife and it would the start of a Dens Park career that would see him pull on the famous jersey 387 times, making him currently eighth in the list of all time competitive appearances for The Dee.

Bobby soon became popular with the Dens Park support with his wholehearted displays and it was no surprise when his leadership qualities saw him appointed as captain of the Club.

In 1980 Dundee, as a First Division side, reached the Bell's League Cup Final against neighbours Dundee United and with the absence of regular captain Stewart McLaren who was injured in the semi final second leg against Ayr United, Glennie was given the job of leading the team out at Dens.

Although Dundee went down 3-0 to their bitterest rivals, Glennie was honoured to have led out The Dee for the first ever all city final. *'Although we lost to our city rivals'*, said Bobby to the Dundee match programme on the twentieth anniversary of the Final, *'that day at Dens was a great occasion. To reach a Final was a great feat for the Club and it was a great occasion for the city to have both teams in a major final.'*

That season did however provide Bobby with some success as Dundee secured promotion back to the Premier Division thanks to a last day win away at East Stirlingshire, which saw Dundee sneak into one of the two promotion places as runners-up behind Hibs. Glennie made the most appearances of any Dundee player that season, starting in every match, turning out forty-nine times for The Dee.

Glennie scored just six goals in his time at Dens but one of his strikes is undoubtedly one of the greatest goals to be scored in the Club's history. Against the side destined to win the Championship, Bobby hit a blistering forty yard screamer into the top corner past Aberdeen and Scotland goalkeeper Jim Leighton and in the press claimed, *'If the net hadn't stopped the ball, they'd have never found it'.*

That goal can be found on You Tube, under the title *'Bobby Glennie Is God'*, while in 2005, Dundee fanzine *The Derry Rhumba* released a Dundee goals DVD entitled, *'It's A Picture Goal For Bobby Glennie'*, which is the S.T.V. commentary on the goal from Jock Brown on their *Scotsport* highlights of the match.

Glennie himself quite rightly still enjoys talking about that goal and at a recent supporters' function proclaimed that, *'Jim Leighton had a cheek moving for that!'*

Glennie's loyalty and service to the Club was rewarded in 1986 with a testimonial against

Manchester City at Dens. Glennie certainly made it a game to remember as first he missed a penalty, then stepped up to score another in a 2-2 draw.

Glennie played in three further semi finals for Dundee, in the Scottish Cup against The Dons at Tynecastle in 1984, again at Tynecastle in the Scottish Cup against Dundee United in 1987 and in the League Cup semi against former club Aberdeen again, this time at Tannadice a few months later.

In his time at Dens, Glennie played under four managers, namely Tommy Gemmell, Donald McKay, Archie Knox and Jocky Scott and made his last appearance for Dundee towards the end of Scott's first spell in charge as boss.

In a Scottish Cup tie against Motherwell in February 1988, although far from fit, Glennie turned out for The Dee due to a shortage of central defenders but he had to limp off after twenty minutes with a recurrence of his groin injury. For him, his season and his Dundee playing career was over but it typified his commitment to the cause that he was prepared to put himself in the front line at considerable risk to himself.

After leaving Dens in 1989, Bobby played briefly for Raith Rovers, Forfar Athletic, Arbroath and Elgin City before a short spell in charge of Forfar and returned to Dens in the late Nineties for a few years as a match day hospitality host.

At the launch the Dundee F.C. Former Players' Association March 2010, Glennie was one of the players who were paraded on the pitch at half time against Inverness Caledonian Thistle and he fully deserved the warm applause that greeted a fondly remembered Dundee hero.

Honours at Dundee:
Bell's Scottish League Cup runner-up: 1980/81
Scottish League First Division runner-up: 1980/81
Appearances, Goals:
League: 303 + 11 subs, 6 goals
Scottish Cup: 26 + 2 subs
League Cup: 43 + 2 subs
Totals: 387, 6 goals

James Grady

James Grady wrote himself into Dundee F.C. folklore when on Sunday 22nd November 1998 he hit a twenty-five yard wonder strike at Tannadice to give The Dee their first victory over neighbours Dundee United in just over six years. Not content with scoring in a winning derby once, Grady did it again a further twice in his Dark Blue career, to earn himself a permanent place in the hearts of Dundee fans everywhere.

James Grady was born in Paisley on March 14th 1971 and he started out in Junior football with Barrhead side Arthurlie before turning senior with Clydebank in 1994. After three seasons at Kilbowie, Grady moved to Dens Park when manager John McCormack paid Clydebank £25,000 for his services, which was a third of the fee Dundee had offered the previous March on transfer deadline day and it soon turned out to be the bargain of the decade.

~ 76 ~

Grady started the first derby of the season at Dens in September when Dundee came back from 2-0 down to rescue a point in the final minute thanks to Darius Adamczuk. It left The Arabs with a sense of injustice and when Dundee made the shortest walk in football in November, United came out fast from the traps and had a goal wrongly disallowed for offside after twelve minutes.

James was amongst eight debutants to turn out for The Dee on the first day of the 1997/98 season at home to Falkirk and he scored his first goal for the Club in his second league match in a 3-0 win away to Partick Thistle.

Dundee had brought in so many new faces in an effort to win promotion back up to the Premier League at the fourth time of asking and the diminutive striker was an ever present as the Dark Blues were successful in their goal. James played in all forty-four league and cup games on the way to the title and his eighteen goals were enough to see him finish as Dundee's top scorer and win the S.P.F.A. First Division Player of the Year.

Grady and his strike partner Eddie Annand had scored thirty-two goals between them to shoot The Dee into the inaugural S.P.L. but in the summer Jocky Scott, who had taken over from 'Cowboy' McCormack in March, decided to bring in Tommy Coyne and Willie Falconer to challenge for the striking positions. It meant therefore that they started together just three times in the S.P.L. but it mattered not as Dundee finished fifth, their highest league position for twenty-five years.

The undoubted highlights of Dundee's triumphant return to the top tier were the two derbies at Tannadice and Jamesie Grady would emerge as a hero in both.

It was all one way traffic towards the Dundee goal for long periods of the game and it took some inspired defending to keep United out. The turning point came with about twenty minutes remaining when Grady, who had missed the last seven games through injury came off the bench to replace Tommy Coyne and with just eight minutes remaining, the 5ft 7in forward ran onto to an Eddie Annand head flick and volleyed a spectacular thirty yarder (it gets further out every time the tale is told) into the top of the net.

Robert Douglas had to make some heroic saves towards the end but to the delight of the Dark Blue fans, Dundee held on in front of the BSKYB cameras for their first Derby success since September 1992.

It was a wonderful winner from Grady and without doubt one of the greatest and most famous goals ever scored in the Club's history. Beating United on their own patch showed Scottish football that Dundee were back and the phenomenal strike from Grady against Dundee's greatest rivals was the best possible way to emphasis this.

By the end of the season, Dundee had achieved their highest placing since winning the Scottish League title in 1962 but of more importance to many Dundee supporters was the fact that Dundee had finished above United for the first time since 1973/74.

The match that this joyous fact was confirmed was ironically at Tannadice with four games to go when a 2-0 win also gave Dundee their first ever double league victory over United away from home.

Over 11,000 turned out on a gloriously sunny May Day and to the delight of their fans, the Dark Blues almost dominated proceedings. Time and again The Dee tore United apart but the breakthrough didn't come until the sixty-seventh minute when Brian Irvine rose high to power home a header from a Hugh Robertson corner.

Grady was again on the bench and he got his chance when Eddie Annand limped off after a shocking foul from United's Northern Ireland defender Darren Patterson, who was shown a red card for the challenge. With full time looming, Grady ran on to a defence splitting pass from Steven Boyack and fired a shot in on goal which after clipping off the United keeper's heel, rolled slowly into the net, to send the Dundee support behind the goal wild.

The following season, Grady did it again against The Arabs in the final derby of the season which this time was at Dens. Having failed to beat United at home since Keith Wright scored a hat-trick in 1989, Dundee were keen to lay that hoodoo to rest and did it in style with a comprehensive 3-0 win.

Grady was once again on the bench and this derby would be long be remembered for Javier Artero's astonishing display in front of the South Enclosure, with his powerful running causing United all sorts of problems. Grady came on at half time for the injured Spaniard Paco Luna and after four minutes played a superb one-two with Artero who crossed for Willie Falconer to head home.

Fifteen minutes later Dundee doubled their lead after fine link up play between Gavin Rae and Steven Boyack left the latter in acres of space in the United penalty box.

Boyack wasted no time picking out Grady, the smallest man on the park, who flashed a pinpoint header past the hapless Alan Combe to give Dundee a 2-0 advantage.

Dundee made it three when Grady unselfishly headed across the goal for Willie Falconer to nod in his second and his contribution after coming on at the interval was a key factor in Dundee's biggest Dens derby success since 1973.

Dundee again finished above Dundee United for the second year in succession but at the end of the season, Dundee dispensed with the services of Jocky Scott and it spelt the end of Grady's Dundee career when the new Italian management team wanted to bring in their own players. There were many Dundee fans however, who felt that Grady had been released far too quickly and could have done a job under the Bonetti regime.

Grady left in the summer to join Ayr United and had spells with Dundee United (we'll forgive him), Gretna, Hamilton and Morton where he was caretaker manager for the 2009/10 season.

Grady's tenacious running, never say die spirit and eye for goal made him a firm favourite on the Dens Park terracing and they were often heard to sing *'The James Grady Macarena'*. *'He's five foot two and his name is Jamesie Grady, He gets the ball and he goes on a mazy.......';* well, you know the rest about a man who goals against the Arabs will always be remembered and made James Grady a true Dundee legend.

Honours at Dundee:
Scottish League First Division winner: 1997/98
S.P.F.A. First Division Player of the Year: 1997/98
Appearances, Goals:
League: 74 + 19 subs, 24 goals
Scottish Cup: 5 + 2 sub, 3 goals
League Cup: 3 + 2 subs, 1 goal
S.F.L. Challenge Cup: 1
Totals: 106, 28 goals

Davie Halliday

Davie Halliday was a phenomenal striker who found scoring as natural as breathing and between the wars, became one of the most prolific centre forwards in the game. He finished top goal scorer on both sides of the borders in the Twenties and set a league goal scoring record for Dundee in season 1923/24 that still stands today.

David Halliday was born in Dumfries on December 11th 1901 and started in local schools football where he featured on the left wing before training as a motor mechanic with car manufacturer Arrol-Johnston. There he played for the works team before having trials with newly created local club Queen of the South and he played for 'The Doonhamers' in their inaugural season after signing for them in January 1920.

With this being Queens first season after formation, their fixtures consisted of challenge games and local cup competitions and soon they had Scottish League clubs enquiring after Halliday. In the summer of 1920, he moved to St. Mirren where he scored twice in thirteen league starts but just twelve months later he was on the move again when he signed for Dundee.

Dundee manager Sandy MacFarlane had been concerned about the lack of height in the Dundee attack and in an effort to rectify matters he signed Halliday from 'The Buddies' and moved him to centre forward. A goal scoring phenomenon was unleashed as sticking the ball in the net became second nature for Davie.

He made his Dark Blue debut in the second game of the season in a 1-0 defeat at Falkirk but his first goal wasn't in long in coming when he scored in a 2-1 defeat at Motherwell in his third start.

To begin with, the powerful Halliday was in and out the side at the start of the season but as the form of the previous season's top marksman Johnny Bell shaded, Davie soon got a regular start and finished the season himself as top goal scorer with twenty-five league and cup goals as Dundee finished fourth.

At the start of the 1922/23 season, Davie's appearances were restricted by injury but he still managed to score fifteen goals alongside new strike partner Davie McLean who had been signed in the summer from Bradford Park Avenue. McLean finished the season as top scorer, netting twenty-three times but it was the following season that the pair started to develop a potent partnership.

The advent of the awkward but hard running Halliday meant McLean switching to inside-right and there he became the 'general' of the team, cleverly controlling play and thrilling the fans with his thunderous long range shots. Perhaps more importantly however, McLean brought the best out of Davie Halliday and that season, the big centre-forward rattled in thirty-nine goals.

Halliday finished as top goal scorer in Scotland and it was an excellent total in an era of the three man offside rule. Remarkably, thirty-eight of those had been in the league in only thirty-six starts and he set a new Club record for the highest number of league goals in a season which still stands today. Tommy Coyne couldn't match his total in 1987/88, despite scoring thirty goals by New Year and even the great Alan Gilzean failed to beat Halliday's record with his best return being thirty-three goals in the league the season Dundee faced Rangers in the Scottish Cup Final.

The following season, Davie himself reached the Scottish Cup Final but like 'Gillie' thirty-nine years later, he too ended up on the losing side to one of the Old Firm when Celtic defeated The Dee 2-1.

On the way to the Final, Dundee defeated Johnstone in the first round when Halliday got a hat-trick in a 5-0 win and after defeating Lochgelly United in the next round, Dundee knocked out high flying Airdrie in round three when Davie got the third in a 3-1 win in front of 22 373 at Dens. In the quarter-final Dundee struggled against lowly Broxburn but with fifteen minutes remaining, the stalemate was broken when Halliday bundled the keeper and the ball into the net to put Dundee into the last four. Hamilton were defeated in the semi after a replay to send Dundee through to Hampden but they endured a painful defeat in the Final when Celtic scored two late goals to cancel out Dundee's halftime lead.

Against the odds, Dundee had dominated from the off and after half an hour took the lead through Halliday's strike partner Davie McLean. After taking a pass from Halliday, McLean slipped the ball to Duncan and when the winger crossed, the Celtic keeper could only palm the ball into the air under pressure form Halliday. Gilmour was first to the lose ball and headed it against the bar before McLean nipped in between two Celtic defenders to give Dundee a deserved lead.

After the break however, Dundee were far too negative and veteran Patsy Gallacher, father of Dundee fifties legend Tommy, started to cause havoc with his exquisite dribbling. Gallacher scored the equaliser with a mazy run which ended with him throwing himself over the goal line with the ball lodged between his feet and then with three minutes remaining won a free kick on the edge of the box from which Jimmy McGrory headed home to win the Cup.

Halliday finished the season as top scorer once again with twenty-four goals and in the summer signed for Sunderland for a Dens Park record fee received of £4000. In March 1924, the twenty-three year old had been capped for the Scottish League in a 1-1 draw with their English counterparts at Ibrox and with a scoring record of 103 goals in 147 games for Dundee, it was going to be hard to stop him becoming the latest in a widespread exodus of top Scots to head to England.

Halliday soon became equally prolific south of the border as north, scoring at least thirty-five league goals in each of the four full seasons he spent at Sunderland. His forty-three goals in 1928/29 made him top scorer in England's top division and this remains Sunderland's highest number of league goals scored by one player in a season in the Black Cats' history. Halliday hit his first 100 goals for Sunderland in just 101 games and has the best strike rate (goals to games ratio) of any Sunderland striker of 165 goals in 175 games.

Halliday returned to his native Scotland in 1937 when he became manager of Aberdeen in 1937 and started to bring national trophies to Pittodrie for the first time in their history after the Second World War. He won the League Cup in 1945/46 and then the Scottish Cup in 1946/47 and in 1954/55, he brought the Scottish League Championship to the Granite City for the first time and is the only manager along with Alex Ferguson to achieve this feat with The Dons.

Unfortunately for Halliday, his goals never brought him full international recognition as a player, being kept out of the Scotland side by Hughie Gallacher who scored twenty goals in twenty-three internationals. He does however remain a Dens Park legend with his league record that has stood for over eighty years and a strike rate of ninety goals in 126 league appearances which has been barely matched since the Club's formation in 1893.

Honours at Dundee:
Scottish Cup runner-up: 1925
Scottish League cap: 1
Appearances, Goals:
League: 126, 90 goals
Scottish Cup: 21, 13 goals
Totals: 147, 103 goals

Alex Hamilton

Alex Hamilton had a party piece where he played keepie-up with a sixpence before flicking it up and catching it in his pocket and he was the joker, the extrovert of Dundee's 1962 League Championship winning team. More than that however, Alex Hamilton was a wonderful footballer, one of the best full backs of his generation and with twenty-four appearances for the full Scotland side, he is the Dark Blues' most capped player in the Club's history.

Alexander William Hamilton was born in the West Lothian mining town of Armadale on April 5th 1936 and after being schooled in nearby Fauldhouse, he joined local juvenile side Westrigg Bluebell where he started his footballing career playing at outside-right.

'Hammy' as he became known at Dundee, joined the Dens Park side on March 6th 1957 despite missing a penalty when the Dark Blue manager Willie Thornton was watching. He had been working as an insurance agent at the behest of his mother but he was destined for great things in the dark blue of Dundee and Scotland.

Hammy didn't have long to wait for his first team debut as just five moths after putting pen to paper on Sandeman Street, he started in a 4-2 defeat at Hearts in the League Cup on August 31st. When his first five appearances all ended in defeat with the loss of twenty-two goals, Hamilton would hardly have envisaged that a League medal and a European Cup semi were only a few years away but by the end of the season, he had made twenty-one appearances at right-back in place of the injured Hugh Reid.

Hammy was a favourite with the fans and popular in the dressing room and his team mates all talk about him with fondness. He was instantly recognisable with his snappy fair-haired crew cut and a cheeky impish smile that was infectious to everyone around him.

At 5ft 7in, he wasn't the best defender in the air but Hammy's skills lay in becoming one of the first over lapping full backs in Scotland, no doubt helped by his education at outside-right with the Bluebells.

With an abundance of pace, he is remembered by Dundee and international team mate Ian Ure as *'a player who oozed talent and flair and was as lively a character as you'll ever meet'*.

Bobby Wishart describes Hammy as *'a livewire, a joker and a trickster'* and says that Hamilton's gang of Hugh Robertson, Ian Ure and Alan Gilzean were always up to something while Gillie himself calls him *'a great character and an unbelievable guy'*.

Off the park, Hammy used to love winding his team mates up, particularly Bobby Cox about how many international caps he had compared to himself and on the pitch, he was often heard to shout to the Dundee fans in the south enclosure, *'here comes the Hammy magic'*, throughout his 359 appearances for The Dee.

The undoubted highlight for Hamilton at Dens came in the 1961/62 season when he was an ever present as Bob Shankly's side lifted the Scottish League Championship trophy and the following season played in all eight ties as Dundee shocked Europe on the way to the Champions' Cup semi-final.

During the title winning season, Hammy made his first international debut when he played for the Scottish League against a star studded Italian League side at Hampden and the same month made his full international debut against Wales in a British International Championship match.

The Daily Record described Hamilton as *'the international find of the season'* and on November 29th 1961, he was one of three Dundee players who along with Ian Ure and Hugh Robertson, lined up against Czechoslovakia in a World Cup play-off match in the Heysel Stadium in Brussels.

It was the only occasion in the twentieth century that three Dundee players lined up together in the same Scotland side and in total, Hammy made thirty-four appearances in the dark blue of Scotland, twenty-four of those at full international level, a record for a Dundee player.

Interestingly, Hamilton lined up against England on seven occasions, three times with the Scottish League and four with the full side and was never on the losing team. He lined up against Bobby Charlton, (who made his Manchester United debut in a 5-1 friendly defeat against Dundee at Dens in 1956) on a number of occasions and told Jim Hendry in his *Dundee Greats* book that after one match at Hampden, a Scotland player shouted to Alf Ramsey, '*if you're looking for Bobby Charlton, you'd best check in our hamper as he might still be in Hammy's back pocket!*'

In May 1964, Hamilton was a team mate of Charlton's when they lined up together for the Rest of Europe against Scandinavia in Denmark and Hammy came on as a second half substitute to replace the Czechoslovakian right-back Bomba. On the bench he sat next to Eusebio and the star studded European side which won the match 4-2, also included Jim Baxter, Dennis Law Jimmy Greaves, Lev Yashin and Paul van Himst, who Hammy had lined up against in Dundee's European Cup quarter-final tie against Anderlecht in 1963.

A month before turning out for the Rest of Europe, Hamilton played in the 1964 Scottish Cup Final against Rangers where The Dee lost 3-1 thanks to two late Rangers' goals and that same season, saw Hamilton score his only goal for Dundee when he netted the winner in a 4-3 win at home to Falkirk four days before Christmas.

Hamilton played for The Dee for eleven years and captained Dundee in the latter stages of his career at Dens but the flamboyant full-backs talents were not restricted to football. Hamilton was also a noted singer and was the front man of a band comprising of Dundee team-mates Hugh Robertson, Andy Penman, Alex Stuart, Kenny Cameron and future Scotland boss Craig Brown.

They called themselves 'Hammy and the Hamsters' and although they released a single, its success was restricted to the local Dundee area.

Hamilton left Dundee in 1967 and had a spell in South Africa playing for Durban United and managing East London United. He returned to the city where he managed Junior side Dundee Violet and returned to Dens Park in 1988 to run the Club's lottery before becoming a match day hospitality host with full-back partner and friend Bobby Cox in 1989.

Alex sadly died in 1993 aged just fifty-seven but his legacy lives on at Dens Park with a hospitality lounge named in his honour and in April 2010, he was inducted in the Dundee F.C. Hall of Fame.

With his Championship-winning team mates Andy Penman, Bobby Cox, Gordon Smith and Hugh Robertson also sadly in the 'High Stand', there is no doubt that the ebullient Alex Hamilton will still be at the centre at all the fun, telling stories and cracking jokes.

Honours at Dundee:	
Scottish League Champions:	1961/62
European Cup semi-final:	1962/63
Scottish Cup runner-up:	1964
Scotland full caps:	24
Scottish League caps:	8
Scotland Trial International appearances:	2
Rest of Europe appearance:	1
Dundee F.C. Hall of Fame:	
Legends Award 2010	
Appearances, Goals:	
League:	261, 1 goal
Scottish Cup:	22
League Cup:	55
Europe:	10
Other:	11
Totals:	259, 1 goal

George 'Pud' Hill

George Hill was a dashing left winger who did much to bring Dundee out of the wilderness at the end of the Second World War and into the forefront of Scottish football. A provisional signing in 1939, he was a terrific servant to Dundee, remaining with the Club until 1955 and he was part of one of the most successful periods in the Dark Blues' history.

As a player, 'Pud' as he was known, was way before his time and he could cross a ball with great accuracy and had an amazing burst of speed. Like many wingers of his age, he was small and had a bag of tricks on the ball and when 'Wee Hilly's' name was announced over the tannoy on a match day, the Dens Park crowd would roar with delight.

Pud signed for Andy Cunningham's Dundee in 1939 after scoring in a trial match for Arbroath against the Dark Blues and made his debut for The Dee in a Scottish War Cup tie against Third Lanark at Dens on February 24th 1940. He played nine times in the Scottish League Eastern Division before Dundee retired for the duration of the conflict during which he returned to his old club, Junior side, Dundee North End.

George returned to Dens Park as soon as the Club started up again in the Scottish League North Eastern Division in 1944 and missed just one match as Dundee won the First Series which was played from August to December.

When the Scottish League resumed properly the following season, Dundee were in the B Division having been relegated in 1938 but as Dundee won the league by ten points, they were denied promotion as the League deemed the season unofficial with so many players still in the armed services.

To get promotion therefore Dundee would have to win it all again and win it again they did in 1946/47 beating Dundee United home and away on route with Pud getting four goals in twenty-two outings.

Within two years Dundee were challenging for the Scottish League championship and Hill was a key figure scampering along Dundee's touchline scoring five times in twenty-eight appearances including the winner against defending champions Hibernian in a 4-3 victory at Easter Road.

On the last day of the season however, Dundee failed to lift the League Flag when they surprisingly flopped at Falkirk in a 4-1 defeat which handed the title to Rangers. It could all have been so different however had the normally deadly Alec Stott converted a first half penalty at 0-0 after Pud was brought down in the box at the end of a mazy run in which he beat three men.

Dundee did however win some silverware in 1951 and 1952 when they twice won the Scottish League Cup but injury denied Hill a winners' medal both times but he did play in the Scottish Cup Final against Motherwell in April 1952.

Having scored twice in the 7-1 second round victory over non-league Wigtown, Pud missed the next round with a broken arm but he took his place in front of 136, 990 at Hampden which remains a record crowd for a final where either of the Old Firm weren't involved. Over 1000 Dundee fans were locked out after their 'special' train arrived late but they were the lucky ones as Pud and his team mates crashed to a 4-0 defeat to the Steelmen.

By 1955, George Anderson was replaced as the Dundee manager by Willie Thornton and when Pud's appearances began to get restricted because of a knee injury, Thornton allowed him to join East Fife after making 257 appearances for The Dee and scoring fifty times.

In 1956 he became manager of Montrose in the year they were admitted into the Scottish League and it was a position he enjoyed at Links Park for three years.

~ 83 ~

George was regarded by many to be unfortunate not to be capped by his country and upon retiring from the game, he ran a newsagent in Dundee's east end. Pud would often be seen in the Boars Rock bar in the city's Arbroath Road regaling his stories about his days at Dens Park playing alongside Billy Steel until he sadly died in 2002 aged eighty-one.

Back in the days when football teams were clearly structured into eleven different positions, it was often the wingers who provided the greatest excitement and George Hill certainly did that during his sixteen years as a Dee. Pud was an outstanding performer for Dundee and although small in stature, he lacked nothing in tenacity, allied to his speed and ability which made him a great favourite with the Dens Park fans.

Honours at Dundee:
Scottish League Championship
runners-up: 1948/49
Scottish Cup runners-up: 1952
Scottish League B Division winners:
1945/46. 1946/47
Scottish League North-East Division (first series) winners: 1944/45
Appearances, Goals:
League: 201, 42 goals
Scottish Cup: 15, 3 goals
League Cup: 35, 3 goals
Other: 6, 2 goals
Totals: 257, 50 goals

Doug Houston

Doug Houston joined Dundee immediately after the Dark Blues won the Scottish League championship and would spend eleven years at Dens Park during which he would play in the 1967 League Cup Final. A versatile player who could play in a variety of positions, Houston would go on to captain the Club and would become the only player to play in two European semi-finals.

Born in Glasgow on April 13th 1943, Doug Houston started his football career as an amateur with Queens Park, which allowed him to combine playing with studying at Jordanhill College to become a P.E. teacher and he would later teach in the City of Discovery.

It was while studying at Jordanhill that Houston met future Scotland manager Craig Brown and Brown, who played nine times in Dundee's championship year, recommended the left winger to Dundee manager Bob Shankly who signed the nineteen year old from The Spiders in the summer of 1962.

Dundee had been crowned Scottish champions the previous April but Houston managed to break into the side straight away and made his debut in the first league game of the 1962/63 season. Dundee however got off to the worst possible defence of their title with a 2-0 loss at home to Hearts but Houston retained his place on the left wing for the next game three days later when Dundee faced Dundee United in the League Cup at Dens. It was a much happier home debut for Doug as The Dee won 2-1 and the goals both came from veteran Gordon Smith who was twice Houston's age.

In his first season, Houston managed to play twenty-three times, with injury to league winning left winger Hugh Robertson giving Doug the chance to make his mark. In the first leg of the European Cup second round tie away to Sporting Club of Lisbon, an injury to Robertson allowed Houston to make his European debut in the Portuguese capital but Dundee went down 1-0 thanks to a last minute winner.

Robertson managed to recover for the second leg 4-1 win at Dens but was out for two months in its aftermath and in that period Houston got a run in the side and was on target for the Dark Blues in a 10-2 home win over Queen of the South, in which Alan Gilzean scored seven.

Dundee progressed to the European Cup semi-final that season and injury again to Robertson meant that Houston was in the line-up in the San Siro against A.C. Milan and again in the second leg at Dens but unfortunately the Dark Blues went out 5-2 on aggregate.

Over the next few seasons, Doug proved himself to be extremely versatile and played in a variety of positions in both midfield and defence. He would play as a left back, sweeper or winger and it was in his forward role that he scored in the European Cup Winners' Cup tie at home to Real Zaragoza in 1964.

By season 1967/68, Houston was an important part of the side and had started the campaign in midfield but when Dundee reached the League Cup Final in October, Doug dropped back into the defence to accommodate Alex Bryce out wide.

In one of the most exciting finals ever seen at the National Stadium, European Cup holders Celtic defeated the Dark Blues 5-3 in front of 66,660 fans with the Parkhead side maintaining a two goal lead for the majority of the game. With just ten minutes played, Dundee were 2-0 down but George Mclean made in 2-1 before the break. With seventeen minutes left, Celtic made it 3-1 before Jim McLean pulled another goal back but a defensive mix-up allowed Bobby Lennox to make it 4-2. Another goal from George McLean with five minutes left gave Dundee hope before Willie Wallace broke away to make the final score 5-3.

It was a huge disappointment for Doug and his team mates but they did have the small consolation of playing in such an enthralling game.

Four days later, Dundee put that disappointment behind them when they defeated Royal Leige 3-1 in the second round of the Inter-Cities Fairs Cup at Dens with Doug back in the midfield and a second leg 4-1 win in Belgium sent Dundee through to the quarter-finals after The Dee received a bye in round three.

Houston didn't play in either the first round match with D.W.S. Amsterdam or the quarter-final match with F.C. Zurich but after two 1-0 win over the Swiss side, Doug was back in the side on the bench for the semi-final first leg tie at Dens against Leeds United.

He didn't get on but three days later he staked a claim for a place in the second leg when he scored the winner in a 4-3 Forfarshire Cup Final match against Dundee United. It worked as Doug lined up against Leeds United at Elland Road but a 1-0 victory for The Peacocks meant that coupled with the 1-1 draw at Dens, Leeds would go through to meet Fenencvaros in Final. Houston's appearance however meant that he became the only Dundee player to play in two European semi-finals.

At the turn of the decade, Houston had been appointed Club captain and he became an influential skipper at Dens leading them out in the famous U.E.F.A. Cup ties against old foes Cologne and A.C. Milan in 1971. Houston was the only survivor from the European Cup clashes of nine years before and after a memorable 5-4 aggregate win over the Germans, Doug lined up once again in the San Siro against the Rossoneri. Dundee gave themselves a mountain to climb after a 3-0 defeat in Milan but they very nearly turned it around with a 2-0 win at home but their constant pressure couldn't get that elusive equaliser.

The following season 1972/73 was Houston's eleventh and last in a Dark Blue jersey as one the last day of the season, he was the subject of a shock £30,000 move to Rangers. Just hours earlier, the popular captain had scored the equaliser in a 2-2 draw with Hearts at Dens but a long standing disagreement between the articulate midfielder who was a qualified coach and manager Davie White over coaching and tactics, hastened his departure.

His time at Ibrox didn't last very long and he joined Dundee United before the year was out and had four years at Tannadice before finishing his playing career with St. Johnstone. Houston stayed in Tayside for his managerial career, taking over the hot seat at Brechin in 1979 and after four years at Glebe Park he took up the reigns at Forfar until 1986.

A great thinker of the game, Doug Houston was a plucky and tenacious performer who served the Dark Blues with distinction and even the most optimistic of Dundee fans would struggle to believe that anyone will ever play in more European semi-finals than he proudly did.

Honours at Dundee:
Scottish League Cup runner-up: 1967/68
European Cup semi-final: 1962/63
U.E.F.A. / Inter-Cities Fairs Cup semi-final: 1967/68
Appearances, Goals:
League: 236 + 1 sub, 16 goals
Scottish Cup: 18, 1 goal
League Cup: 66, 3 goals
Europe: 16, 1 goal
Other: 5
Totals: 342, 21 goals

John 'Sailor' Hunter

1910 was a year which saw General Election debate, that like one hundred years later, embroiled in expenses, hung parliaments and a possible coalitions. It saw the death of King Edward VII and the coronation of his son George V and the death of Mark Twain not 'greatly exaggerated' on this occasion. On April 20th it saw the return to Earth of Halley's Comet during its seventy-five year orbit and on the very same day that the comet became visible to the naked eye, 1910 also saw John 'Sailor' Hunter write himself into Dundee Football Club folklore when he scored the winning goal in the Scottish Cup Final to bring the trophy to Dens for the first and to date only time in the Club's history.

John Bryson Hunter was born in Johnstone, Renfrewshire on April 6th 1978 and after a youth career with Paisley Junior side Westmarch, he signed for the town's original Scottish League members Abercorn, aged 18 in 1897.

At the turn of the century, John tried his luck down south and went to Liverpool where he was part of their first ever side to win the English League Championship in 1901 but a year later moved back to Scotland to join Hearts for £300 where he was a Scottish Cup runner-up in 1903 when the 'Jambos' lost out in the Final 2-0 to Rangers.

In 1904 he joined Woolwich Arsenal in a £165 transfer, playing twenty-two times for them in 1904/05 before joining Portsmouth of the Southern League and in 1907 he was back in Scotland when he signed for Scottish League runners-up Dundee in pre season.

Nicknamed 'Sailor' because of his rolling gate, John was a strong centre forward who became a prolific goal scorer in his three years at Dens Park. He became an instant hit with the Dark Blue support when he scored on his debut away to Falkirk on August 17th 1907 and he became the first Dundee player to score back to back hat-tricks when he got a treble against Clyde in a 6-1 home win in October and did it again a week later when The Dee beat Queens Park 5-0 at Dens.

By the end of the season, John was top scorer with eighteen goals and in his second season repeated that feat with an impressive thirty-two goals in thirty-five games as Dundee very nearly won the Scottish League Championship. By April Dundee were top of the league, having held that position since the turn of the year but by the end of the season missed out on the Championship to defending champions Celtic despite John's twenty-nine league goals beating the Scottish League record by five strikes.

The undoubted turning point came in March when Hunter was called up to play for Scotland in a Home International match with Wales in Wrexham and while John was winning his only international cap in a 3-2 defeat, Dundee also went down in his absence 2-1 to Morton at Dens. That failure proved fatal as Celtic took six points from their last four games in a five day spell and Dundee failed to win their first major honour by a solitary point.

That first honour however was just twelve months away and 'Sailor' Hunter was to be at the heart of it. By April 1910, Dundee had reached the Scottish Cup Final for the first ever time after a marathon eight game campaign and were favourites to defeat Clyde at the 75,000 capacity Ibrox Stadium being used instead of Hampden which suffered serious damage after riots in the 1909 Old Firm Final.

In the first round, Dundee defeated non-league Beith after a replay and in the second round defeated Falkirk 3-0 at home with Hunter scoring Dundee's third. In the next round, a Sandy Hall hat-trick helped Dundee progress to the semis 3-1 at Motherwell where they would meet Hibernian in a repeat of their 1903 quarter-final meeting.

In what proved to be an epic tie, Dundee went through to the Final after the second replay with the first two matches at Dens and Easter Road ending goalless and with Parkhead the neutral venue for the third match Dundee won 1-0 thanks to a typical headed counter from Hunter.

Dundee's final opponents Clyde had beaten Rangers and Celtic on the 'road to Ibrox' and by half time were 2-0 ahead against the Dark Blues in front of 60,000 fans on April 6th. As the minutes ticked away, The Dee showed little sign of making a comeback and the Dundee fans started streaming for the exits as the Clyde ribbons were being tied to the trophy.

With just under four minutes left however, a long ball was sent down the middle which Hunter diligently chased and as the Clyde keeper attempted to clear, the ball rebounded off the inrushing 5ft 10in striker and into the net to put Dundee back in the hunt. Caution was then thrown to the wind and with just thirty seconds remaining the Dark Blues' efforts were rewarded when George Langlands crashed a Bellamy corner high into the net.

The replay took place a week later on Saturday 16th April but a no scoring draw meant that the sides had to do it all again midweek on Wednesday the 20th. Just like the first match, Clyde shocked Dundee early on when Chalmers gave them the lead in only three minutes but just twelve minutes later Dundee drew level when Jimmy Bellamy headed home from a corner.

But then came the moment when John Hunter would immortalise himself into Dundee's history with a goal that would live long in the memory. *'Dundee had played some brilliant football'* reported the *Glasgow Herald* and with the clock running down and another replay looming in these pre penalty shoot out days,

Hunter took advantage of a blunder by the Clyde defence to run in on goal. After beating former Dens Park centre-half McAteer, he sent the ball high into the net past McTurk from a narrow angle to give Dundee a lead in the tie for the first time.

Clyde laid siege to the Dundee goal but The Dee managed to hold on and win the oldest trophy in the world 2-1. *'At last the hitherto elusive Scottish Cup has been brought to Dundee',* exclaimed *The Courier* the morning after Dundee's victory as 'Jute City' celebrated like it had never celebrated before.

A 20,000 crowd awaiting the returning heroes at the Dundee West train station at eleven o'clock at night and the names of the cup winning side would be long remembered especially that of John 'Sailor' Hunter, whose winning goal ensured that the Cup would come east to Dens Park.

Hunter only played twice more for The Dee in the first two games of the 1910/11 season but after moving ironically to Clyde in September, he failed to make an appearance for the Shawfield club as he was forced to retire through injury six months later.

Almost a year to the day from the cup winning triumph, Hunter became Motherwell's first ever manager and would lead them to the Scottish League Championship in 1931/32 during a thirty-five year managerial reign. He would stay on as club secretary until his retirement in 1959 at the age of 80 when the club granted him a weekly pension and he sadly passed away on January 12th 1966.

In a year which saw Winston Churchill elected as a Liberal M.P. for Dundee in the December General Election, saw Portugal become a republic, Japan annexe Korea, the first commercial flight took place, Dr. Crippon arrested and the RMS Olympic launched, at Dens Park, it will always be remembered as the year that John 'Sailor' Hunter was the man who scored the winning goal for Dundee to win the Scottish Cup and their first major honour after a seventeen year wait.

> Honours at Dundee:
> Scottish Cup winner: 1910
> Scottish League Championship runner-up: 1908/09
> Forfarshire Cup winner: 1908/09
> Scotland full caps: 1
> Appearance, Goals:
> League: 90, 53 goals
> Scottish Cup: 17, 7 goals
> Totals: 107, 60 goals

Brian Irvine

'I hope you write Brian Irvine was rubbish today', Brian Irvine told reporters when he signed for Dundee in the summer of 1997, *'and not Brian Irvine, committed Christian and MS sufferer.'* Brian Irvine was no ordinary footballer and when he joined the Dark Blues after being surprisingly released by Aberdeen, he had successfully resumed his career after being diagnosed with multiple sclerosis in June 1995. He now hoped that the press would concentrate on his football performances with The Dee and not his illness or religious faith.

Born in Bellshill on May 24th 1965, Irvine started his career with Falkirk, where he played alongside his brother and in 1985 he signed for Alex Ferguson's Aberdeen for a fee of around £80,000 and would make almost 400 appearances for 'The Dons'. The centre-half had to be patient for first team opportunities with Alex McLeish and Willie Miller established at the heart of defence for club and country but when he forced his way into the side, Brian would become a firm favourite with the fans and wrote himself in Dons' folklore when he scored the winning penalty in the shoot-out in the Scottish Cup Final victory over Celtic in 1990.

Brian won nine international caps with Scotland during his twelve years at Pittodrie and was awarded with a testimonial against Wimbledon in 1997. At the end of his testimonial year however, Brian was surprisingly released by manager Roy Aitken, despite being back to playing thirty games a season after overcoming the mild form of M.S. that he had contracted two years before.

Irvine now had to weigh up the best move for himself and his family and so despite interest from Premier League Motherwell, he decided to join First Division Dundee as he could commute from his home in the Granite City. Brian had met Dundee manager John McCormack in the summer while undertaking the A License course at the S.F.A. coaching centre at Largs and 'Cowboy' McCormack wanted the centre-half at the heart of his defence as Dundee tried to return to the top tier at the fourth time of asking.

Brian's time at Dens however didn't get off to the best of starts when a newspaper chose to run an article with the headline *"Would you sign a footballer with MS?"* and the Dundee board got jumpy and sought to change the terms of the contract Irvine had agreed. Instead of £600 a week that had been agreed with McCormack, Brian was now offered a £200 basic wage and £400 each time he played, confirming that the enemy Irvine would often have to fight was not just the disease, but the perception of it.

The Dundee board needn't have worried however as Irvine was immense as the Dark Blues marched to the First Division title by mid April. Brian an ever present, playing in all forty-four league and cup matches and he struck up a terrific partnership with Barry Smith at the back. Both players lead by example and wore their hearts on their sleeves and it was clear to all Dundee supporters watching, how much playing for The Dee meant to Brian.

~ 89 ~

In his biography *Winning Through*, Brian confirmed this when he said, *'I cared so much about playing well and winning that I would often stay in a hotel the night before a game to make sure I could give my best. I did this at my own expense, although my home in Aberdeen was only an hour away.'*

And play well Brian did, none more so than in the Scottish Cup quarter-final tie with Rangers at Ibrox. Up against thirty-goal Marco Negri, Brian showed the live television audience that he was still good enough for the big time when he turned in a superb performance to snuff out the Italian and help Dundee earn a replay against the Scottish champions.

That big time came as Dundee entered the inaugural Scottish Premier League but it was a season that Dundee off the field were in a continual fight against adversity, expulsion, bankruptcy and takeover fears. The S.P.L. wanted to see Dens Park as a 10,000 all seated stadium within twelve months and Dundee United attempted a takeover and merge the clubs but the players got on with it and turned in some terrific performances.

On the field, Dundee showed a gritty determination and fighting spirit to retain their top flight status and no one epitomised this more than Brian Irvine. By the end of the season, Brian had missed just three matches as The Dee finished in fifth place, their highest league position for twenty-five years and never bettered since they were Scottish champions in 1962.

Dundee had also failed to finish above their rivals Dundee United during the same period but now they managed to achieve this thanks to a memorable derby victory on May 1st in which Brian was the hero.

The derby at Tannadice had an extra edge to it due to the recent takeover talk involving 'The Terrors' and 11,000 turned up on a gloriously sunny day with United still in serious danger of relegation.

Straight from the off, Dundee dominated and time and again tore United apart but became frustrated as they couldn't make the breakthrough. On sixty-seven minutes however, the frustration disappeared when a Dark Blue hero was born as Brian rose majestically to meet a Hugh Robertson corner and power a header down into the net. Irvine ran to the Dundee support behind the goal and joined in with their wild celebrations as he added himself into folklore at Dens, just as he had done at Pittodrie as Dundee confirmed themselves as the city's top dogs.

James Grady added a second in injury time for a 2-0 win and the following week returned from Brian's old stomping ground with their first win over Aberdeen for eleven years.

Seven days later Dundee defeated Dunfermline at Dens, with the stands behind the goals now under construction but at the end of the match Brian went to the crowd, kissed the Dundee badge and waved at Dundee fans who began to suspect that he might be leaving. He did the same again the following week at Perth as it was confirmed that he was indeed leaving the Club, having only been offered a one year deal to stay, instead of the two he wanted.

Many fans were upset that the Club had put money before loyalty offering Irvine less than his initial basic rate and he had shown that he still had mush to offer. His two years at Dens had given Dundee two of the best years on the pitch the Club had enjoyed in ages and it was a big disappointment that he was allowed to leave, having played such a big part in the success.

Hibs, Aberdeen and Dunfermline all showed interest but Brian instead signed for Second Division Ross County. In an in-depth interview in *The Courier* he explained, *'That was so I didn't come up against Dundee. I had a tear in my eye after the St. Johnstone game and that night I couldn't sleep. I want to say a big thank you to the Dundee fans who now have as special a place in my heart as those of Aberdeen. I am going with good memories and I sincerely hope the supporters enjoyed what we achieved as much as I did.'*

We certainly did Brian and did the press ever get to write, *'Brian Irvine was rubbish today'?* Absolutely not! You were magnificent and a genuine Dundee legend.

Honours at Dundee:
Scottish League First Division winner: 1997/98

Appearances, Goals:
League: 69, 4 goals
Scottish Cup: 5
League Cup: 3
S.F.L. Challenge Cup: 1
Totals: 78, 4 goals

Albert Juliussen

Albert Juliussen was a real 'Roy of the Rovers', post war hero to the Dundee support when he scored an incredible ninety-five goals in seventy-three top team games and was top goal scorer for Dundee for three years in a row from 1945/46 to 1947/48. He was part of a free scoring Dundee side which won back to back B Division Championships and has the best goal ratio of any Dundee striker who has played more than twenty games for the Club with an average of 1.3 goals per game.

Juliussen was born in Blyth, Northumberland and began his senior football career with English top division side Huddersfield Town, joining them from Cramlington Black Watch in 1938.

However, the outbreak of war was to prevent 'Julie' making his mark in England and he found himself stationed in Dundee and Perth with the Black Watch. He soon became part of their all-conquering regiment team, which played most of their games at that time at Dens Park.

City rivals Dundee United were first off the mark to spot his potential and he officially joined the Tannadice side on loan for the remainder of the War years. His goal scoring prowess was immediately displayed to the Dundee public when he scored six in one match against St. Bernards in a Scottish League North-East Division match and scored five against Rangers in a game in which he was carried off.

Dundee boss George Anderson soon had the giant centre-forward in his sights upon the Club's resumption towards the end of the War and in August 1945 was signed for a Club record fee of £3000 from his parent club Huddersfield.

He had signed for The Dee on the morning of the first game of the new season and made an astonishing start to his Dark Blue career when he scored with the first touch of the ball in a 2-1 victory over East Fife.

The powerful Juliussen was typical of centre-forwards of that era. Exciting to watch and possessing a tremendous left-foot shot, the Englishman's shoot-on-sight policy brought him forty-six goals out of Dundee's seasonal tally of 146 as The Dee won the Scottish League B Division by ten points from East Fife.

Dundee had been relegated to the B Division on the eve of the Second World War in 1938 but the first full season back upon the cessation of hostilities was considered by the Scottish League to be 'unofficial' as club's were given a year's grace to 'put their house in order'. With so many guest and loan players at most clubs and many players still in service with the armed forces, it was decided that there was to be no promotion and relegation in 1945/46 and if Juliussen and Dundee wanted to return to the top flight, they would have to win the league all over again.

Incredibly however, Dundee did just that and this time bettered the previous season's goal tally scoring 134 goals in 35 league and cup games.

On the way to winning their second Championship, Dundee put themselves into the record books with astonishing back to back 10-0 victories. On Saturday 8th March, Dundee ran up a 10-0 win over Alloa Athletic at a muddy Recreation Park and Juliussen, who had recently been playing at outside-left, celebrated his return to the centre with six cracking goals.

This was a Dens Park club record but incredibly, the 10-0 score line was repeated in the next game a fortnight later at home to Dunfermline and once again Juliussen was in sensational form by going one better with seven goals! If you read that as a story line in *Roy of the Rovers*, you wouldn't have believed it.

Dundee were back in the big league but they had already confirmed their top flight credentials when they defeated A Division side Celtic 2-1 in the Scottish Cup on Burns Day in front of 36,000 at Dens.

In the quarter-final Dundee drew another A Division side in the guise of Aberdeen who had already knocked the Dark Blues out of the League Cup at the same stage and it was a match in which Dundee were keen for revenge. The match however went down in the record books as the first British cup tie to be decided on a 'golden goal' when the sides decided to agree to a sudden death scenario to avoid a replay due to a fixture pile up after they were level one each after thirty minutes extra time.

It was The Dons who got that historic goal when Williams scored with 129 minutes on the clock but Dundee were unlucky with the deadly Juliussen taking considerable punishment from Aberdeen's close marking tactics.

Juliussen finished top scorer for the second season in a row but this time he shared that honour with strike partner Ernie Ewan having scored thirty-three goals each although 'Julie' had played twelve games less through injury.

It wasn't just in the league that the big Englishman was prolific when he scored four goals unusually in two Forfarshire Cup Finals in the same season. In April, Juliussen scored four in a 6-1 win over Forfar in a Final had been held over from the previous season and then a month later, scored four again in the 1946/47 Final in a 5-0 win over Dundee United in front of 14,000 at Dens.

Dundee's first season back in the A Division saw them finish a credible fourth and 'Julie' was again top scorer with twenty goals in all competitions. Towards the end of the season, he had indicated to George Anderson that he wished to return down south and just after his twentieth strike he signed for Portsmouth for a fee of £10,000; £7,000 more than Dundee had paid for him three years before and a record fee received for a Dundee player at that time.

'Julie' had scored many spectacular goals and was a big favourite amongst the Dundee support but although his departure sparked off a barrage of criticism, George Anderson was adamant that there was no room for unhappy players at Dens.

~ 92 ~

Albert Juliussen was a goal scoring machine in his time in Dark Blue and his seven goals against Dunfermline is a joint club record (with Alan Gilzean) for most goals in one match. He brought hope and joy to a war weary Dundee footballing public who were grateful for the goals that got Dundee back into the big time.

> Honours at Dundee:
> Scottish League B Division Champions: 1945/46, 1946/47
> Forfarshire Cup winner: 1945/46, 1946/47
> Appearances, Goals:
> League: 53, 79 goals
> Scottish Cup: 3, 1 goal
> League Cup: 11, 7 goals
> Other: 6, 8 goals
> Totals: 73, 95 goals

Temuri Ketsbaia

Once in a generation, a club may be lucky enough to have a player slide through their ranks for a short spell but do enough to earn themselves the status of hero or legend and for fans of Dundee, they were lucky enough to see it happen twice in the space of twelve months, in the early years of the third millennium.

With the Dundee fans craving a new idol in the wake of Claudio Caniggia's departure to Rangers, the 'Bald Eagle', Temuri Ketsbaia became the Argentinean's Dark Blue 'hair apparent' when he joined Dundee in October 2001 with the Bonetti Revolution in full flow.

Ketsbaia arrived at Dens with an impressive pedigree with forty-five Georgian international caps under his belt and as his country's leading goal scorer and he would represent them while plying his trade in the City of Discovery. Temuri became the third Georgian to join up at Dens alongside Zurab Zhizanishvili and Giorgi Nemsadze and he later claimed that his international captain Nemsadze had been instrumental in persuading him to go to Tayside to join the 'Tayzurri'.

The 'road and the miles to Dundee' were long for Ketsbaia for having been born on March 18th 1968, in Gali, Abkhazia, an autonomous republic of the Soviet Union within the Georgian S.S.R., he was forced to flee his home near the Turkish border as a teenager and moved to Sukhumi where signed for local football club Dinamo Sukhumi.

Next stop was his country's biggest club Dinamo Tbilisi in the Georgian capital where he picked up a league championship medal, then to the Cypriot port of Famagusta where he met his wife, Katerina, and together they have kept on moving. First to Athens, where he won the Greek Cup with A.E.K. and then they landed in England, and Newcastle, before moving to Birmingham, where they lived while he played for Wolverhampton Wanderers.

Joining Newcastle in the summer of 1997, the newly signed Ketsbaia scored a goal in extra-time against Croatia Zagreb and won a place for The Magpies in the U.E.F.A. Champions League for the first time in their history and he played up front with Alan Shearer in the 1998 and 1999 F.A. Cup Finals which Newcastle both lost 2-0 to first Arsenal then Manchester United.

Although a popular player with the 'Toon Army' it wasn't his goals he was remembered for at St James' Park but rather his bizarre celebrations. After scoring against Bolton for Newcastle in January 1998, the bulging-eyed midfielder-cum-striker ripped off his shirt, and proceeded to clatter the offending board with his boot, as his team-mates attempted to restrain him and while Ketsbaia was not lacking in passion, even for casual observers of the beautiful game, a mere mention of his name conjures up only one image - the most vicious assault on an advertising hoarding you are ever likely to see.

And so onto Dens, after an unsuccessful spell at Molineux as Dundee bought out the remaining six months of his contract and it was another major transfer coup for Ivano Bonetti for a player he had been chasing for months. Temuri made his debut for Dundee at Easter Road on October 27th 2001 when a last minute winner by substitute Steven Milne gave The Dee a 2-1 win but it was three days that Ketsbaia made his mark in his home debut against Motherwell.

Wearing a sky and white vertical striped shirt, the colours of one of Dundee's founding clubs East End which Dundee wore in their first ever match in 1893 against Rangers (although the cynics suggested it looked more like an Argentina shirt, cashing in on the popularity of Cannigia, Caballero, Sara and Caranza), Ketsbaia turned in a man of the match performance in a 3-1 win when he first netted with a typical surging run and then set up Caballero who scored with a fine curling shot.

Very soon, Dundee's balding number six became a major influence in the side and his drive and shooting power made him a big favourite with the fans. As Dundee's performances failed to live up to the promise of the previous season, the form of Ketsbaia was one of the few highlights for the demoralised Dark Blue fans and with a fine goal at Rugby Park and a blistering low shot against The Dons at Dens, it seemed he was often holding the side together on his own.

Dundee were certainly not helped with long term injuries to key players while Temuri was at Dens and amongst them were fellow Georgians Khizanishvili and Nemsadze. Zurab tore a cruciate ligament at Parkhead in December which ruled him out for the remainder of the season while a similar injury to Nensadze meant that the Georgian midfield maestros never played together in a Dundee shirt.

Dundee fans can only dream at how good that would have been.

At the end of the season, Bonetti was away and the press were full of speculation that a new management dream team of former boss Jim Duffy and Ketsbaia would take over. Duffy did come back to Dens but Temuri was off, returning to his wife's homeland where he signed again for Anorthosis Famagusta.

Ketsbaia did go into management however but it was with the Cypriot side in January 2004 and after leading Famagusta to the Cypriot league title and into the Champions League group stages for the first time in their history, he was inducted into Cyprus Football Hall of Fame.

Ketsbaia is now manager of the Georgian national side but was a star signing of the Bonetti era. His passion, drive and never say die attitude won him an army of fans at Dens who in April 2002 awarded him with Dundee's Player of the Year trophy. He was a worthy successor to Caniggia who had won it the season before and while Dundee fans had worn blond wigs in honour of the Argentinean, there were soon plenty of Dundonian men who claimed that their lack of hair wasn't genetic but was in fact in deference to Temuri Ketsbia, the balding genius with the ferocious shot and the heart of a lion who sadly graced a dark blue jersey for all too short a time.

Honours at Dundee:	
Georgia International caps:	1
D.S.A. Player of the Year:	2001/02
Appearances, Goals:	
League:	22, 6 goals
Scottish Cup:	2 + 1 sub
Totals:	25, 6 goals

Pat Liney

Pat signed for Dundee in 1957 from junior side Dalry Thistle after catching the Dark Blues' attention by saving five penalties in a cup tie and altogether made 121 appearances for The Dees before leaving for his hometown team St Mirren early in 1964.

Pat made his debut for Dundee on the last day of the 1957/58 season at Ibrox against League Champions Rangers and was thrust into the fray after regular keeper Bill Brown had been sent home with a virus.

Pat became Dundee's regular number one after Brown's departure to Tottenham and it is his contribution as an ever present in Dundee's Championship side that he will always be fondly remembered at Dens. Indeed Dundee record goal scorer Alan Gilzean stated that *'Pat Liney's contribution to Dundee's Championship season should never be underestimated and the fact that he was an ever present that year speaks for itself. He was rock solid and never let us down.'*

Pat will most likely be remembered by Dundee's supporters of a certain age for a crucial penalty save in the penultimate game of the season at home to St Mirren. Going into the match Dundee were still a point behind leaders Rangers but by half time Dundee were one up thanks to an Alan Cousin strike and Rangers were losing 1-0 at Pittodrie.

With twelve minutes left however disaster struck when the referee awarded St. Mirren a penalty after an alleged handball from Gordon Smith and it looked like Dundee's chances of winning the League Flag were about to evaporate.

Dundee had earlier in the season been knocked out the Scottish Cup by eventual runners-up St Mirren and in the build up to the game Pat's father, himself a Buddie supporter, gave him some advice that would prove crucial a few months later. He told Pat that if St Mirren got a penalty, Clunie takes them and always hammers ot towards the top right hand corner.

Although St Mirren never got a penalty in that game Pat always remembered that advice from his father. When a nervous looking Clunie steeped up to take the kick, he did exactly what Pat's father had predicted and hit it towards the top right corner, only to see Liney Jnr. twist in mid air and parry the ball to safety before collecting it.

Pat then threw the ball out to Gordon Smith on the wing and Smith then went down the wing beating two players, before looking up to see there was no one there, as the forwards were still patting Pat on the back. Smith then brought the ball back to the halfway line still beating men until the forwards could get back up field, which Pat describes as *'an amazing sight and something only Gordon Smith could have done like that.'*

Dundee scored a crucial second minutes later and when news filtered through that The Dons had held on to beat Rangers at Pittodrie, Dundee were now in pole position, needing a victory in their final game at Muirton to win the League.

At the time Pat didn't realise the significance of the penalty save until Gordon Smith spoke to him after the game. Gordon told Pat *'You realise that if we win the League on Saturday you will be famous in Dundee forever.'* He was correct as no matter what Pat did before or after he was always remembered for that penalty save in Dundee, without which the League Flag might not have come to Dens.

Pat was unlucky to only make two more appearances for Dundee after winning the League and so just two years later left Dens to join his boyhood team St. Mirren where he made forty-eight appearances before moving to Yorkshire in 1966.

Pat first played for Bradford Park Avenue for a season before moving to Bradford City where he made 147 appearances between 1967 and 1972

Pat stayed in Yorkshire until 1978 when he moved back to Blairgowrie but in the move back north he unfortunately lost his Championship medal. Thankfully in 2005 the medal appeared in an auction house in Yorkshire and after contacting the police, Pat was reunited with his prize possession.

Fellow Championship team member Bobby Wishart remembers Pat as a great character and great to have around the dressing room and that he fancied himself as a bit of a crooner. This was backed up at the Dundee FC Fortieth Anniversary Championship Dinner in 2002 at the Hilton Hotel, when Pat grabbed the microphone and led the assembled Dees in a chorus of, *'Hail, Hail, The Dees are Here.'* Legends are made of such stuff!

Pat's popularity at Valley Parade was in evidence years after he finished playing where he worked as a host in the pre match hospitality, a role he now fulfils at Dens.

Honours at Dundee:	
Scottish League Champions:	1961/62
Appearances:	
League:	102
Scottish Cup:	3
League Cup:	16
Other:	5
Total:	126

William 'Plum' Longair

William Longair is one of the original legends of Dundee F.C. as he had the honour of captaining Dundee in their very first match against Rangers in 1893 and gave the Club almost thirty years service.

Longair was born in the city on July 19th 1870 and was known to his family as Will although he was often referred to in the press as Bill or Billy. To the footballing public in Juteopolis however he was known as 'Plum', a nickname he could never explain and actually disliked but it stuck with him throughout his career.

By the age of 17, Longair was playing for a local Junior side Rockwell F.C. who played on a pitch on the north side of The Law and in 1888 he signed for local senior side East End F.C., where he quickly became a prolific goal scorer.

In November 1890 however, the path of his career was changed when he replaced the injured McCarthy at centre half and it was in this position he was to play for the remainder of his career and represent his country.

In 1893 an application was successfully made to the Scottish League for two of the city's leading clubs, East End and Our Boys to merge and join the three year old competition and the newly amalgamated club was to be called Dundee Football Club.

William Longair officially signed for the new club on August 1st 1893 and had the honour of leading out Dundee in their first ever match the following day in a 3-3 draw with Rangers at West Craigie Park. He would also have the honour of captaining Dundee in their first match at Carolina Port in 1894 and would be in the first side to play in the new Dens Park in 1899.

Longair would go on the play for Dundee with distinction for 136 appearances and but for a two year stint in England would stay with the Club until his death in 1926. He signed for Newton Heath (Manchester United) in 1895 making just one appearance in four months before returning to Dundee in June 1895 and then the lure of big wages saw him leave Dundee again in 1896 for short stints at Sunderland (where he was hampered by injury) and Burnley before returning to Dundee in the autumn of 1897.

Financial problems at Dundee saw several players forced to leave the Club in 1898 and again Longair headed south to this time sign for Brighton United. Longair however had recently married his wife Janet before leaving for Brighton and while he headed for the English Riviera, Janet remained in Scotland and so it was no surprise to see him back at Dundee in June 1899, this time for a fourth and final time.

In was during his first spell at Dundee, that Longair won his one and only cap when he represented Scotland against Ireland in Belfast in 1894, alongside team mates Francis Barrett and Sandy Keillor who were the first Dundee players to receive international recognition.

He was unfortunate not to add to his solitary cap as he was selected for Scotland on two further occasions but injury prevented him for turning out again for his country.

During his time with Dundee, he was to set many milestones and would play in a number Dundee trophy winning sides at a time when local cup competitions held much prestige.

In Dundee's opening season, Longair captained the side which won the Forfarshire Cup with a 4-0 win over Dundee Harp in front of 10,000 fans at 'neutral' Carolina Port (it became Dundee's home ground two months after the Final) and would captain the side again a year later as Dundee retained the trophy beating Lochee United in the Final at Gayfield.

He would win the Forfarshire Cup again in 1901 and would also win the Dewar Shield the same year, a competition played between the winners of the Forfarshire, Aberdeenshire, Stirlingshire and Perthshire cup competitions.

In national cup competition, the furthest Longair was to reach as a player was the Scottish Cup semi-final in 1895 against Renton and he played in both the 1-1 draw at home and then the replay at Hampden in which Renton progressed to the final 3-0.

Longair however was part of the backroom staff at Dens when Dundee won their first major honour with the Scottish Cup in 1910 as he had by then retired from playing and was by now the team's trainer.

Within a year of returning to Dundee in 1899, Longair took on the job of training the team and when he retired from playing two years later, he was kept on as trainer and continued in that position for another twenty years.

In April 1896, Longair was part of the Dundee team that played in front of a new British record crowd of 60,000 in a friendly away to Corinthian F.C. in London but was unfortunately also part of the Dundee side that went down to a record score of 11-0 to Celtic at Parkhead on October 25th 1895.

The embarrassing score of 11-0 however does not tell the full story as Dundee played the second half with just nine men. In the first half, full back Bill Ferrier broke his leg twenty minutes into the game and Longair and a Celtic forward were involved in a clash of heads in which 'Plum' came off by far the worst.

Advised to leave the field, he bravely played on but had to be assisted off at half time. In the dressing room he lost consciousness and it took two doctors an hour to bring him round so that he could travel home to Dundee where another two doctors kept him under observation overnight.

In the spring of 1922, Will missed his first game in twenty years when he became seriously ill with acute pneumonia and though he recovered fully, he was never the same physically.

In 1924 therefore, the club very gently offered him the post of Curator of Dens Park on the same salary and effectively became what would be a modern day groundsman but it was a decision that hurt the very proud man. Just two years later, he died aged 56 on November Street to the Eastern Cemetery, the route was lined was lined by crowds five deep on either side of the road with an estimated 20,000 honouring a true city legend.

Eighty-three years later, the Club that he had loved and dedicated most of his adult life to honoured him once again when he was inducted into Dundee F.C.'s inaugural Hall of Fame with his great, great nephew (also called William) receiving the Heritage Award on his family's behalf. Considering he was never awarded with a testimonial for his long service, it was a final fitting tribute for a Dundee great.

Honours at Dundee:
Dundee F.C. Hall of Fame:
Heritage Award 2009

(As Player):
Scotland full caps: 1
Forfarshire Cup winner:
1893/94, 1894/95, 1900/01
Dewer Shield winner: 1900/01
Scotland full caps: 1

(As Trainer):
Scottish Cup winner: 1910
Scottish League Championship runner-up: 1902/03, 1906/07, 1908/09
Forfarshire Cup winner:
1902/03, 1904/05, 1908/09, 1911/12, 1912/13
Dewar Shield: 1902/03, 1904/05

Appearances, Goals:
League: 114, 3 goals
Scottish Cup: 22, 1 goal
Totals: 136, 4 goals

Sandy MacFarlane

Sandy MacFarlane is a legendary figure in the annals of Dundee F.C. with a career that spanned over a quarter of a century as both a player from 1901 to 1913 and as manager where he had two spells between the Wars. His time at Dens saw him win eight international honours, be a Scottish League Championship runner-up three times and was a key figure in Dundee's 1910 Scottish Cup win.

Alexander MacFarlane was born in Airdrie in 1878 and began his career with his home town team Airdrieonians with whom he enjoyed two spells between 1895 and 1898. In between times, Sandy turned out seven times for Woolwich Arsenal but it was second move south of the border which was more successful when he joined Newcastle United in 1898 and became their first-choice inside-left.

In four seasons in the north-east McFarlane made eighty-four First Division appearances, scoring seventeen goals in three consecutive top six finishes, as well as two FA Cup appearances.

In 1901 the clever inside-forward signed for Dundee and he would go onto to make 333 appearances for the Dark Blues, scoring seventy-one times and provide The Dee with over a decade of dedicated play.

Signed in November, Sandy made his debut at home to Celtic and by the end of the season had turned out nine times as Dundee finished a disappointing second bottom with just thirteen points. Expansion to Division One meant that Dundee didn't have to apply for re-election and in the new twelve team top tier, Dundee managed a remarkable turnaround by finishing second behind champions Hibernian who they knocked out in the quarter-final of the Scottish Cup.

Unfortunately Hearts knocked Dundee out in the semi-final after a replay with Sandy playing in all twenty-eight league and cup matches, scoring five times. Dundee did however win both the Forfarshire Cup and the Dewar Shield to give Sandy his first winners' medals and he would win the Forfarshire Cup a further three times as a player and once as manger.

In 1904 Dens Park hosted its first full international when Scotland played Wales in a British International Championship match and Sandy made his Scotland debut in the 1-1 draw. When Dens hosted its second international four years later, also against Wales, Sandy was again in the line up and he would win five full caps and three Scottish League caps over a seven year period while at Dundee.

In March 1909, Sandy scored his first international goal in a 5-0 win over Northern Ireland at Ibrox and thirteen months later, Ibrox was again the scene of celebration for Sandy when he was part of Dundee's Scottish Cup winning side after they beat Clyde 2-1 in a second replay. Having finished as runners-up in the league in both 1907 and 1909, Dundee finally managed to win their first piece of silverware with that Scottish Cup victory and the sturdy inside-forward played in all three Final ties.

It was a night to remember for all concerned with Dundee and in a marathon ten games to win the trophy, Dundee were watched by a whopping 214 000 fans on the road to glory. It proved a real money spinner for the Club and Sandy and the players received a healthy bonus of £40 per man.

Sandy played for Dundee for another three years and was part of the side which went on an incredible thirty-nine unbeaten run at Dens between 1908 and 1911. He left for Stamford Bridge in 1913 but he returned to Dens Park after the First World War to become the Club's first full time manager.

Dundee had gone into a two year abeyance towards the end of the conflict and when they returned for the 1919/20 season, William Wallace announced his resignation from the manager's post and Sandy was invited to take over the Dens Park hot seat.

Unlike his predecessor, MacFarlane would be full-time and he faced a daunting task of re-establishing the Dark Blues amongst Scotland's elite and in their first three seasons back, The Dee finished a credible fourth.

In 1923, Sandy led Dundee on their first overseas tour when a lengthy boat journey took them to Spain where they won four of their seven matches.

Amongst those wins was a 2-0 triumph over the famous Real Madrid and with the tour being deemed a great success, Dundee returned the following year. This time Dundee enjoyed two victories over Barcelona with 2-0 and 2-1 wins and became the first non-Spanish sides to defeat both Real Madrid and Barcelona on their own patches.

After such a bright start to the tour, Dundee once again met Real Madrid but after taking a 1-0 half time lead, the game exploded when the Spanish referee, who had officiated from the shade, with a lemon in his hand, awarded Real a dubious penalty.

The Dundee players were furious and when the referee came out of the shade and placed the ball on the spot, an exasperated Willie Rankine kicked it into the net. At this the referee tried to strike Rankine but was quickly pushed away by the Dundee centre-half who was then sent off for his trouble. Rankine refused to leave the field of play and when he was escorted off the pitch by six armed policemen, the whole Dundee team followed suit.

There was uproar amongst the Spanish crowd and only the intervention of MacFarlane ensured the completion of the game which finished 1-1. The sides met again the following day and recorded a most satisfying 2-1 win meaning that Sandy had led his side to three wins and a draw in four matches against the Spanish giants.

It was of course the Roaring Twenties but when the Dark Blues failed to roar onto any tangible success, MacFarlane resigned after a poor start to the 1924/25 season. By the end of the season, the side which he had built reached the Scottish Cup Final in April but they lost 2-1 to Celtic after two late goals from 'The Bhoys' cancelled out Dundee's half time lead. Just over two years later, in October 1927, MacFarlane returned to Dens Park for a second spell in charge but his renewed love affair with Dundee proved to be short lived when he resigned the following May following a disappointing run of form. He did however enjoy a Scottish Cup victory over Dundee United in the clubs first ever national cup meeting with a 1-0 win at Dens in a replay after a 3-3 draw at Tannadice.

Sandy MacFarlane gave eighteen years loyal service to Dundee Football Club and as the Club's first full time manager and as a member of the legendary 1910 Scottish Cup winning side, he was nominated for the Dundee F.C. Hall of Fame Heritage Award one hundred years after that Ibrox triumph

Honours at Dundee:
Scottish Cup winner:
1910
Scottish League Championship runner-up:
1902/03, 1906/07, 1908/09
Forfarshire Cup winner:
1902/03, 1908/09, 1911/12, 1912/13
Dewar Shield:
1902/03, 1904/05
Scotland full caps: 5
Scottish League caps: 3
Appearances, Goals:
League: 293, 68 goals
Scottish Cup: 40, 3 goals
Totals: 333, 71 goals

Managerial Record with Dundee:
(1919 - 1924, 1927 - 1928)

	P	W	D	L	F	A	Pts
League:	244	107	58	79	381	339	272
Scottish Cup:	26	12	8	6	39	22	
Total:	270	119	66	85	420	361	

Bill Marsh

Giant goalkeeper Bill Marsh spent thirteen years at Dens Park between 1924 and 1937 and amassed a total number of 417 appearances for the Dark Blues, making him fourth on the list of most competitive appearances. He turned out 386 times in the league, which is a Dundee club record for most appearances in the league and it could have quite easily been more had he not spent his first two years at Dens Park in the reserves or shared the goalkeeping duties during a couple of seasons.

Marsh was born in Woodhouse in Yorkshire and began his career with Eckington Works of Sheffield before joining Chelsea in December 1921 and spent two and a half years at Stamford Bridge before signing for Dundee in the summer of 1924. The 6ft 2in goalkeeper was a formidable figure between the posts but he had to wait until April 15th 1925 to make his debut for Dundee at home to St. Mirren, four days after Dundee had lost 2-1 to Celtic in the Scottish Cup Final.

It was Bill's solitary first team appearance that year and the following season made only seven starts but when regular number one Jock Britton was transferred to Tottenham Hotspur in the summer of 1926, Marsh was to take over in goal at the start of the next campaign.

It was a successful first full season in goal for Marsh as he was an ever present with Dundee finishing fifth in the Scottish League Division One, their best placing for four years. There were plenty of highlights throughout the campaign including 5-0 and 7-2 wins over Dundee United and against both sides of the Old Firm, Bill kept a clean sheet on Dundee's visits to Ibrox and Parkhead.

The popular Englishman was a great personality and at well over fourteen stone he was an imposing figure who dominated his goal area. He was renowned for having enormous hands and was well known for clutching the ball, rain-sodden or not, one handed.

The following year saw The Dee's good form continue against relegated neighbours Dundee United by beating them 4-3 in the Forfarshire Cup and knocking them out of the Scottish Cup 1-0 at Dens after a 3-3 draw at Tannadice but league form was disappointing as Dundee slipped to fourteenth place with Marsh playing thirty-nine times.

Marsh continued to be the Dark Blue's first choice keeper for the next four years and enjoying life in the city, he opened a greengrocer's business in Ann Street just off the city's Hilltown. Marsh was extremely popular with his customers and enjoyed talking about what was going on at Dens both on and off the park and fans were as likely to pop in for a chat as they were as they were to have him cut a slice of ham.

Season 1932/33 saw Bill share the goalkeeping duties with Dave Edwards who turned out nineteen times to Marsh's twenty-three and had lost his place after a 6-1 defeat at Motherwell in November. By the end of the season, Bill was back in the side and in the following year he had well and truly seen off the youngster's challenge as he was again an ever present.

After twelve years with Dundee, Marsh was awarded with a benefit match for his services and on October 5th 1936, a healthy crowd of 12 000 turned out to watch a 3-0 win over Portsmouth for which Bill received £500.

In his time at Dens, Marsh kept ninety-seven clean sheets for Dundee in league and cup and when he started to reach the veteran stage, he started to share again the goalkeeping duties this time with promising nineteen year old Johnny Lynch.

At the start of the 1937/38 season, Marsh must have felt that that the writing on the wall as he sold his greengrocer's business in Ann Street and in December, he was sold to Kilmarnock with whom he had a nightmare debut, conceding eight against Celtic on Christmas Day.

He made the last of 417 appearances on November 13th 1937 in a 4-1 home defeat to Falkirk and although he finished his Dundee career twenty-nine games short of Doug Cowie's Club record, he played forty-five more times in the league than the legendary half-back, giving him the Dens Park record for most appearances in the league.

Marsh's 386 appearances in the league is eighteen more than the Club's second highest total of 368 games by Barry Smith and considering the it took Barry eleven years to achieve his total and with the constant movement of players between clubs in the modern game, Marsh's record is one that is unlikely to be beaten for a long time, if indeed ever.

Appearances:	
League:	386
Scottish Cup:	31
Total:	417

Neil McCann

'It's a flash of genius from the Dundee youngster which looks like earning his team a cup final place', proclaimed B.B.C. commentator Jock Brown after Neil McCann scored a sensational goal against Airdrie in the last few minutes of the 1995 Coca-Cola Cup semi-final. It was a goal which meant so much to everyone connected with Dundee as it not only sent The Dee into their first major cup final in fifteen years, but it also gave the Club a much needed financial lifeline and the gave the fans a night to remember after being in the doldrums in recent times.

There was a lot more to Neil McCann's Dundee career however than his sensational cup semi-final goal and by then he had been in the first team for two years and was a key man in the Dark Blues' side. Born in Greenock on November 8th 1974, Neil Docherty McCann broke into the Dundee side while still in the Premier Division and made his debut aged eighteen at home to Partick Thistle in a 2-2 draw on October 5th 1993.

By the end of the season Neil had established himself on the left wing and had all the skills of a traditional winger. He repeatedly demonstrated his electrifying pace in beating full backs before putting in a telling ball and at the end of his first season he chosen as Dundee's player of the year and became the first recipient of the De Vries Memorial Trophy.

Despite Dundee's relegation, McCann had quickly made a name for himself in the Premier League and at the end of the season, he was called up for the Scotland Under 21 side who were taking part in the prestigious Toulon Tournament in the south of France.

Neil played particularly well in Toulon where a number of top clubs had expressed an interest but Dundee managed to keep a hold of their starlet as they started their assault on the First Division. They started their promotion campaign well, and McCann was influential as Dundee won their first four games but when Neil had to miss a number of games through injury, Dundee started dropping points with a defeat to Ayr and draws with Dunfermline and Raith Rovers.

Neil was back in the starting line up on October 18th for the B&Q Challenge Cup semi-final against league leaders Dunfermline at East End Park and he marked his return to the side with the winner in a 2-1 floodlit thriller.

The Final at McDiarmid Park three weeks later however was a big disappointment as Dundee lost 3-2 to Airdrie after extra time and there was an even bigger disappointment at the end of the season when Dundee missed out on the title by just one point and the play-offs with the second bottom side in the Premier Division on goal difference.

In the third last game of the campaign, Dundee handed their rivals from Fife the momentum when they lost 1-0 in Paisley to St. Mirren and it was a match which McCann had missed due to a virus he had contracted while away with the Scotland Under-21s in San Marino midweek. It was more points dropped in Neil's absence and it was to prove vital as Dundee missed out on promotion by the narrowest of margins.

Jim Duffy had built a good attacking side in which McCann was pivotal and now they faced a tough challenge for promotion with newly relegated Dundee United as well as Dunfermline who had lost out to Aberdeen in the play-off.

However Dundee made a good start with a 2-0 win over St. Johnstone and in the second match of the 1995/96, McCann hit the headlines when he scored four in a 6-0 rout of East Stirlingshire in their opening match in the League Cup.

Now sponsored by Coca-Cola, it was Dundee's first match on the 'Road to Hampden' which would take Dundee all the way to the League Cup Final. In the quarter-final at home to Hearts, Dundee won a pulsating match 5-4 on penalties after an extraordinary 4-4 draw and McCann was one of the heroes when he netted one of the pens.

In the semi-final, Dundee were fortunate to be paired with fellow First Division side Airdrie while Rangers faced Aberdeen in the other tie and Dundee had the chance to exact revenge on The Diamonds for the B&Q Cup Final defeat at the same venue almost twelve months before.

Of greater concern however was the current financial plight of The Dee and on the eve of the match in Perth, manager Jim Duffy was privately told that Dundee had to simply reach the Final to survive. With so much at stake on a windy night, where the Dark Blues enjoyed over three quarters of the crowd, they started well with a number of chances and eventually broke the deadlock just before the interval when Paul Tosh rammed home a Tommy McQueen cross.

With only seven minutes left, Dundee looked like they might be home and dry but they received a stunning blow when Paul Duffield stooped to head home the equaliser. The Diamonds then looked the stronger side and more likely to score but then enter Neil McCann who was about to write himself into Dundee folklore.

With just two minutes remaining, George Shaw sent the ball wide to Neil McCann and the 5ft 10in winger sped the ball into the box with everyone expecting a cross. However he lobbed the ball over John Martin's head before it dipped into the net off the inside of the far post and after a moment's hesitation, the Dundee fans went wild as they realised what McCann had just done with his audacious effort.

Dundee were in their first final since 1980 and their first final at Hampden since the year before McCann was born but it was to be an ultimately frustrating occasion against Aberdeen who cruised to a 2-0 win. Too many of the Dundee players did not perform while McCann himself had declared himself fit on the morning of the match having suffered a thigh strain three days before but he was clearly not at his penetrating best.

For the rest of the season, McCann was dogged with injury as Dundee again failed to return to the Premier League. Towards the end of the season, he was the subject of an unsuccessful £500, 000 bid by Dundee United but failure to achieve promotion meant that they had to sell him for a cut price fee of £250 000 to Hearts before he could join Sturm Graz under freedom of contract. It was clearly only a fraction of what the tricky winger was worth but when he joined Rangers two years later for £1.8 million,

Dundee received another £350 000, thanks to a sell on clause inserted by Jim Duffy.

In six years at Ibrox, McCann would win three S.P.L. titles, two League Cups and fours Scottish Cups, including a winners' medal against Dundee in 2003 and he would establish himself into a full internationalist, winning twenty-six caps with Scotland.

At Dens, he will also be remembered for that goal and a host of terrific, exciting displays and when he left Dundee he told that the press that, *'I signed for Dundee when I was thirteen and I would like to thank everyone at Dens for what they did they did for me'.* However, it is the Dundee support who should be thanking Neil and we do so from the bottom of our hearts.

Honours at Dundee:	
Coca-Cola League Cup runners-up:	1995/95
B&Q Challenge Cup runner-up:	1994/95
Scotland Under 21 caps:	10
D.S.A. Player of the Year:	1994
Appearances, Goals:	
League:	73 + 4 subs, 5 goals
Scottish Cup:	6
League Cup:	7, 5 goals
S.F.L. Challenge Cup:	4, 1 goal
Totals:	94, 11 goals

Tosh McKinlay

Tosh McKinlay was a popular full back with Dundee who is probably best remembered for his stunning goal in a famous derby win over Dundee United at Tannadice in 1984.

Thomas Valley McKinlay was born in Glasgow on December 3rd 1964 and as a left winger with a deadly shot, he represented Scotland at schoolboy level. In 1981 Tosh joined Dundee from Celtic Boys' Club and turning professional with the Dark Blues saw him change his position to full back where he spent seven years playing for The Dee.

Tosh broke into the Dundee first team as a teenager and made his debut in the penultimate game of the 1982/83 season in a 2-1 defeat to St. Mirren in Paisley. He started the first match of the following season against Aberdeen at Pittodrie and quickly became a mainstay in the side making forty-six appearances by the end of the term.

Tosh was an attacking left back who liked to attack and his apprenticeship as a winger served him well as he was able to fire in telling crosses into the opponent's box at regular intervals.

He chipped in as well with the odd goal and netted his first strike for the Club at Tynecastle in a 3-1 win over Hearts in October.

Towards the end of Tosh's first full season with Dundee, Tynecastle was also the venue for a Scottish Cup semi-final against cup holders Aberdeen but despite having the ball in the net three times, referee Brian McGinlay chopped them all off and Aberdeen progressed to the Final where they retained the trophy with a 2-1 win over Celtic.

Tosh played in three semi-finals during his time at Dens and his second one also came in the Scottish Cup at Tynecastle when in April 1987 The Dee lost out 3-2 to Dundee United where an exciting match. Just over four months later Dundee again reached the last four of a cup competition when they faced Aberdeen in the Skol League Cup semi-final at Tannadice but like three years earlier in Edinburgh, The Dons went through to the Final with a 2-0 win.

Tannadice however was to be the scene of one of Tosh's finest moments in a dark blue shirt when he scored a fabulous goal in a 4-3 victory over Dundee United in September 1984.

Dundee had failed to win any over their opening four matches of the season and had been knocked out the League Cup by Hearts at Dens the previous Wednesday but suddenly Archie Knox's clutch of summer signings all came good at the right time and secured a famous victory over their local rivals.

Of Dundee's four scorers in the match, three, namely Derek McWilliams, Colin Harris and John Brown had all been recently brought to the Club by Knox but it was nineteen year old McKinlay who scored the best goal of this and almost any other derby.

Having gone in level at half-time, Dundee came out quickly in the second half and took a 2-1 lead when Tosh scored his wonder goal. Just inside the United half, John McCormack played a long ball forward into The Arabs' box and when picked up out on the left by Robert Connor, he fired a low cross into the six yard area which Paul Hegarty could only half clear. The ball bounced outside the box about twenty yards out and when Tosh McKinlay came rushing in, he controlled the high, bouncing spinning ball on his chest before sending a sweet, powerful volley high over Billy Thomson and into the top right hand corner of the net.

'McKinlay – there's a great goal', exclaimed B.B.C, commentator Archie McPherson on *Sportscene* at night. *'That's one of the best goals I've seen in this local derby.'*

It was Tosh's second victory over United, having been part of the side to record their first win over The Arabs in four years the previous November and he would go on to have an excellent record against United over the next few years. In total he was undefeated in thirteen derbies with six victories and seven draws but his special goal in that 4-3 win was his only goal against The Terrors.

Tosh would win six Scotland Under-21 caps while at Dens and was given the first of those by Andy Roxburgh against East Germany in 1983 and got the last of those against Iceland in 1985.

The same month Dundee had earlier missed out on European qualification by a point despite defeating Dundee United 1-0 on the last day of the season and the following year, it was same again for Tosh and Dundee when a 2-0 win over Hearts denied the Edinburgh side the League title but saw Dundee finish sixth, a point behind both St. Mirren and Rangers.

In January 1988, Tosh was part of the Dundee side which won the Tennents' Sixes, the indoor football tournament contested annually by the Scottish Premier Division clubs, having just come back from a ten week lay off with damaged ankle ligaments.

In the summer, Dave Smith replaced Jocky Scott in the Dens Park hot seat but within a few months of his reign, Tosh was one of a number of players who handed in a transfer request along with Graham Harvey, Alan Lawrence, Stuart Rafferty and Vince Mennie. Two bids from Hearts had already been turned down for the 5ft 9in left back and when his agent Bill McMurdo intimated Tosh's intention to move when his contact expired the following June, the board felt it was in their best interests to sell.

Tosh therefore was on his way to Hearts for a £300,000 fee and after six years in the capital he moved to boyhood heroes Celtic. At Parkhead, Tosh won his first major honours with Scottish Cup and League Championship winners' medals and he represented Scotland at both Euro 96 and World Cup 98 while collecting twenty-two caps.

At Dens, the classy left-back with the attacking flair served Dundee F.C. with distinction and at the 2010 Player of the Year Dinner, he was welcomed back as a guest speaker and entertained the crowd with humorous tales. Needless to say, after the dinner, there were plenty of Dees looking to get Tosh's autograph and looking to ask him about his famous goal at Tannadice for which they will forever be grateful.

Honours at Dundee:	
Tennents' Sixes winner:	1988
Scotland Under 21 caps:	6
Appearances, Goals:	
League:	161 + 1 sub, 8 goals
Scottish Cup:	23
League Cup:	18 + 1 sub, 1 goal
Totals:	204, 9 goals

George McLean

When Dundee signed George McLean in 1967, there was no doubt that manager Bobby Ancell had picked up a player of quality. Having been released by Rangers in the wake of their embarrassing Scottish Cup defeat to Berwick Rangers, big 'Dandy' as he was affectionately known oozed class on the ball, liked the finer things in life, had a wife who was a model (who once kicked off a testimonial at Dens), had a jaguar car and was a dapper dresser, hence the nickname.

George Tomlinson McLean was born in Paisley May 26th 1943 and in 1959 joined local senior side St. Mirren after turning out for Drumchapel Amateurs. He was part of The Buddies' side that reached the Scottish Cup Final in 1962 and on the 'Road to Hampden', they beat eventual league champions Dundee 1-0 in the second round at Dens, thanks to George's winner.

Although Rangers won the Final 2-0, McLean impressed the Ibrox management enough to persuade them to part with a then Scottish record fee of £27,500 the following January and in five years in Govan, he won two league championships, two League Cups and three Scottish Cups including a winners' medal against Dundee in 1964.

However following a disastrous 1-0 Scottish Cup defeat to Second Division Berwick Rangers in January 1967, Jim Forrest and George McLean were made scapegoats and were transfer listed, never to play for the Light Blues again and it initially looked like it was Forrest who was going to join Dundee in exchange for Andy Penman, who himself had handed in a transfer request at Dens. Forrest however joined Preston North End but in April, the £55,000 rated Dundee championship winner Penman, joined Rangers in exchange for George McLean plus £30,000.

The twenty-four year old McLean had scored eighty league and cup goals for Rangers but the inside-forward was ineligible for Dundee's remaining games having signed after the transfer deadline. He had to wait therefore to the first game of the 1967/68 season to make his Dark Blue debut and he did so coming off the bench to replace Billy Campbell in a 0-0 League Cup sectional tie with Hibernian at Dens.

It was the start of a dream debut season for McLean which would see the forward finish as top scorer with thirty-five goals as Dundee reached a major cup final and the semi-final of a European competition.

His first goal for Dundee came in his first start at home to Motherwell in a 2-1 League Cup win and it was part of a League Cup campaign that would take Dundee all the way to the Final. Having topped a section which included Motherwell, Hibs and Clyde, Dundee defeated East Fife over two legs in the quarter-final and St. Johnstone in the semi-final at Tannadice with McLean scoring five en route to Hampden.

In the Final against Celtic in October, McLean was on target again, scoring twice but it only earned 'Dandy' a runners-up medal as Dundee lost out 5-3 to the Lisbon Lions in an exciting but from Dundee's point of view, ultimately disappointing match.

The Dark Blues also found themselves in the Inter-Cities Fairs Cup having profited from the rule which stated the only one club could enter per city which denied Clyde a place with Rangers finishing higher in the league the previous year. Dundee took full advantage of Clyde's misfortune by going all the way to the semi-final where they lost out to Leeds United 2-1 on aggregate.

McLean was on target in the first round in the away leg against D.W.S. Amsterdam in the Olympic Stadium but it was in the away leg in the second round that George really made his mark.

Drawn against Royal Leige from Belgium, Dundee won the home leg 3-1 just four days after the League Cup Final defeat but in the second leg, they recorded a stunning 4-1 win, with George McLean scoring all of Dundee's goals.

Although essentially a great team display, 'Dandy' had taken star billing by scoring all four of Dundee's goals and set a Club record for most goals in a European match, which still stands today.

McLean was a great character both on and off the park and after his double brace in Leige, he suggested to Dundee manager Bobby Ancell that his number should be replaced on his shirt with an 'S' for Superman!

A great season was literally 'capped' for McLean when he made his one and only appearance for Scotland in a goalless draw against Holland in May 1968 in the same stadium where he had earlier scored his Fairs Cup quadruple.

However less than twelve months later, he was on his way out of Dens when he failed to thrive on the different style of play introduced by new manager John Prentice. He joined Dunfermline for £22,000 in March 1969 but not before he scored another eleven goals including a hat-trick against Stranraer in the League Cup quarter-final when Jocky Scott also got a treble in a 6-0 win and a strike in the semi-final at Tynecastle when Dundee narrowly missed out on a second successive final, losing 2-1 to Hibs.

He later played for Ayr United and Vancouver Whitecaps before retiring from the game after one substitute appearance for Hamilton in 1975.

His time at Dens had been mercurial to say the least and he was a player who the fans never knew what he was going to do next. He could be frustrating one minute then brilliant the next but there was no doubting that George McLean was popular with the support, who remember his brilliant moments with relish.

Honours at Dundee:
Scottish League Cup runner-up: 1967/68
U.E.F.A. / Inter-Cities Fairs Cup semi-final: 1967/68
Scotland full cap: 1
Appearances, Goals:
League: 52 + 2 subs, 25 goals
Scottish Cup: 4
League Cup: 16 + 1 sub, 16 goals
Europe: 8, 5 goals
Totals: 86, 46 goals

George Merchant

When the great Dundee side of the early fifties began to break up, it gave the chance for promising youngster George Merchant to emerge who would go on to become Dundee's top goal scorer three seasons in succession and equal the Club record for most goals in a Scottish Cup match.

In 1953/54, Dundee still had players like Bill Brown, Tommy Gallacher and Doug Cowie and of course that season was the last time that the Dens Park faithful would see the legendary Billy Steel strut his stuff in the Dark Blue. Later that season however, the fans would see an emerging youngster in George Merchant and despite not making an appearance until as late as January, he would finish as top goal scorer with eleven goals to his credit.

Merchant was a big, fast bustling centre-forward when centre-forwards were indeed meant to be just that. What George lacked in finesse, he more than made up for in pace and aggression and he was a handful for any defence.

However, George hadn't always been a centre-forward and in fact had made his first team debut a couple of seasons earlier as a centre-half. In season 1951/52, George made eleven appearances deputising for the injured Doug Cowie and again made three starts in the same position the following year.

George made his first top team appearance as a striker at Palmerston Park against Queen of the South on January 16th 1954 and scored Dundee's goal in a 5-1 defeat.

Three weeks later in the Scottish Cup against Albion Rovers in Coatbridge, he netted for Dundee in a 1-1 draw and then in the replay scored all four goals as Dundee romped to a 4-0 win. This equalled a Club record for most goals in a Scottish Cup match set by Alec Stott in against St. Johnstone in 1949 and matched by John Duncan against Stranraer in 1973, it remains a Club record today.

Whilst eleven goals in thirteen games in his first season up front was impressive, George seemed determined to make certain that it was no flash in the pan and in the following season in the League Cup, Merchant netted five times in his opening three games. He scored against Celtic in a 3-1 victory at Dens before a crowd of 29, 000 and three days later, he whacked in a hat-trick against Falkirk in another 3-1 success.

A week later, on August 28th, George was again on the score sheet against Hearts in front of 29, 500 at Dens as Dundee ran out 4-1 winners but it was to be his last game until November as he got injured against The Jam Tarts. However he still finished the season as top scorer with sixteen goals which included the winner against Rangers at home in January in a 2-1 win.

In season 1955/56, despite only making twenty-four starts, Merchant finished as top scorer for the third season in succession with

~ 108 ~

Merchant notched his customary goal as the teams fought out a 2-2 draw on a snow covered Tannadice and the general consensus was that the pitch had been a great leveller. For the replay the following Wednesday however, Dundee made no mistake when their lower league neighbours were put to the sword 3-0 and George scored the first in front of a 17,000 afternoon crowd.

At the end of that season, George also curiously scored in two different Forfarshire Cup Finals when he first scored a brace in a 2-1 win over Arbroath at Dens and then two weeks later scored four in a 6-0 rout of Montrose in the Final for the previous year's competition.

Season 1956/57 was the last time the Dens support would see George sport a D.F.C. badge on his shirt and he managed eleven goals in thirteen starts before falling out of favour and being transferred to Falkirk. There, along with left-back Andy Irvine, he won a Scottish Cup winners' medal at the end of the season after he scored the first in a 2-1 replay win over Kilmarnock at Hampden.

George Merchant became known as 'The Merchant of Menace', and his goal scoring record suggests that he should not have been transferred from The Dee so soon. He was a real old fashioned centre-forward, a real Dundee man and his dashing style will always be remembered at Dens Park.

fourteen goals in all competitions. In the Scottish Cup, Dundee were paired with Second Division Dundee United at Tannadice and the city's underdogs gave their more illustrious opponents a bit of a fright.

Appearances, Goals:	
League:	65, 31 goals
Scottish Cup:	8, 7 goals
League Cup:	16, 14 goals
Totals:	89, 52 goals

Giorgi Nemsadze

When 500 or so Dees went to watch Dundee pre season in north-east of England in 2000, they hardly expected that they were about to witness something special. Dundee had appointed a new manager during the summer in Ivano Bonetti and the Italian had arranged a friendly against his old club Grimsby Town and the Mariners' Brundell Park was about to play host to a moment of pure magic.

Giorgi Nemsadze was Ivano Bonetti's first signing for Dundee and the well travelled Georgian international captain came to Dundee with a vast experience of European football and fifty-two international caps behind him. After pulling on a Dundee shirt for the first time at Raith Rovers, he was now about to show what he was truly capable of in the in the seaside town of Cleethorpes where Grimsby play their games.

With Dundee trailing 2-1, Nemsadze picked up a pass from Javier Artero and then started to dance through a packed penalty area, beating four players (one of them twice) before nonchalantly slotting the ball home as if he did this every day of the week.

Those who had journeyed south to see the game spread the word that something exciting was happening at Dens and at the first day of the season, over 2000 Dees travelled west to Motherwell to see what all the fuss were about and weren't disappointed when Giorgi made his competitive debut in a 2-0 win.

The following week, Dundee hit the top of the S.P.L. with a 3-0 win over Dunfermline and Nemsadze was at the heart of it with his surging runs from midfield and his dancing feet which won the Dark Blues two penalties.

Dundee's results sometimes didn't match the scintillating football on display but the feast of football on offer more often than not had Dundee's Georgian number ten at the heart of it.

His dazzling footwork was again on display in the first derby of the season at Dens when Giorgi's close ball skills helped set up Juan Sara's hat-trick in a memorable 3-0 win.

He sense of moment and theatre returned in the second derby in November when at Tannadice, Giorgi scored one of the most breathtaking goals in the Club's history. With Dundee leading 1-0 at half-time through Argentinean legend Claudio Caniggia, Giorgi set about upstaging the superstar with a goal that lives long in the memory. Barry Smith collected the ball form Rocatti in the Dundee goal and played a neat ball up to Caniggia near the half way line but the ball he played to Nemsadze was slightly behind the 5ft. 11in. midfielder. Giorgi however simply dragged the ball into his path leaving three Arab defenders in his wake and from a tight angle on the left of United's box, he sent a sublime chip over Alan Combe in the Terrors' goal who could only turn round and put his hands on his hips as he watched the ball land into his net.

It was a purely stunning goal and a Dundee legend was born and it meant as much to Giorgi as to the fans who idolised him in the stands.

'Dundee was the best, it was my second home,' Nemsadze told the Sunday Herald in 2007. *'I loved it very much. Scotland will always be my second home. I was there for three-and-a-half years. For me, my best moment was the chip I scored in the derby against Dundee United.'*

By the end of the season Dundee had secured an S.P.L. post-split, top six finish which had been cemented by a 2-0 win at Pittodrie when Giorgi's sense of occasion again came to the fore as he opened the scoring against Aberdeen.

The following season brought a serious injury for Giorgi which kept him out for months but he had found himself a home on Tayside that other locations in his diverse career just could not provide. Prior to coming to Dens, Nemsadze's path had taken him to Germany with F.C. Homburg, to Turkey with Trabzonspor, Switzerland with Grasshoppers and Italy with Reggiana to name but a few and having five different clubs in the twelve months before coming to the City of Discovery, Dundee provided Giorgi with stability and a platform to show off his wares.

At Reggiana, Nemsadze had had high hopes as Italy is supposed to be the El Dorado for professional footballers, but for Giorgi it was hell. Reggiana had plunged to two successive demotions, and when Nemsadze got there in 1998, their Serie B status was just about to expire and he had to buy out his contract because Italian labour laws do not permit foreigners to play in Serie C. He had returned to his homeland to play for Dinamo Tbilisi after Italy and from there to Dens Park and he was now determined to repay Dundee for their faith when he returned from injury.

By then Dundee had a new manager in Jim Duffy and he was about to embark with Dundee on a 'Road to Hampden' in the Scottish Cup that would take Dundee on the 'Road to Europe'.

Giorgi helped pave that road by appearing in all five matches on the way to the Final and contributed with goals in the third round victory away to Partick Thistle with a wonderful free kick and a goal against Inverness Caledonian Thistle in the semi.

Not since 1964 had Dundee graced a Scottish Cup Final and they booked their place in the big day when Giorgi slid home a low shot from the edge of the box with twelve minutes to go to give Dundee a 1-0 win. With League Champions Rangers waiting in the Final, Dundee were guaranteed a place in next season's U.E.F.A. Cup and it was Giorgi's goal that had sealed Dundee's passport to Europe for the first time in twenty-nine years.

That passport would take Dundee to Albania in the preliminary round where no Scottish side had ever won but with Giorgi in his natural environment with more room to play, he dazzled against K.S. Vllaznia dictating the tempo throughout. A superb ball to Steve Lovell set up the opener and the 2-0 first leg win was supplanted with a 4-0 victory in the second leg to take Dundee through to a glamour first round tie.

That glamour came in the Italian region of Umbria where over 2000 Dees made the pilgrimage to Perugia. Unfortunately they were to be disappointed when Dundee couldn't overturn the 2-1 first leg deficit and went down 1-0 to the Intertoto Cup holders.

More disappointment was to follow a month later when Dundee plunged into administration and Nemsadze was one of fifteen players released in an effort to cut the wage bill.

Giorgi's three and a half years at Dens however provided many highlights for the Dundee support and the man with the dazzling skill made seventeen appearances for Georgia while at Dens.

He retains his affection for the Club at which he played the most games and spent the most time and that affection was returned when he was inducted into the Dundee F.C. Hall of Fame in April 2010 being the recipient of the International Award.

His skill and goals are legendary, especially that chip in the derby and if you haven't seen that goal at Grimsby yet, check it out on *You Tube* where you'll be one of over ten thousand hits to marvel at the man with the dancing feet.

> Honours at Dundee:
> Tennents' Scottish Cup runners-up: 2003
> Georgia International caps: 17
> Dundee F.C. Hall of Fame:
> 2010 International Award
> Appearances, Goals:
> League: 76 + 3 subs, 3 goals
> Scottish Cup: 10, 2 goals
> League Cup: 2 + 1 sub
> Europe: 4
> Totals: 96, 5 goals

Nacho Novo

Nacho Novo's time at Dundee experienced the most extreme highs and lows as he enjoyed a Scottish Cup Final and a European campaign to the ignominy of administration where Nacho survived the cull and in all probability scored the goals which literally helped the Club to survive.

Ignacio Javier Gómez Novo, simply known as Nacho Novo (Gomez being the first family name and Novo the second) was born on March 26th 1979 in Ferrol, Galicia in the north-west of Spain near the port of La Coruna and started his football career with local side Racing Ferrol. In 2000 he signed for Sociedad Deportiva Huesca in the Spanish Tercera Division (the fourth tier of Spanish football) and after twenty-two league goals in his debut season, he took a gamble to 'up sticks' and move to Scotland, where he joined First Division club Raith Rovers.

Soon his goal scoring record in Kirkcaldy alerted S.P.L. side Dundee and in the summer of 2002, he joined the Dens Park side for a fee of £100, 000. Given squad number seventeen, Nacho made his debut for Dundee on August 3rd against Hearts at home and with the successful partnership of Caballero and Sara, starting up front, Novo made his first start playing out wide on the right.

Before the end of the month, new manager Jim Duffy brought in striker Steve Lovell from Portsmouth to bring a dash of power to the forward line and Nacho was often given a roving commission in the side as The Dee often played with three up front. He scored his first goals for Dundee with a brace away to Dunfermline on August 17th and his first home goal a month later against Livingston in a 2-1 win.

On January 25th 2003, Dundee started an impressive fourteen match unbeaten run which helped Dundee secure a top six finish with Nacho scoring seven league goals in twenty-five starts.

That unbeaten run started away to Partick Thistle in the third round of the Scottish Cup and it was the first match on the Road to Hampden that would ultimately lead to a Cup Final appearance in May. In the fourth round at home to Aberdeen, Nacho scored Dundee's second in a 2-0 win over Aberdeen and in the quarter-final, he scored an even more crucial goal when he netted a late equaliser at Brockville to earn Dundee a replay with First Division leaders Falkirk.

With Falkirk defeated 4-1 at Dens and Inverness dispatched in the semis, Dundee were in their first Scottish Cup Final for thirty-nine years but Nacho would start on the bench against Rangers on May 31st. Loan striker Mark Burchill was preferred ahead of the 5ft 9in Spaniard and when Nacho came on in the second half to replace to former Celtic man, he couldn't help prevent Rangers from winning 1-0 and completing the domestic treble.

Nacho's second season saw him return to prolific best and he would score three goals in the U.E.F.A. Cup for which Dundee qualified for through their Scottish Cup Final appearance. After a twenty-nine year European absence, Dundee became the first Scottish side to win on Albanian soil when they defeated K.S. Vllaznia 2-0 with Nacho scoring the second and in the preliminary round home leg, he was again on target with a double as Dundee ran out comfortable 4-0 winners.

The first round proper saw Dundee draw Intertoto Cup winners A.C. Perugia from Serie A and a near capacity crowd turned out to watch the biggest match at Dens in over thirty years. Perugia went ahead five minutes after half-time but in sixty-three minutes Lee Wilkie made it 1-1 when he headed home a corner with the predatory Novo trying to claim the final touch.

Perugia however grabbed a second late on but it didn't deter 2500 Dees making the pilgrimage to Umbria to Perugia's Reni Curi Stadium. Dundee had a number of chances from Rae, Sara and Novo but they couldn't make the break through and Perugia booked their package into round two with a goal nineteen minutes from time.

It was an enjoyable experience for The Dee but just a month later Dundee plunged into administration with debts nearing £20 million and fifteen members of the playing staff were released. Nacho however was one of the lucky ones who retained his job but there was enormous pressure on the experienced players who remained, with only thirteen experienced first teamers left.

Nacho however stepped up to the plate and continued to perform, often playing up front on his own through sheer lack of selection options for manager Jim Duffy and by the end of the season, he had performed admirably scoring twenty-five times as Dundee secured seventh place against all the odds. Novo finished as Dundee's top goal scorer and deservedly won the Supporters' Association Player of the Year and without his goals, there is every chance Dundee might have been relegated which would surely have seen the Club close down for good.

Amongst those goals was a strike in a derby against Dundee United in January which was crucial in Dundee's bid for survival. Having endured a miserable run since going into administration, the 2-1 win on Burns Day gave the whole Club a lift and showed the nation watching live on BBC that Dundee were a club worth saving and Nacho's goal was crucial in drawing Dundee level.

At the end of the season it was obvious that Novo would have to be one of the players sold to help balance the books and having fended off interest from Rangers in the January transfer window, he now headed to Ibrox for a £500,000 fee. The Dark Blues had got the money they wanted for Novo but only after the Spaniard, who had rejected overtures from Celtic, waived his £50,000 fee to ensure that he joined former team mates Zurab Zhizanishvili and Gavin Rae in Glasgow.

Novo's old club Raith Rovers were due 15% of the fee but with Dundee in administration, they were regarded as an unsecured creditor under the terms of the Enterprise Act and had to accept a much smaller compromise figure which was offset by Dundee with the money Novo himself gave up.

Novo's never say die attitude and eye for goal made him a popular figure with the Dundee support and while many were disappointed with his Rangers badge kissing exploits on his return to Dens, history will record that his goals went a long way to staving off liquidation as well as giving up a substantial sum of money himself.

Honours at Dundee:
Tennents' Scottish Cup runner-up: 2003
D.S.A. Player of the Year: 2003
Appearances, Goals:
League: 59 + 11 subs, 27 goals
Scottish Cup: 6 + 2 subs, 3 goals
League Cup: 3 + 1 sub, 1 goal
Europe: 4, 3 goals
Totals: 86, 34 goals

Andy Penman

When you enter through the main reception at Dens Park, you are greeted with a picture with the simple caption 'The Penalty King' and inside the frame is a photo of the boy genius of Dundee, Andy Penman, who made his debut for the Club at the tender age of fifteen and won a Championship medal aged just nineteen after scoring the goal which clinched the title.

Andy Penman was a wonderful midfield player with startling vision and a fine passer of the ball who could clip balls precisely through, round and over defences to give his forwards clear, unhindered runs at goal. He was a genius, a child prodigy in the art of football who went down to Everton straight from school in Dunfermline and turned out for their reserve side in a Merseyside derby at just fifteen years of age.

Born in Rosyth on February 20th 1943, the son of a Fife miner was homesick down in Liverpool and it didn't take much for manager Willie Thornton to persuade Andy to come back north to Scotland and sign an amateur contract with his Dundee side in 1958.

Thornton knew he had signed someone special and it took just two games in the reserves to convince the Dundee management that they had a real talent and was pitched him into the first team against Hearts at Tynecastle, just thirteen days before his sixteenth birthday, making him the youngest player to ever to turn out in the Scottish League.

Within twelve months Andy was a regular in the Dundee side and wearing the number seven shirt, he made twenty-one appearances in the 1959/60 season. It was towards the end of that campaign that Andy showed his goal scoring potential with a hat-trick against Hibs in a 6-3 win at Dens but it wasn't until the following year that Penman started to earn his 'Penalty King' nickname when he scored his first spot kick for the Club.

That historic strike came in a League Cup quarter-final second leg tie at home to Rangers but it wasn't enough to see The Dee into the semi-final as the Dark Blues lost 4-3, to be knocked out 5-3 on aggregate. Sharing the penalty duties with Doug Cowie and Bobby Cox, Penman managed three that term but the following season saw Andy take over the responsibility full time and scored five on the way to Dundee winning the League Flag.

At the start of the 1961/62 season, the arrival of Gordon Smith meant that Andy moved to inside-forward and the pair forged a formidable right-wing partnership which was to bring Dundee the Scottish League Championship and then European glory. Having scored twelve goals in the previous two campaigns, Andy's new position saw him now contribute seventeen goals on the way to the title which included his second hat-trick for The Dee at home against Kilmarnock in October and the third goal in the 3-0 win against St. Johnstone which saw Dundee become Champions of Scotland in April.

The Championship season saw Dundee go on a Club record twenty games undefeated and amongst those matches was a friendly against Swedish champions Elfsborg Boras when Andy scored five in an 8-1 win at Dens and a Dewer Shield 4-2 victory over St. Johnstone in which Andy scored from the spot. Andy also scored three goals pre season which meant that Dundee's title winning year saw Penman score an impressive twenty-six goals.

Winning the title meant European competition for the first time in the Club's history and Andy was an ever present throughout the season as Dundee reached the Champions' Cup semi-final.

In the preliminary round against Cologne, Andy was part of a tie that he would never forget when in the first leg at Dens, he scored in the remarkable 8-1 win and then in the second leg in Germany, he ended up in goal after Bert Slater was stretched off in the twenty-seventh minute.

'Whoever put Andy Penman in goal have made better decisions', claimed Ian Ure on the fortieth anniversary of the tie but the youngster was brave enough to take over the number one shirt. Already 1-0 down on the night, Andy let in two further goals before half time and it was a relief to everyone connected with Dundee, when Bert Slater returned between the sticks early in the second half to help Dundee see out the tie 8-5 on aggregate.

That European Cup season would see Andy play fifty-two times, scoring fourteen goals and was the only player to play in every match throughout the 1962/63 campaign. He would again hit fifty appearances the following season but his goal scoring record was more that double the year before scoring a terrific thirty goals in all competitions but astonishingly was only the second top scorer behind fifty-two goal 'Gillie'.

He did however finish top scorer the next two seasons with thirty-three goals in 1964/65 and nineteen the following year.

Season 1963/64 saw Andy and Dundee reach the Scottish Cup Final but he collected a runners-up medal after a 3-1 defeat to future employers Rangers. The Championship win two years before turned out not only to be Andy's only winner's medal at Dundee but was also the only winners' medal of his entire career. Considering that he signed for Rangers for £30,000 plus George McLean in 1967, it is a surprise he didn't collect another winner's medal but these were barren years for Rangers as Celtic dominated and he missed out on the European Cup Winner's Cup triumph in 1972 through injury.

Before he left for Ibrox, Andy was called up for Scotland in 1966 when he made his full international debut against Holland to add to the Under-23 and Scottish League caps he won while at Dens. It is a tragedy that he only won a further two full caps but and it meant he had been capped at every level by Scotland from schoolboy upwards.

After leaving Rangers in 1973, Andy joined Arbroath who were then in the top flight and then after three years at Gayfield, it was off to the Highlands to become player / manager of Inverness Caledonian where he received a testimonial when an Inverness Select played a Dundee XI in 1979.

Andy was a tireless worker in midfield and contributed a terrific 141 goals as one of only ten players to hit over a century for Dundee as the Club's fifth top scorer of all time. A dead ball expert, his forte was from the penalty spot where he rarely missed, scoring twenty-five times from twelve yards in eight years at Dens.

Sadly, Andy died in 1994, aged just fifty-one but his legacy lives on at Dens Park. Not only are you greeted by Andy's image when you enter the main door but there is also a hospitality lounge that bears his name showing that 'Boy Kings' never grow up and they never die, at least not in the memories of those who were lucky enough to witness the skills and genius of Andy Penman.

Honours at Dundee:	
Scottish League Champions:	1961/62
European Cup semi-final:	1962/63
Scottish Cup runner-up:	1964
Scotland full caps:	1
Scottish League caps:	4
Scotland Under 23 caps:	4
Appearances, Goals:	
League:	215, 100 goals
Scottish Cup:	17 + 1 sub, 10 goals
League Cup:	46, 18 goals
Europe:	10, 1 goal
Other:	17, 12 goals
Totals:	306, 141 goals

Iain Phillip

Iain Phillip was a real classy defender who turned out for Dundee 261 times in two spells over a ten year period which saw him pick up one of the three League Cup winners medals that he won during his career.

Born in Broughty Ferry on Valentine's Day 1951, the quiet unassuming Grove Academy schoolboy who put pen to paper for Dundee in November 1968 was considered to be one of the best signings ever made by manager John Prentice.

Iain Phillip was a Scottish Schoolboy international by the time he signed at Dens and he made his debut for The Dee when he came on for Jocky Scott in a 2-1 League Cup defeat at Kilmarnock in August 1970.

He went on to play thirty-four times in his debut season as Dundee finished fifth, which gave the Dee their highest league finish since winning the Championship nine years earlier and they would go on to finish fifth again in the following three seasons.

During that time, Iain was part of the side which beat such European giants as Cologne and A.C. Milan in the U.E.F.A. Cup and although not capped at full international level, he represented his country for the Scottish League against the English League in 1972 and played for the Scotland Under 23 side against a West German Olympic XI in the same year.

After having an outstanding match against the English League, Scotland manager Tommy Docherty offered Iain the chance to go on the Scotland tour of Brazil but he turned it down having just returned from Dundee's tour of Australia and New Zealand, thus giving up the chance of winning a full cap.

International recognition did however bring Iain to the attention of Bert Head at Crystal Palace and later that year, the twenty-one year old left Dundee for a Club record fee of £105 000 to join the London club.

It was not only the highest fee the Dark Blues had received at that time but it was also the second highest transfer fee received by a Scottish club to date, being trumped only by the £125 000 Aberdeen received from Manchester United for Martin Buchan.

Iain however couldn't quite settle at Selhurst Park under the flamboyant Malcolm Allison and Davie White swooped to bring him back to Tayside for a cut price fee of £40, 500 after just thirteen months in the capital.

It was a great move for both White and Phillip as within two months of his return, Iain became part of the side which shocked Scottish football in the 1973 League Cup Final by beating league champions and strong favourites Celtic 1-0 at Hampden. He played in both legs of the quarter-final against Clyde and in the semi-final against Kilmarnock and in the Final, Iain was outstanding and helped keep Kenny Dalglish quiet in the snow, sleet and driving rain.

The League Cup win was Iain's only major honour at Dens as Dundee were unable to get past Celtic at the semi-final stage in the Scottish Cup where the sides met five times in the seventies and Iain was part of two of those unsuccessful semis.

He was however part of the Dundee side which won promotion back to the top tier after being relegated from the inaugural Premier Division in 1975/76. Dundee gained promotion by winning the Scottish First Division in 1978/79 and in that season, Iain scored one of his only two goals for the Club in a 1-1 draw at home to Montrose in August with his other coming in a 3-1 home win over Airdrie in April 1977.

It was midway through that season however that Iain left Dundee when he stepped back up to the Premier Division before his team mates by making the short walk down Tannadice Street for a fee of £25, 000.

He had by then lost his place in the team as sweeper to Willie Watson and put in a transfer request, feeling that he wasn't the type of player manager Tommy Gemmell liked but he found an admirer in Jim McLean across the road.

Iain was at Dundee United for just over five years where he won a further two League Cups both at his former home of Dens Park, one of which at his former employers expense and he was also part of the United side which won the Scottish League Premier Division in 1983.

After leaving Tannadice, Iain spent three years at Raith Rovers before bringing down the curtain on a eighteen year playing career with Arbroath in 1988.

Known as 'Aggie' for his liking of Agatha Christie novels, Iain Phillip was a strong, elegant centre-half who holds a unique place in the history of football in the City of Discovery as the only man to win major honours both for Dundee F.C. and Dundee United.

Honours at Dundee:	
Scottish League Cup winner:	1973/74
Scottish League First Division winner:	1978/79
Scottish League cap:	1
Scotland Under 23 appearance:	1
Appearances, Goals:	
League:	189 + 6 subs, 2 goals
Scottish Cup:	18
League Cup:	34 + 2 subs
Europe:	7
Other:	5
Totals:	261, 2 goals

Billy Pirie

Being brought in to replace fans' favourite Gordon Wallace might have seemed a daunting task to many but not for Billy Pirie who went on to establish himself as a Dundee legend by scoring over 100 goals in his four seasons at the Club and topping the Dundee scoring charts three years on the trot.

There cannot have been a more prolific in Dundee's history than Billy Pirie and his 106 goals in 138 games is a phenomenal ratio which sees him ninth in Dundee's all time goal scoring list and while critics may point towards the fact that the majority of his goals were in the second tier, at his peak he looked one of the sharpest strikers around.

A stocky figure, likened by many as in the Gerd Muller mould, Billy started his career with South African side Arcadia Shepherds where he could count among his team mates such legends of the English game as Johnny Byrne and Johnny Haynes.

After a short illness however, Billy returned to Scotland where he signed for Highland League side Huntly and then Arbroath before being lured to his home town team, Aberdeen for £30,000 in 1974.

Surprisingly, Billy never became a first team regular at Pittodrie and he agreed to join North American Soccer League side New York Apollos after being given a free transfer by Dons boss Ally McLeod.

By then Dundee were on a look out for a new striker after Wallace's high profile departure and Dundee manager Davie White spotted the man he wanted when Billy scored a hat-trick for Aberdeen against Dundee in a Reserve League Cup Final which the Reds won 4-1.

Dundee had been relegated at the end of the first Premier Division and Davie White persuaded Billy that he was the man to spearhead the promotion push and agreed to put pen to paper for the Dark Blues.

Dundee agreed to allow him to play for the American side during the summer and Pirie rewarded their faith in him with an incredible forty-four goals in forty-five appearances in his debut season.

Billy netted thirty-eight of Dundee's ninety goals in the First Division but it wasn't enough to secure promotion as The Dee could only finish in third place behind St. Mirren and Clydebank but it did win Billy the Scottish First Division Player of the Year.

Failure to win promotion meant that the tracksuit-clad Davie White resigned in April 1977 and the following season, now under the managerial charge of Tommy Gemmell, Pirie continued to delight the home support by finding the back of the net.

Early results included a Pirie-inspired 5-3 victory over St. Johnstone, with the striker converting an injury time penalty and an even later strike to secure his hat-trick and with Pirie and Eric Sinclair now forming a deadly partnership, the side topped the division by the New Year.

Pirie kept on scoring, grabbing four in a 6-0 drubbing of Alloa, as Hearts, Morton and the Dundee tied at the top of the division and it proved to be a rollercoaster end to the season. Pirie scored a last-minute winner against Morton to make the score 3-2 and both players and fans thought the Dundee side had won promotion. However, minutes later it transpired that Hearts had also scored in the final stages to take second place, leaving Dundee facing heart break and another season in the First Division.

By now attacking defenders with his iconic premed hair-do, Pirie was to play a pivotal role as Dundee returned to the Premier Division at the third attempt in 1979. The Dark Blues' goal machine scored sixteen times, as the side put the turmoil of the previous season behind them and returned to the top tier as champions.

While both Pirie and the club found the net less frequently than in previous seasons, a tighter backline was the catalyst for their title win. The attacking role was now shared with Ian Redford and Eric Sinclair and both Pirie and Redford each scored sixteen league goals. Billy's two cup goals however saw him crowned leading goal scorer for the third season in succession becoming the first Dundee player to achieve that since Alan Gilzean in 1964.

In the Premier Division, Billy missed the start of the season with an ankle injury and scored six goals in just twelve outings before departing for Australia before the season ended to join up with former Dens Park coach Willie Wallace at Sydney club Apia.

These days Billy runs the Albert Bar in Montrose but was welcomed back to Dens in early 2010 for the founding of the Former Players' Association when he was warmly applauded onto the pitch at half time.

Billy's record speaks for itself as a prolific goal getter not just in Dundee's history but also in Scottish footballing history and his forty-four goal haul in his first season with Dundee, has yet to be bettered by any player who has followed. His 1.3 goals per game ratio did much to alleviate the sense of doom and gloom then prevailing at Dens Park with the Dees having just been relegated from the newly formed Premier Division and the memories of him terrorising First Division defenders live long in the mind of all who saw him.

Honours at Dundee:
Scottish League First Division winner: 1978/79
S.P.F.A. Scottish First Division Player of the Year: 1977/78
Appearances, Goals:
League: 111 + 1 sub, 93 goals
Scottish Cup: 11, 5 goals
League Cup: 15, 8 goals
Totals: 138, 106 goals

Gavin Rae

When Scotland manager Craig Brown was asked in a press conference why he called up Dundee midfielder Gavin Rae for an international friendly against Poland in Bydgoszcz in April 2001, he replied that it was because '*he played for Dundee*'. While he was attempting with tongue in cheek to show his fondness for the club with whom he won a Scottish League championship medal, Brown failed to give credit to popular Dark Blue midfielder who had become Dundee's first Scottish internationalist in fifteen years.

Aberdonian Rae was born on November 28th 1977 and made his debut for The Dee aged eighteen in front of just 828 fans at Broadwood Stadium when he came off the bench in 1-0 win over Hamilton Accies in March 1996.

It was Dundee manager Jim Duffy who gave Rae his debut but when he left to join Hibs nine months later, Gavin found his chances limited under new manager John McCormack who was very close to letting Rae to Brechin City for a nominal fee.

When McCormack was sacked in February 1998 however, his replacement Jocky Scott said that all players in the squad would get a chance to prove themselves and Gavin managed to force his way back into the first team squad as Dundee went on the win the First Division and secure promotion into the inaugural Scottish Premier League.

It was in the S.P.L. that Gavin started to flourish and in Dundee's first season back in the top flight, he made twenty-three starts, two more than his total in the previous three campaigns. By the end of the season, he had established himself in the side, starting the last ten matches as Dundee finished strongly and secured a fifth place spot, their highest league placing in twenty-five years.

The following term Gavin missed just one match, making the most appearances of any of the Dundee squad and in November 1999, he scored a famous injury time winner in a 2-1 triumph over Rangers at Ibrox to cement his popularity with the Dens Park support.

Rae had been used as both a right-back and an attacking midfielder during his time at Dens and his philosophy of hard work coupled with his excellent attitude was now paying dividends. Gavin had sought to improve his fitness and his dedication had begun to pay off as he was now employed as a deep-lying midfielder and broke through into the Scotland Under-21 side.

It was all change for the Dark Blues in the summer of 2000 however when Jocky Scott was replaced by Ivano Bonetti in the Dundee hot seat and while the Italian brought in a host of international talent to Dens Park, including Argentinean superstar Claudio Caniggia, Gavin was one of the few Scots who managed to hold onto their place in the side.

Rae now became highly influential in the Dark Blues' midfield and was rewarded for his performances in an exciting Dundee side which secured a top six finish side by being called up for that Scotland international against Poland. He made his debut from the start in the 1-1 draw and in the process became the first Dundee player to play for Scotland since Robert Connor was capped against Holland in 1986.

At the start of Bonetti's second season in charge, Gavin opened the campaign with a goal in a 2-2 draw with Dundee United at Tannadice. In his eight years at Dens, Gavin had a terrific record in the Dundee derby, playing in six wins and six draws and he revelled in the big game atmosphere.

The undoubted highlight of his time at Dens however came the following season when Dundee reached the Scottish Cup Final and qualified for Europe for the first time in twenty-nine years. On route to the Final, Dundee's number eight played in all five games and scored in the 2-0 win over Partick Thistle in the third round and having made his debut in front of 828 fans in Cumbernauld, he now lined up in front of 47 136 fans at the National Stadium.

Dundee however lost out in the final 1-0 to Rangers but as S.P.L. champions, the Ibrox side qualified for the Champions' League which allowed Dundee to enter into the U.E.F.A. Cup for the first time since 1974.

In the preliminary round in August, Dundee drew the unknown K.S. Vllaznia from Shkoder in Albania but a terrific performance in the first leg, saw Dundee become the first Scottish side to win in Albania with a 2-0 victory.

In the second leg at Dens, Dundee were comfortable 4-0 winners and the highlight of a very enjoyable night for the 8254 crowd was a terrific goal from Gavin when he thundered in a ferocious volley from just outside the box which flew into the top of the Albanian net.

In the first round proper, Dundee faced Serie A side Perugia but the European adventure went no further as Dundee went out 3-1 on aggregate after over 2000 Dees travelled to Italy to watch their side in action.

A month later, Gavin won his eighth Scotland cap in the Euro 2004 play-off against Holland in Amsterdam but on returning home from the Netherlands, he was greeted with the devastating news that Dundee had plunged into administration.

It was the beginning of the end of Gavin's Dark Blue career as his consistent performances had made him one of Dundee's most saleable assets. In December, Rangers displayed little festive spirit with a derisory £50, 000 offer and tried to get the Scottish internationalist on the cheap with further bids of £100, 000 and £125, 000. Dundee however refused to bow to Rangers bully-boy tactics and by the end of the month got the quarter of a million pound fee they had been holding out for.

Rae had been a grand servant in his ten years with the Dundee and his driving midfield play would be missed.

Before departing, he posted an emotional thank you letter to the fans online for all their support and did the club a great service by stating a willingness to go anywhere so that the Club would receive as big a fee as necessary in their hour of need. The fans were grateful and administrator Tom Burton echoed the supporters' appreciation by stating, *'Gavin recognised that his move could ease our situation and his professionalism has been exemplary.'*

However the fans were not just grateful for Gavin's help in such desperate times but also for his commitment, hard work and terrific performances which will be fondly remembered by all Dee4Lifers.

Honours at Dundee:	
Tennents' Scottish Cup runners-up: 2003	
Scottish League First Division winner: 1997/98	
Scotland full caps:	8
Scotland B/Future caps:	1
Scotland Under 21 caps:	6
Appearances, Goals:	
League:	186+23 subs, 24 goals
Scottish Cup:	17, 2 goals
League Cup:	9 + 1 sub
Europe:	6, 1 goal
S.F.L. Challenge Cup:	1
Totals:	245, 27 goals

Hugh Robertson

Hugh, better known to many as 'Shug' or 'Shuggie' was a key member of the Dundee squad who brought the League Flag to Dens in 1962 and reached the European Cup semi the following year and in a Dundee career spanning eight years, would go on to play 292 times for The Dee.

Robertson's appearances make him twenty-first on Dundee's all time list and curiously he is also currently number twenty-one in Dundee's all time goal scoring chart with sixty-one goals and he was a constant threat from his outside-left position on the wing.

Hugh was born in Auchenleck on November 29th 1939 and he played his early football for the local side Auchenleck Talbot. It was from Talbot that Hugh was signed for Dundee at the age of seventeen in 1957 by the then Dundee manager Willie Thornton and made his debut two weeks before his eighteenth birthday later that year in a 5-0 win at home to Partick Thistle in which he managed to get on the score sheet.

Originally a miner in his native Ayrshire, Hugh initially signed part-time at Dens, combining his football career with his mining job but that soon changed to full time after a good impression on his goal scoring debut.

By 1960 Bob Shankly had joined the club and the Championship side was beginning to take shape. Two years later of course Dundee enjoyed their finest hour when they lifted the Scottish League Championship for the first time and Hugh Robertson was very much an important part of that success.

Standing at 5ft 9in tall, with short dark hair parted on the left side, Hugh, who regularly wore the number 11 shirt, would miss just one match in the title winning year, scoring seven goals in forty appearances including the fourth in a 4-1 derby win over Dundee United.

He would also be responsible for setting up many a goal throughout the title winning year, including the goal which sealed the win at Muirton on the last day when he squared the ball across the eighteen yard line from the left wing, for Andy Penman to fire an unstoppable shot via the crossbar into the St. Johnstone net.

In was during that Championship season that Robertson would make his one and only appearance for the full international side and it was a match in which the Scotland side would feature three Dundee players in the starting line up for the only time in the twentieth century.

Helped no doubt by the Club's climb to the top and by the recent 5-1 win over Rangers at Ibrox, Hugh was joined by Ian Ure and Alex Hamilton in the Scotland side which took the field against Czechoslovakia in November 1961 in a play off match to qualify for the 1962 World Cup Finals in Chile. It was however an ultimately disappointing night for Shug and the Scots as they lost out to the Czechs 4-2 after extra time in the Heysel Stadium in Brussel.

Unfortunately for Hugh he was one of five players dropped for the next Scotland match and he was never again to play for the full international side again.

Hugh did however win two Under-23 caps against England and Wales in 1962 but can consider himself unlucky to never to win another full cap. He was never given a proper chance to recreate his club form at international level and he suffered from the fact that there were so many good wingers in Scotland at the time with the likes of Wille Henderson and Jimmy Johnstone regularly filling the wider roles throughout the Sixties.

While his international impact for the national side was limited, it was anything but at club level, as Hugh would feature in Dundee's run to the European Cup semi-final the year after winning the league as The Dee took Europe by storm.

Hugh played in five matches in that fabulous run and in the famous first match at home to second favourites Cologne, he scored the third goal in the twelfth minute in an 8-1 win.

Missing the first leg in Lisbon against Sporting, Shug returned to help overturn a first leg deficit at Dens to help reach quarter finals and he was then able to overcome any lingering disappointment from that Scotland defeat in Heysel when he returned to the same ground with Dundee against Belgian champions Anderlecht and help Dundee secure a stunning 4-1 win.

Hugh also played in the 2-1 second leg win at Dens but injury ruled him out of both semi final legs against A.C. Milan but he would feature in one more European tie for the Dark Blues in late 1964 in a European Cup Winners Cup second round tie, against Fairs Cup holders, Real Zarragoza from Spain.

Shug lined up for the 2-2 first leg at Dens and in the second leg he gave Dundee the lead before Zarragoza fought back with two goals to give the Spaniards a 4-3 aggregate win.

Dundee had qualified for the Cup Winners' Cup that season by virtue of reaching the 1964 Scottish Cup Final. In what became known as 'The Bert Slater Final', Dundee they lost out narrowly 3-1 to League Champions Rangers and as they had qualified for the European Cup, Dundee were entered into U.E.F.A.'s secondary competition. Robertson lined up in his usual left wing position on that sunny cup final day at Hampden and could only watch in disbelief as Rangers scored two injury time goals to lift the trophy.

Less than a year after that cup final, Bob Shankly left Dens to take up the reigns at Easter Road and within two months, new manager Bobby Ancell allowed Shuggie to join Dunfermline for a £10,000 fee. There was no doubt he was allowed to leave Dundee prematurely and he would come back and haunt his former Club on several occasions.

While at East End Park, Robertson won the Scottish Cup in 1968 when The Pars overcame Hearts 3-1 in the Final and the following year made up for missing out on a European semi with Dundee by playing in the Cup Winners' Cup semi final against eventual winners Slovan Bratislava who knocked The Pars out 2-1 on aggregate.

Robertson left Dunfermline to join Arbroath in 1971 but after just forty matches for the Gayfield side was forced to retire on medical grounds and took up the post of coach.

He returned to Dens a few years later as first a coach and then chief scout and on the eve of Dundee's Scottish Cup tie away to Celtic in 2009, Celtic manager Gordon Strachan recalled his fondness to his time at Dens and mentioned what a fabulous coach Hugh Robertson was and how he '*picked up so many good habits*' from him.

On the fortieth anniversary of Dundee's Championship win, Alan Gilzean remembered Robertson as '*a little terrier, who had lots of skill, was very tricky and could turn on a sixpence.*'

Hugh Robertson is a legend at Dens Park and not just because his name is comes first in the list of players in the famous Hector Nicol, "Dundee Song" but because he was a fabulous player who will be fondly remembered by all who saw him wear the Dark Blue with pride in the Club's most successful era.

Honours at Dundee:	
Scottish League Champions:	1961/62
Scottish Cup runner-up:	1964
Scotland full caps:	1
Scotland Under 23 caps:	2
Appearances, Goals:	
League:	223, 48 goals
Scottish Cup:	14, 3 goals
League Cup:	39, 8 goals
Europe:	7, 2 goals
Other:	9
Totals:	292, 61 goals

Bobby Robinson

Bobby Robinson was a classy midfielder in the excellent Dundee side of the early seventies and was one of the real gentlemen of football. Nicknamed 'Trigger' by his team mates because of his turn of pace, he graced Dens Park for six years where he picked up a League Cup winners medal and was part of Scotland's 1974 World Cup squad.

Born in Gorebridge, Midlothian on November 10th 1950, Robert Sharp Robinson started his career in junior football before signing for Falkirk in 1969 but was a surprise free transfer three years later when Dundee picked him up from 'The Bairns'.

Bobby made a scoring debut for The Dee in the first game of the 1972/73 season in an 8-2 away win over East Stirlingshire in the League Cup and he would rarely miss a game that term.

That particular season was perhaps best known for the epic cup battles with Celtic and Bobby played in all five games against 'The Boys' who were in the middle of their nine in a row league titles. In the League Cup quarter-final, Dundee beat 'The Hoops' 1-0 at Dens in the first leg but after losing 3-2 in the second leg at Parkhead, a replay would be required after extra time couldn't separate the sides.

Played at neutral Hampden, Dundee's hopes were high having also beaten Celtic 2-0 in the league at Dens but in wasn't to be as Celtic progressed to the semis 4-1 before losing to Hibs in the Final.

Robinson and Dundee had a chance for revenge in the Scottish Cup when the sides met at Hampden in the semi-final but after drawing 0-0 in the first match, a replay was again required in which Celtic won again 3-0 after extra time with the score goal less after ninety minutes.

Dundee did get revenge however the following year when Dundee won the League Cup Final 1-0 over Celtic in December 1973 and it was the highlight of Robinson's time at Dens as Dundee lifted to date their last major title.

The same season again saw Dundee again draw Celtic in the Scottish Cup semi-final and it was the Glasgow side's turn for revenge as they emerged as 1-0 victors and would then lift the trophy against Dundee's deadly rivals United in the Final.

Robinson played fifty-three times in the League Cup winning season and included in those appearances was the third round Scottish Cup tie at Pittodrie when 'Trigger' scored Dundee's second in a 2-0 win over Aberdeen. In the next round, Bobby was instrumental in Dundee's stunning 3-0 win over Rangers at Ibrox and then in the quarter-final wore the number eight shirt in both the first match against Hibs which finished 3-3 and then the replay at Dens in which Dundee won 3-0 in front of a terrific crowd of 30,888.

Bobby's performances in these high profile matches alerted Scottish manager Willie Ormond to his ability and he was called up for a friendly with West Germany in Frankfurt just before the 1974 World Cup in the same country. He earned the first of his four caps when he came on as a substitute for Kenny Burns in the 2-1 loss and did enough to persuade Ormond to include him in the World Cup squad of forty for the Finals in the summer although he failed to make it into the final twenty-two which went to West Germany.

Bobby was also capped for the Under 23s against Wales in 1974 but he made his first full start for Scotland in a friendly away to Sweden in April 1975. He won two further caps before the end of the season against Northern Ireland at Hampden in the British Championships and came off the bench to replace Lou Macari in Romania in a Euro 76 Qualifier in Bucharest in June.

Bobby played in two U.E.F.A. Cup campaigns for Dundee and in season 1974/75 the ginger haired midfielder scored seven goals in forty-seven appearances but the following year he played just half that total. When in 1976/77, he was being increasingly used as a substitute, it became clear to 'Trigger' that he would have to continue his career elsewhere and he did that in August 1977 when his former coach at Dens Jim McLean took him across the road to Tannadice as part of a swap deal for Billy Williamson.

Two years later, he left Dundee United for Hearts when his former international manager signed him for Hearts for £20, 000 and then in 1981 another former colleague, Gordon Wallace, who had played with Robinson on both sides of Tannadice Street took him to Raith Rovers where he finished his playing career.

Bobby played most of his time as a part-timer, preferring to study for a degree at Dundee University and this stood him in good stead when he gave up professional football to become a school teacher in Kirriemuir in Angus while still playing for a string of a string of Junior clubs.

Bobby Robinson scored twenty goals for the Dark Blues and one of them, described by commentator Archie McPherson as a *'peach of a goal'* featured weekly on the opening credits to BBC Scotland's Sportscene show.

Sadly Bobby died aged just forty-six on Christmas Eve 1996, after a long battle with cancer. In a tribute to the midfield star, his former team mate, manager and friend Gordon Wallace said that, *'You could not have met a nicer person than Bobby'* while the Dundee fans that saw him play will remember him as a great player who wore the Dark Blue of Dundee with distinction.

Honours at Dundee:
Scottish League Cup winner: 1973/74
Scotland full caps: 4
Scotland Under 23 caps: 1
Appearances, Goals:
League: 131 + 18 subs, 15 goals
Scottish Cup: 18 + 2 subs, 2 goals
League Cup: 34 + 3 subs, 3 goals
Europe: 4
Other: 8
Totals: 218, 20 goals

Juan Sara

'Juan Sara, Sara, whatever will be, will be, he gave United three, Juan Sara, Sara' was sung to the *'Que Sera'* tune every time Juan Sara took to the field for Dundee after the famous derby against Dundee United on Wednesday 20th September 2000. He wrote himself into Dundee folklore where he scored that treble against The Arabs but there was much more to Sara's Dark Blue career as he finished top goal scorer in two different seasons and scored for Dundee in two separate European competitions.

Like many young South American boys, Juan Manuel Sara always wanted to be a professional footballer. Born in Buenos Aires on October 13th 1978, he was always ready for a game of football with his friends and from an early age it was obvious that he had a talent for the game. It was no surprise when Argentinean club Alte Brown offered the teenage Sara the opportunity of full time football then in 1999 he crossed the border to join Cerro Porteno in the Paraguay League.

At Porteno Sara played in the Copa Libertadores, the South American equivalent of the Champions League and was the third top scorer in the Paraguayan League but playing in Europe is the ambition of many a South American footballer and Juan was no different. His break came when Ivano Bonetti was appointed manger of Dundee and one of the Italian's first acts was to offer Sara a short term loan deal at the Club, where The Dee would pay a Players' Agency £80,000 for his services for one year.

He signed for Dundee on July 17th 2000 and on that very evening made his debut for the Dark Blues in a pre season friendly away to Raith Rovers. Immediately Sara opened his account for The Dee, playing up front with new strike partner Fabian Cabellero who was also signed that day from Paraguayan football for a similar deal and who scored Dundee's other goal that night in a 2-1 win.

Four days later Sara scored his second goal in a Dundee shirt in another pre season friendly away to Grimsby and already the powerful Argentinean showed he had a good first touch, a poacher's instinct and an eye for goal.

When the season kicked off at the end of the month Sara was part of the side that played some scintillating football in a 2-0 win at Motherwell and in his competitive home debut the following week at home to Dunfermline, Dundee shot to the top of the S.P.L. with a 3-0 win with Sara getting Dundee's second from the penalty spot.

Scored in front of the Bobby Cox Stand, Sara first showed off his trademark celebration to the Dundee spot when he ran behind the goal and lifted up his number nine Dundee shirt to reveal a t-shirt which said *'Jesus Loves You'*. A committed Christian, Sara got the idea from a few players who did the same in South America and in the coming months as the goals flowed, Sara also displayed biblical messages on his t-shirts from a verse from Philippians 4:16 and that old sporting favourite John 3:16.

Sara's second competitive goal also came from the spot at Love Street against St. Mirren and his first goal from open play came at home to Rangers in early September when he came off the bench to rob Lorenzo Amoruso at the edge of the box before slipping the ball under Klos in goal.

'He's here to score goals and convert souls', said Scotsport commentator Archie Macpherson in the highlights of the 1-1 draw but it would be his next goals in a Dundee shirt that would convert a few souls to the merits of the 6ft 1in striker.

On September 20th, fifth placed Dundee entertained bottom of the table Dundee United who had failed to win any of their opening seven games.

Dundee however had won only one home derby in the last eleven years but it would become a derby long remembered and a derby for which the name of Juan Sara would be forever linked.

For long spells, Dundee were on the defensive but soon after the break, Sara netted from a tight angle after Combe could only parry a powerful Caballero shot from twenty-five yards.

Not long after however Caballero was stretchered off after a horrendous double tackle but his replacement Javier Artero soon started causing United all sorts of problems out wide with Sara now ploughing a lone furrow up front. Dundee continued to press and in seventy-nine minutes got their reward when Sara headed home after Giorgi Nemsadze had weaved his way past three men.

The Dundee support were in raptures and with just two minutes left were in complete delirium when Sara completed a memorable hat-trick as he headed home from an Artero cross to make himself an instant Dundee legend.

The Dundee club shop had started selling t-shirts with the slogan *'Sara says Jesus Loves You'*, on the front and *'Jesus Saves while Sara nets the rebound'* on the back and sales of these shirts rocketed after his derby hat-trick. The t-shirts however weren't popular with everyone when he was booked by the referee at Paisley in February for revealing a t-shirt which said, *'I can do everything through Christ'* and after putting Dundee ahead with a superbly executed overhead kick was later sent off for an innocuous handball.

By then Dundee had signed Argentinean superstar Claudio Caniggia and with Sara getting the chance to play with one of his idols, the goals continued to come.

As Dundee secured a top six finish, Sara finished the season as the Dark Blues top goal scorer and his seventeen goals saw him finish as the second highest scorer in the S.P.L. behind Celtic's Henrik Larsson. It is a tragedy that Juan didn't win any of the nominations for Scottish Player of the Year or Young Player of the Year after a terrific debut season.

His goals also persuaded manager Ivano Bonetti that Sara was worth signing on a long term contract and his services were secured on a three year deal for a transfer of £500, 000, the second highest fee paid in the Club's history.

In the summer, Dundee took part in the U.E.F.A. Intertoto Cup and in the first round were drawn in the F.K. Sartid from Yugoslavia. The winners of the tie were due to play 1860 Munich in the Olympic Stadium but it was the Serbians who went through when they defeated Dundee 5-2 in the second leg after a 0-0 draw at Dens.

Dundee's second goal in the away leg was scored by Sara as he started his second season in the same goal scoring form as his first and he would again finish as Dundee's top marksman with thirteen goals.

The summer of 2002 saw a managerial change at Dundee with Jim Duffy replacing Bonetti and with the addition of Nacho Novo and Steve Lovell to the squad, Sara was allowed to go on loan to Coventry City but not before another four goals.

He returned to Dundee before the end of the season in time for the Scottish Cup Final but didn't make it into the Hampden sixteen as The Dee lost 1-0 to Rangers. With Rangers winning the league however, Dundee qualified for the U.E.F.A. Cup for the first time in twenty-nine years and Juan was back in the side for the Preliminary Round first leg match against K.S. Vllaznia where he came off the bench in Albania in a 2-0 win.

Juan was on the bench again for the second leg and came on for fellow Argentinean Beto Carranza in the first half to score Dundee's second in a 4-0 win as Dundee made a triumphant European return.

Juan's second European goal, this time in a different U.E.F.A. competition, was enough to give him a starting place in both legs of the First Round match against Italian side A.C. Perugia but it was an ultimately disappointing experience for the Club as they exited the competition 3-1 on aggregate.

Just a month later however, Dundee plunged into administration and Sara was one of fifteen players axed in a cost cutting cull and a disappointed Sara would play the rest of the season with Serie A side Reggina who finished two places above the U.E.F.A. Cup opponents Perugia.

Becoming a bit of a soccer nomad playing his career in Italy (twice), Ireland, Argentina, Liechtenstein, Switzerland, Spain, Paraguay and Puerto Rico since leaving Dundee, his longest and most successful spell of his career was undoubtedly at Dens, where he will always be remembered for that derby hat-trick, the first overseas player to do so and scoring thirty-five goals in 107 appearances.

Juan Sara – Dundee legend? It was as easy as 'Juan, two three!'

Appearances, Goals:
League: 64 + 25 subs, 28 goals
Scottish Cup: 6 + 1 sub, 3 goals
League Cup: 4 + 1 sub, 2 goals,
Europe: 4 + 2 subs, 2 goals
Totals: 107, 35 goals

Jocky Scott

When history looks back on the life and times of Dundee F.C., there will be a few who will claim a right to have a locker in the Dark Blue Hall of Fame with a list of entertainers, ball-players, match winners, goal scorers, coaches and managers with brilliant tactical brains but Jocky Scott is a man with a claim better than most, fitting all of the aforementioned categories.

In Dundee career spanning almost half a century, Jocky Scott has been all those things in a time that has spanned the peaks and the troughs from the heady, hopeful days of 1964 through to his departure from his third spell in the managerial hot-seat in 2010 while Dundee were top of the Scottish First Division.

John (Jocky) Alexander Scott was born in Aberdeen on January 14th 1948 but surprisingly it was English club Chelsea who first spotted his prowess in front of goal and duly took him down to Stamford Bridge as a schoolboy. London however wasn't for the young Scott and when Dundee manager Bob Shankly heard of the striker's home sickness, he approached Chelsea boss Tommy Docherty to secure Jocky's signature and so began a love affair that would continue off and on for the next forty-six years.

After impressing in the pre season public trail, Jocky made his debut at sixteen years of age on August 26th 1964 at home to Motherwell in a League Cup sectional tie. Dundee were by then unable to qualify from their section and so Shankly decided to field a host of youngsters, including Scott and they did him proud with a 6-0 win.

Jocky in particular was impressive and kept his place in the side for the next match and scored his first goals for the Club in the best possible circumstances with a double in a 4-1 win over deadly rivals Dundee United at Tannadice a fortnight later.

This was the start of a Dens Park playing career that would see the rugged and robust striker turn out 433 times for The Dee making him joint second in the list of those players who have made the most competitive appearances for Dundee and score 154 goals which is a total bettered by only Alan Gilzean and Archie Coats.

It took Jocky a couple of seasons to become a regular in the team but in the 1967/68 season, he made twenty-eight starts for the side which culminated in lining up against Leeds United in the semi-final in the Inter-Cities Fairs Cup. Jocky was on the bench in the 1-1 first leg draw at Dens but started the second leg at Elland Road where Leeds progressed to the Final with an Eddie Gray winner nine minutes from time.

That same season, Jocky was left out of the side which lost out to Celtic in the League Cup Final in October but six years later more than made up for it when he played in the 1973 League Cup Final where Dundee famously defeated Celtic 1-0 thanks to a Gordon Wallace winner.

The League Cup was a competition that was to be good to Jocky which he won again with Aberdeen in 1976 under Ally McLeod after scoring a hat-trick against Rangers in the semi-final, would win it again with the Dons as co-manager in 1989 and also take Dunfermline to the Final in 1991 where they lost to Hibs.

Before he left Dundee to join his hometown team in 1975, Jocky was top scorer for Dundee in four different seasons and gained two international caps for Scotland when he was picked to play against Denmark and Soviet Union in 1971.

After spells at Pittodrie and in the N.A.S.L. with Seattle Sounders where he won the 1977 Soccerbowl defeating George Best's L.A. Aztecs, Jocky returned to Dens in the autumn of 1977 in time to be part of the side who won the Scottish First Division the following season. Three years later he joined the coaching staff in 1980 following the departure of former Lisbon Lion Willie Wallace who emigrated to Australia and in season 1980/81 helped Dundee win promotion back to the Premier League as runners-up before having a testimonial against Aberdeen the day after they went back up.

A year on, Jocky became first team coach under then manager Donald McKay and when McKay left, Jocky wanted the top job but saw it go to Archie Knox who kept Scott on as number two.

Jocky got his chance however in 1986 when Knox joined Alex Ferguson at Aberdeen and just two years later, Jocky made the same journey north himself to become co-manager with Alex Smith.

His two years in charge saw Dundee play some exciting attacking football, scoring 100 goals in all competitions in 1986/87 and also reaching the Scottish Cup semi final after signing goal scoring legends Keith Wright and Tommy Coyne. In his second season he led his Dundee side to the League Cup semi-final and victory in the Tennents' Sixes and those two seasons memorably saw Dundee achieve three victories over Dundee United, including a famous League Cup quarter-final final win in front of almost 20 000 at Dens.

After leaving Dundee for a second time, Jocky's coaching and managerial career took around Scotland via Aberdeen, Dunfermline, Hibs, Dundee United and Arbroath before returning to take charge of Dundee for a second time in February 1998 to see them over the First Division finishing line after the sacking of John McCormack.

In Dundee's first year back in the top flight after a four year absence, Jocky took the Dark Blues to their highest ever Premier position, finishing fifth which equalled Dundee's highest league placing since Dundee won the Scottish Championship in 1962.

At the end of the following season however, Scott was disappointed to find that his contract wasn't being renewed as the Club were moving in a completely different direction under the Bonetti brothers but it wasn't the end of his time at Dens.

In November 2008, Jocky returned to Dundee for a fourth time to start his third spell in charge of the Club and twelve months later led Dundee to victory in the ALBA Challenge Cup with a 3-2 win over Inverness in Perth, making him the first manager to win all three cup competitions in Scotland having won the League and Scottish Cups with Aberdeen.

Four months later however, Jocky was again the victim of the board's decision to take a new direction when he was sacked despite being top of the First Division thus ending a period of service spanning almost forty-six years.

While standing on the touchline urging his players on as manager is how the younger generation will remember Jocky Scott, it's with the cuffs of his jersey clutched in his hands scoring a barrow load of goals that the older Dees will fondly remember one of the most naturally gifted players ever to wear the dark blue.

While some might claim to deserve a place in Dundee's Hall of Fame, there is no arguing the case of Jocky Scott and he was rightly entered into Dundee's inaugural Hall of Fame in 2009 to sit proudly among the elite of the Club's great history.

Honours at Dundee:
Dundee F.C. Hall of Fame:
2009 Legends Award

(As Player)
Scottish League Cup winner: 1973/74
U.E.F.A. / Inter-Cities Fairs Cup semi-final: 1967/68
Scottish League First Division winner: 1978/79
Scottish League First Division runner-up: 1980/81
Scotland full caps: 2

(As Manager)
Tennents' Sixes winner: 1988
Scottish First Division winner: 1997/98
ALBA Scottish League Challenge Cup winner: 2009/10

Appearances, Goals:
League: 298 + 11 sub, 117 goals
Scottish Cup: 28, 8 goals
League Cup: 70 + 1 sub, 28 goals
Europe: 13 + 1 sub, 1 goal
Other: 11
Totals: 233, 154 goals

Managerial Record with Dundee:
(1986 - 1988, 1998 - 2000, 2008 - 2010)

	P	W	D	L	F	A	Pts
League:	224	90	51	83	303	296	286
Scottish Cup:	24	8	10	6	35	24	
League Cup:	15	10	0	5	38	16	
S.F.L. Challenge Cup:	4	4	0	0	11	3	
Total:	267	112	61	94	387	339	

Bobby Seith

When Bob Shankly secured Bobby Seith's signature for Dundee in the summer of 1960 for a fee of £7500, it was a case of 'coming home' for the Burnley artistic right half, having been brought up in Monifieth and signed for the Lancashire side as a sixteen year old from the local juvenile side.

Having spent eleven years at Turf Moor, where he had just won a League Championship title, Bobby became part of the formidable half back line of Bobby Wishart, Ian Ure and Seith which was the backbone of Dundee's success in the early sixties where The Dee won the Scottish League Championship in 1962 and then reach the European Cup semi-finals against A.C. Milan were Bobby had the honour of skippering the side.

Born in Coatbridge on March 9th 1932, Robert 'Bobby' Seith was a seasoned twenty-eight year old professional when he joined up at Dens as Bob Shankly tried to add some experienced heads to the promising youngsters such as Gilzean, Penman and Ure who were emerging through ranks.

Bobby made his debut in the opening game of the 1960-61 season in a 5-0 home win over Raith Rovers in the League Cup but a tenth place finish nine months later in the league gave little clue to the glory that was just around the corner.

His debut season saw the skilful Seith play forty-two competitive matches and in his first four seasons at Dens, he would never play less than forty games for the Club. In his second season, Bobby would be ever present, playing forty-one times and was a key figure as Dundee went on to win the Scottish League Championship for the first time in their history.

It would be a record breaking season in more ways than one for The Dee as they would set a Club record of ten successive wins from September 23rd 1961 to November 25th 1961 and would go a Club record nineteen games unbeaten in the league and twenty games in all competitions on the way to winning the League Flag.

It was during this spell that Bobby scored one of his two goals in the Championship season with a crucial strike that went a long way to seeing the league trophy come to Dens.

Having recorded a famous 5-1 win at Ibrox on November 11th 1961, Dundee were firm favourites to pick up two points at home to Raith Rovers the following week but with twenty-seven minutes left found themselves 4-2 down to the men from Fife.

Roared on by the 15,000 crowd, two cracking shots by Bobby Wishart and Bobby Seith levelled the scores at 4-4 and just two minutes from time, Dens erupted when Gordon Smith made it 5-4 with a dramatic winner.

The win signalled Dundee's intentions to challenge for the title and had Bobby not equalised, their title credentials would have been seriously challenged. Those two matches in November 1961 against Raith and Rangers are listed by Bobby as key in Dundee's Championship challenge and high among his highlights at Dens.

One of his other highlights is of course the last day of the season at Perth when Dundee beat St. Johnstone 3-0 to give Bobby his second league title in three years.

'We required only a draw for the Championship' wrote Bobby in a letter to this author in 2003, *'but we wanted to win the title in style, which we did winning 3-0 and at the same time producing one of our best performances.*

When I reflect on these days, it is not so much individual performances I recall but the camaraderie and team spirit that was present both on and off the field.

If you were looking for the secret of our success, this would be high on the list. Of course there was a lot of skill and talent in the team but it was that team spirit which pulled us through when we were a bit off key.'

The following season, that team spirit, allied to the skill and talent took Dundee to the European Cup semi-finals in a run which saw Cologne, Sporting Club of Portugal and Anderlecht dispatched on route.

Bobby played in all eight games in the campaign and in the semi-final against A.C. Milan was given the honour of being captain for both legs in the absence of the injured Bobby Cox. Seith therefore led Dundee out in the San Siro against a side which included nine full internationalists and with double Brazilian World Cup winner Altafini, Cesare Maldini, Giovanni Trappatoni and Italian golden boy Gianni Rivera in their ranks defeated The Dee 5-1.

Milan were a top side but according to Bobby not as good as Cologne or Anderlecht. Indeed there was every indication that Dundee had been cheated for the Spanish referee was found to have accepted extravagant gifts from the Italians and was subsequently banned on various other charges of bribery.

Dundee did however have the consolation of a second leg win, when Bobby again had the armband as Alan Gilzean gave The Dee a 1-0 win.

Twelve months later, Dundee were again on the glory trail as they reached the Scottish Cup Final against Rangers at Hampden in April 1964 but it was a runners-up medal for Bobby as the Light Blues went on to win 3-1 with two injury time goals.

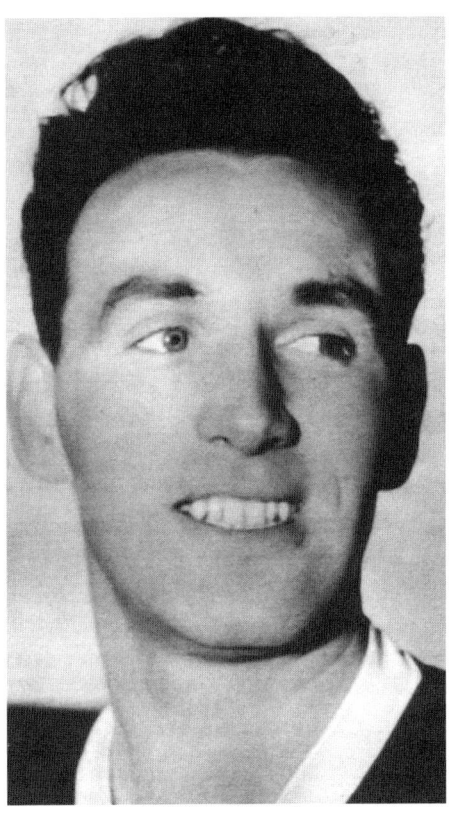

By then the Championship side had already begun to break up and in February 1965 Bobby played his last game for Dundee at the scene of his greatest Dark Blue moment in Perth where The Dee went down 1-0 to St. Johnstone.

During his time at Dens, Bobby was unfortunate not to gain any full caps for Scotland as he was in the frame to be picked for a World Cup qualifying tie but a broken wrist put paid to that. He did however make one appearance for the Scottish League against the full Scottish side in 1962 when these matches were used as 'trial' internationals but the full honours never came despite his good form at Dens.

Upon retiring however Bobby remained at Dens as part of the coaching staff under new manager Bobby Ancell, having gained coaching certificates from both the English and Scottish F.A.s but it was not long before his qualities were realised elsewhere and Scott Symon tempted him to Ibrox to fulfil a similar role with Rangers.

Bobby however resigned his position in 1967 in protest at the unceremonious sacking of Symon who was replaced by future cup winning Dundee manager Davie White and he headed back down to Lancashire to take up his first managerial post at Preston North End.

Bobby left Deepdale in 1970 and following a short spell in charge of the Scottish national youth team took up the reigns at Hearts where he stayed for five years before leaving the game for good to set up a chiropodist business in Broughty Ferry having trained in that particular branch of medicine while at Burnley.

Despite winning the league at Burnley in 1959/60, Bobby was denied a league medal at the time due to a dispute with the then chairman Bob Lord which had subsequently prompted his move to Dens but in October 1999 was belated presented with a medal in a public ceremony prior to a home match against Bristol City.

One of the gentlemen of the game who was never booked, Bobby is listed on Burnley's website as one of their all time greats and holds a similar place in the history of Dundee F.C. as one of the men to make Dundee, Champions of Scotland.

With a passing game ahead of its time, Bobby will always be remembered as one of the lynch pins who supplied the ammunition for the likes of Gilzean and Cousin and co. and is a Dark Blue legend in is own right who is regularly welcomed back to various functions at the Club.

Honours at Dundee:	
Scottish League Champions:	1961/62
European Cup semi-final:	1962/63
Scottish Cup runner-up:	1964
Scottish League appearance:	1
Appearances, Goals:	
League:	134, 5 goals
Scottish Cup:	6
League Cup:	13
Europe:	8
Other:	11
Totals:	197, 5 goals

Bob Shankly

1910 was an historic, even seminal year in the history of Dundee Football Club. It was the year in which Dundee won the Scottish Cup for the first and to date only time and it was also the year in which Bob Shankly, the architect of Dundee's Scottish League Championship victory in 1962 was born. Shankly is a name which is legendary in the annals of football but for Dundee fans, it means only one thing, that of Bob Shankly, the manager who took the Dark Blues to the height of their glories by becoming champions of Scotland, then reaching the European Cup semi-final in scintillating style.

Born in Glenbuck, in Ayrshire on February 25th, two months before Dundee lifted the Scottish Cup, Robert Shankly was the second youngest of five brothers who all played for the local village team Glenbuck Cherrypickers, before Bob himself joined Junior club Auchinleck Talbot.

By the time he joined Dundee in 1959, Bob had been in the senior game for twenty-nine years, having emerged from the coal mining pits to sign for Alloa Athletic in 1930.

Both he and his brother John scored on his Alloa debut in a 2-1 Penman Cup win over Dundee and he combined his work as a miner with playing centre-forward for The Wasps.

Bob transferred to Falkirk for £100 after three years at Recreation Park and played for The Bairns for fifteen years before hanging up his boots and taking on a coaching position at Stenhousemuir. He returned to Brockville as manager in 1950, astutely leading them for seven years before moving to Third Lanark and leading the Hi-His to the League Cup Final which they lost 2-1 to Hearts in the wake of his departure.

Shankly gave up the chance to lead the Cathkin Park side out at Hampden in order to join Dundee after Willie Thornton had resigned but there was an abundance of young talent at Dens to entice the ambitious forty-eight year old. It could quite easily have been his brother Bill who took charge at Dens after he sent in a late application while he was at Huddersfield but Bob, with his quiet, unassuming efficiency, who was seen cutting his grass in his garden in Nelson Street before 9am the morning after

~ 134 ~

Dundee had won the league, made The Dee into an outstanding team which his brother would have struggled to match.

Shankly relished the challenge ahead of him and the prospect of building on the youth policy Thornton had established which had already produced the likes of Gilzean, Ure, Hamilton, Cox, Robertson, Cousin, Gabriel and Penman. There was much work to be done however as Dundee had started the 1959/60 season badly having winning only three out of thirteen matches and his baptism of fire saw Dundee go down 3-1 at home to Rangers.

Shankly was Dundee's tenth manager and although initially languishing in mid-table when he arrived, his influence saw them climb to fourth place by the end of the season.

The 1960/61 campaign began brightly but injuries to Doug Cowie, Andy Penman, and George McGeachie took their toll and Dundee could only finish eighth. By then, Shankly was resident in the city after almost two years of commuting from Kincardine but on the park there were clear signs that he was close to a winning combination. He realised the importance of adding experience to the youthful talent and that term he had signed right-half Bob Seith from Burnley with inside-left Bobby Wishart arriving from Aberdeen.

Shankly was a down-to-earth character, described by Alan Gilzean as *'an honest man who would call a spade a spade.'*

He was a real working manager for whom there was no public flamboyancy, no red carnation or rich cigar and he wasn't just one of those football bosses who just talked a good game. He would rather get his jacket off and get down to the gruelling business of football with his players and if there was one man who could rid Dundee of their 'nearly men' reputation (having finished as Scottish League runners-up on four occasions and in the top five seventeen times), it was Bob Shankly.

One thing that did concern Bob at the start of his third season was the supply line to his forwards Gilzean and Cousin and at the third time of asking, he secured the services of Gordon Smith who had won league medals with both Hibs and Hearts. However at thirty-seven years old, many Dundee fans wondered how much mileage there was in the 'Gay Gordon's' legs but it proved to be a masterstroke from 'Shanks' as Smith's clever prompting and deadly crossing became a major factor in Dundee embarking on a nineteen game unbeaten league run from September 23rd 1961 until February 3rd 1962.

Included in that Club record run was a coupon busting 5-1 win over Rangers at Ibrox on November 11th, arguably Dundee's greatest ever league result as Dundee set down a marker for their championship aspirations. The following week, Dundee came back from 4-2 down with twenty-seven minutes to go to win 5-4 at home to Raith and at the end of the campaign, Shankly singled this match out as a key moment in their Championship winning year, saying, *'Dundee's terrific fight and last gasp winner are surely among the greatest feats recorded all season.'*

At one point, near the end of January 1962, Dundee held an eight-point advantage over the Ibrox title favourites before enduring a six-game slump without a win. Just as Shankly had produced a winning blend, he now used all his vast experience and refused to be panicked into changes. In the end his judgement was vindicated with only fifteen players used as Dundee went on to win the Scottish League Championship with seven straight wins, the last, a 3-0 triumph over St. Johnstone at a sunny Muirton Park on April 28th 1962.

As well as their wonderful, flowing football, it had required great resilience to take the title and the Dark Blues would now play in the 1962/63 European Cup. West German champions Cologne were first to be put to the sword, going down 8-1 at Dens before Dundee were made to survive a rough-house return leg to qualify 8-5 on aggregate. Sporting Lisbon, who had pipped Benfica, the European Cup holders, to the Portuguese championship, were brushed aside 4-2 on aggregate, before Anderlecht, conquerors of five-times winners Real Madrid, were defeated 6-2 over the two matches in the quarter-final. That had involved a magnificent 4-1 victory at the Heysel Stadium in Brussels and now Dundee were taken very seriously indeed.

However, the dream of playing in a European Cup Final at Wembley final was to end with a 5-1 defeat to A.C. Milan at the San Siro, although the 1-0 win in the Dens return restored a measure of pride.

The following year, Shankly took Dundee to the Scottish Cup Final where they were unfortunate to lose 3-1 to Rangers but less than a year later, he resigned and moved to take over at Hibs after being frustrated at the sale of top players such as Alan Gilzean, Ian Ure and Charlie Cooke.

After four years in Edinburgh, a similar problem prompted him to resign from Easter Road but football was in his blood and in 1971 he returned as manager of Stirling Albion, later becoming general manager and then a director. Four years later he and his great friend Jock Stein were seriously injured in a motorway car crash. Both recovered but in May 1982, just a year after the death of his younger brother Bill, (72), Bob collapsed and died of a heart-attack whilst attending an SFA meeting.

At Dens Park the following Saturday against Airdrie, the Dundee fans chanted his name and in 1999 they ensured his name will live on forever when they voted to call one of the new stands, the Bob Shankly Stand. In 2010, Bob was again honoured by the Club when he was inducted into the Dundee F.C. Hall of Fame as the recipient of the Heritage Award.

He was a man with a sharp, if somewhat dry sense of humour, often telling the press on a Friday that wife Greta hadn't yet picked the team for the Saturday. However, Dundee fans are in no doubt who to thank for making them champions of Scotland and while Dundee's title success in 1962 was the greatest achievement of Bob Shankly's footballing life, it was also the greatest in the history of Dundee Football Club.

Honours at Dundee:
Scottish League Champions: 1961/62
European Cup semi-final: 1962/63
Scottish Cup runners-up: 1964
Dundee F.C. Hall of Fame: 2010
Heritage Award

Managerial Record with Dundee: (1959 – 1965)

	P	W	D	L	F	A	Pts
League:	188	96	36	56	410	279	228
Scottish Cup:	16	8	2	6	49	27	
League Cup:	34	18	3	13	80	55	
Europe:	10	5	1	4	23	18	
Other:	11	3	5	3	21	20	
Total:	259	130	47	82	583	399	

Eric Sinclair

Eric Sinclair emerged from his time at Dens as a player who was wholeheartedly committed to the cause who played for the jersey and he enhanced his popularity and reputation when he scored the goal which returned Dundee to the Scottish Premier Division in May 1981. The tall blond, striker never gave anything less than 100% during games and was a regular goal getter for The Dee, netting ninety five times and finishing as leading goal scorer twice.

Eric Sinclair joined the Dark Blues in 1974 from Kilsyth Rangers and his early days at Dens Park were spent as a part-timer where he combined his day job as a crane driver, with training twice a week with Falkirk at Brockville, only seeing his Dundee team mates on a match day.

'Sinky' made his debut on the final day of the 1974/75 season wearing the number eleven shirt as Hearts were defeated 2-0 and the following term, he made thirteen appearances in the inaugural Premier Division, from which Dundee were relegated on goal difference behind both Aberdeen and Dundee United. Eric however started the last five games in which Dundee were undefeated, and he started to cement his legendary status with the fans when he scored his first goal for The Dee with the winner in a 2-1 derby win over Dundee United.

In the First Division, Eric established himself in the Dundee starting line up making thirty-nine appearances, scoring fourteen times. He scored his first hat-trick for the Dark Blues in a 6-1 home win over Montrose and formed a good understanding with strike partner Billy Pirie, who netted an astonishing forty-five goals that season. Pirie and 'Sinky' formed the highest scoring partnership in Britain but unfortunately their goals couldn't fire Dundee back to the top tier as they finished third behind St. Mirren and Clydebank.

Season 1977/78 was a carbon copy of the previous year as Dundee again finished third despite the Sinclair / Pirie combination scoring fifty-three goals.

However, it was third time lucky for Dundee the next year when they won the Scottish League First Division title and 'Sinky' contributed thirteen goals as Dundee returned to its rightful place in Scottish Football.

However, the Dark Blues found it tough in the top flight and at the end of the campaign finished ninth, a relegation spot, despite a famous 5-1 win over runners-up Celtic with three games to go, in which Eric scored.

It was one of fourteen goals Sinclair scored in the 1979/80 season to finish as Dundee's top goal scorer and in March, he was rewarded for his good individual form with a cap for the Scottish League against the League of Ireland in Dublin. The game turned out to be the penultimate inter-league match that the Scottish League would ever play and Eric marked his only international honour with a goal in the 2-1 defeat.

Back in the First Division, Eric once again finished as Dundee's top scorer as Dundee finished runners-up which was enough to secure promotion behind champions Hibernian and his twenty-two goals helped him win the S.P.F.A. First Division Player of the Year.

The most important of these goals undoubtedly came in the final game at East Stirlingshire when Dundee completed a terrific comeback after a dreadful start to the campaign and the 1-0 win sent Dundee back to the Premier League. The famous goal came in the thirty-second minute when a Jimmy Murphy corner drifted beyond the far post and when Bobby Glennie headed the ball back across goal, the hard working Sinclair was on the spot to head home.

Eric, whose speciality was shielding the ball with his back to goal, scored another fifteen goals in the Premier Division before leaving to join St. Mirren in September 1983 in a swap deal which brought Lex Richardson to Dens, whom Eric had played with in that Scottish League match three years before.

His final goal tally of ninety-five puts Eric Sinclair twelfth on Dundee's all time leading goal scoring list and the extent of the popularity 'Sinky' is still held in a Dens was evidenced in March 2010, when he was giving a rousing reception after coming on the pitch at half-time in a match against Inverness as Dundee launched their Former Players' Association.

That season also saw Dundee reach the Bells' League Cup Final after Eric scored the winner in the semi-final against Ayr United. It was an historic City of Discovery final as Dundee met Dundee United at Dens Park but it ended in disappointment for the Dark Blues when they lost 3-0 to their local rivals. It could have been so different however if Dundee had not had a goal disallowed in twenty-two minutes when 'Sinky' headed home after Hamish McAlpine fumbled an Eric Schaedler cross or if city referee Bob Valentine had given The Dee a penalty when Ray Stephen was sent sprawling in the box.

> Honours at Dundee:
> Scottish League First Division winner: 1978/79
> Scottish League First Division runner-up: 1980/81
> Bells' Scottish League Cup runner-up: 1980/81
> Scottish League cap: 1
> S.P.F.A. Scottish First Division Player of the Year: 1980/81
> Appearances, Goals:
> League: 214 + 23 subs, 76 goal
> Scottish Cup: 10 + 1 sub, 5 goal
> League Cup: 35 + 1 sub, 13 goal
> Other: 5. 1 goal
> Totals: 289, 95 goals

Bert Slater

Bert Slater wrote his name into Dundee folklore when his magnificent performance in the 1964 Scottish Cup Final meant that the match would forever be known as the 'Bert Slater Final'. It was however by no was means his first heroic display in the goal for Dundee as his performances in the European Cup run in the previous season had already earned him legendary status.

Slater was born in Musselburgh, East Lothian on May 5th 1936 and was signed by Bob Shankly, who was to be his manager at Dens when he was seventeen years old on a part time contract. This allowed Bert to finish his apprenticeship as an electrician and in 1957, he won a Scottish Cup winners' medal with The Bairns when they defeated Kilmarnock in the Final.

He had been capped at Scotland Under-23 level while at Brockville and toured Denmark with the full Scotland side in 1959 and in the same year, Bert joined Liverpool in a swap deal for

Tommy Younger and played a big part in Liverpool's successful promotion winning campaign in 1962.

Liverpool Second Division title winning side was managed by Bill Shankly and at the same time his brother Bob was leading Dundee to the Scottish League Championship. Bob had been a long term admirer of Slater, not only at Falkirk but also when he turned out for Liverpool against The Dee in a friendly to hansel the Dundee floodlights in March 1960 and midway through Dundee's championship year had tried to sign Bert in January. That time Bob's brother Bill said no but in the closed season, Bob tried again to get his man and persuaded his brother to part with Slater in exchange for £2500.

Most expected Slater to be back up for league winning keeper Pat Liney but in the first match of the season, Bert was surprisingly in possession of the yellow number one jersey in a League Cup tie at Tannadice against Dundee United.

A month later, Bert got his introduction to European football when Dundee entered the Champions' Cup and in the preliminary round were drawn against second favourites Cologne. Unbelievably Dundee were five up by half-time and went on to win 8-1 and Cologne only got the one because of an own-goal by Alex Hamilton.

To be fair to Cologne they lost their goalkeeper to injury at half-time but the Germans thought the challenge was a bad one and rumour had it, were targeting Slater for reprisal in the second leg.

If they were, by the twenty-seventh minute they got their man as Slater took a boot to the head which opened up and oozed blood from behind his ear.

He was replaced in goal by inside-forward Andy Penman in these pre substitute days as the German medics tried to get Slater into an ambulance which had taken up position behind Slater's goal at kick off but he refused to be taken to hospital. By half-time, the Germans were three up and the Dundee dressing room was in disarray but Slater diffused the situation by suggesting that his bandaged head made him look like American actress Lana Turner.

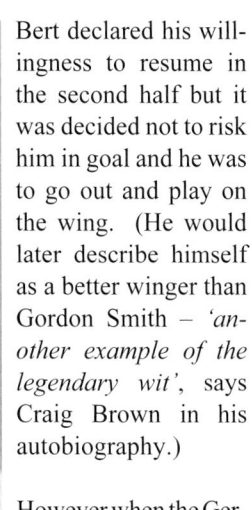

Bert declared his willingness to resume in the second half but it was decided not to risk him in goal and he was to go out and play on the wing. (He would later describe himself as a better winger than Gordon Smith – *'another example of the legendary wit'*, says Craig Brown in his autobiography.)

However when the Germans got a fourth goal and looked like they had a chance to produce the greatest turnaround in two-legged football, Slater went back in goal and saw the Germans miss a penalty as Dundee held on for a famous victory.

In the next two rounds, Slater was again outstanding in the four matches against Sporting Lisbon and Anderlecht and in the semi-final was unfortunate to be on the end of a 5-1 defeat in the San Siro to A.C. Milan as flashbulbs were distracting Bert every time a high ball came into the box.

Slater's performances Europe and in particular his defiance in Germany gave the Dark Blue faithful a new hero between the sticks. At 5ft 9in, he was short for a keeper but what he lacked in height, he more than made up for with agility. He was nicknamed 'Punchy' by team mates because he looked like a boxer with so many thick ears and scars from kicks about the face and he was a brave, hard keeper who wasn't afraid to go in where it hurt.

The following season, Dundee reached the Scottish Cup Final against Rangers at Hampden and were unlucky not to earn a replay when two last gasp goals gave Rangers a 3-1 victory. Time and again, Slater had almost single-handedly defied Rangers with a series of miraculous saves and despite the Light Blues lifting the trophy, the match became known as 'The Bert Slater Final'.

In total, Slater would make 114 appearances for Dundee between 1962 and 1965 and kept a clean sheet in twenty-one of them in, including in the European Cup semi-final second leg 1-0 win over Milan at Dens. Bert left Dundee in 1965 to join Watford with whom he would later become assistant manager but he would return to Dens Park twenty-two years later as chief scout with coaching responsibilities and set up an invaluable network of scouts which covered the country while working with managers Jocky Scott, Dave Smith and Gordon Wallace.

Bert sadly died aged seventy on July 21st 2006 when he collapsed during a round of golf in Brechin and he will be fondly remembered as a heroic keeper from Dundee's glory years.

One lesser known story of Bert is that he once appeared in a television commercial for Wagon Wheels, the big round chocolate biscuit. The scene kind of resembled Custer's last stand, and Bert was one of the soldiers who fell to the ground having been hit by an arrow and it's a wonder he didn't just put a bandage on it and carry on!

Honours at Dundee:
European Cup semi-final: 1962/63
Scottish Cup runner-up: 1964
Appearances:
League: 70
Scottish Cup: 13
League Cup: 18
Europe: 8
Other: 5
Total: 114

Barry Smith

Barry Smith is a Dundee legend in every sense of the word having captained The Dee to the First Division Championship, a Scottish Cup Final and a return to senior European competition after a twenty-nine year hiatus in his eleven years at Dens.

Born in Paisley on February 19th 1974, Barry Martin Smith signed on an S-form with Celtic while still at school and at seventeen made his debut for The Bhoys in his first year as a professional in a 4-3 defeat to Falkirk. He made twenty-two first team appearances for the Parkhead side, including two outings in an Old Firm derby but there are few who would have imagined when left Celtic to join Dundee as part of the deal that would see Morten Weighorst go in the opposite direction, that he would become a distinguished Club captain and rack up 433 appearances to come joint second in Dundee's all time appearance list.

Barry made his debut for Dundee on December 9th 1995 in a 4-2 home defeat to Dunfermline and at the end of the season was appointed captain by manager Jim Duffy when skipper Neil Duffy crossed Tannadice Street to join Dundee United. It was a role which he immediately revelled in and at the end of his first full season with the Club, he was awarded with the Player of the Year trophy.

Barry would play in a variety of positions while wearing a dark blue shirt but it was his partnership in the centre of defence with Brian Irvine that formed the rock on which Dundee's promotion winning defence was built in 1998.

It was in the title winning season when Smith scored his first of four goals for The Dark Blues when he scored a vital last minute winner at Stirling Albion and at the end of the season, he proudly held aloft the First Division trophy after making forty-two appearances, missing only the last two games of the campaign with the championship wrapped up the month before.

Dundee spent seven seasons in the S.P.L. with Barry as captain and in his first year he led Dundee to fifth, their highest ever finish in the Premier League. This also equalled Dundee's highest position since Bobby Cox lifted the same trophy Barry did the previous year, when it was used as the Scottish League Championship trophy in 1962.

That fifth placed finish was under the management of Jocky Scott but after Scott's departure in 2000, Barry became the Scottish heart in Ivano Bonetti's continental superstars and continued in his role of captain.

When Bonetti left, the man who had signed Barry for Dundee, Jim Duffy returned for a second spell in charge and in an inspired move, changed Barry into a central midfielder where he became a revelation. In 2003 Barry captained The Dee to their first Scottish Cup Final since 1964 and were a millimetre away from winning it when Barry hit the post in the first few minutes.

Ultimately the day would end in disappointment as Rangers ran out 1-0 winners but with the Glasgow side also winning the S.P.L. championship, Dundee had qualified for the U.E.F.A. Cup for the first time since the year Barry was born.

Smith had played in the two U.E.F.A. Intertoto Cup matches in the summer of 2001 but this for Dundee, was the real deal as Dundee looked to add to their impressive European pedigree. Smith led Dundee out in the Loro-Borici Stadium in the north of Albania when they took on K.S. Vllaznia Shkoder in the U.E.F.A. Cup preliminary round and he became the first skipper to captain a Scottish side to victory in Albania with the 2-0 win therefore achieving something the Celtic Lisbon Lions and the Aberdeen Gothenburg Greats had failed to do.

A comfortable 4-0 win in the second leg at Dens meant that Dundee were next drawn a glamour tie against Serie A side Perugia and over 2000 Dees made the trip to Umbria to see Barry lead his Dundee close to defeating the Intertoto Cup winners who ultimately progressed with a 3-1 aggregate win.

Just a few weeks after the memorable European adventure, Dundee plunged into administration and Barry was lucky enough to be one of the playing staff retained by the Club. The Bonetti era had brought many wonderful footballers to Dens but at a horrendous cost and as Dundee struggled to maintain its very existence, Barry was an exemplary leader who represented the heart and soul of Dundee Football Club.

After two months of administration, Dundee had failed to win any league games and with relegation likely to serve as a death-knell to the Club, the match against Partick Thistle was as big a must win game in any of Dundee's 110 year history. As usual Barry led from the front and in injury time struck a ball from outside the box which flew into the top of Thistle's net to secure a vital 2-1 win and no one who was in the away end that day will ever forget it.

Staying up at the end of the 2003/04 season meant that Dundee could regroup and put a long term plans for survival into place and in his tenth year at Dens, it was announced that Barry would be awarded with a testimonial. The following season however ended in relegation and with The Dees in the First Division, Barry graciously turned down as testimonial match as the fundraising continued at a premium under the new Dee4Life Supporters Trust, of which Barry was a huge supporter.

That season didn't go as planned however and when Dundee weren't able to regain promotion, manager Alan Kernaghan was sacked and Barry was made caretaker manager with team mate Bobby Mann with two games remaining.

The final match of the season was to be Barry's 433rd and last match for the Club and under his and Bobby's guidance the team won 3-1 away to Queen of the South which the Doonhamers boss Ian McCall described as *'like watching Real Madrid.'*

At the end of the season, Barry took the chance to play abroad for the first time in his career and joined Valur in Iceland. During the mid season break, he returned to Scotland to play for Partick Thistle on loan in 2007 and Greenock Morton in 2008 but towards the end of that year, he finally came 'home' when he was welcomed back to Dens as part of Jocky Scott's backroom staff and take charge the Under 19s; a role he still enjoys today.

Barry's time at Dens has experienced the most incredible highs and lows and while journalists often used phrases such as dependable, reliable or hard working to describe Barry, such faint praise comes nowhere close to defining his value to the team of the Club.

From his early performances at right-back, then centre-half and latterly in midfield, Barry developed into perhaps Dundee's most influential performer. Few Dundee fans expected, following a memorable man-marking performance against United's Charlie Miller, that Barry's then unfamiliar midfield role would become the one for which he was best known.

As captain, he was simply the modern day 'Mr Dundee' and he encompassed everything that our great club looks for in a leader and there is no doubt that he will one day take over the manager's hot seat full time. A true Dundee legend if ever there was one.

Honours at Dundee:
Tennents' Scottish Cup runners-up: 2003
Scottish League First Division winner: 1997/98
D.S.A. Player of the Year: 1997
Dundee F.C. Hall of Fame: 2009
Legends Award
Appearances, Goals:
League: 360 + 8 subs, 4 goals
Scottish Cup: 32
League Cup: 20 + 1 sub
Europe: 6
S.F.L. Challenge Cup: 6
Totals: 433, 4 goals

Managerial Record at Dundee: (caretaker co-manager with Bobby Mann: 2006)

	P	W	D	L	F	A	Pts
League:	2	1	0	1	3	2	3

Gordon Smith

Gordon Smith was a hugely important member of the 1961-62 Championship winning squad and is regarded by many as the final piece in the successful jigsaw that manager Bob Shankly pieced together.

In trying to build a team, Shankly was concerned about the supply to his big forwards and made a third and this time successful attempt to secure the services of Gordon Smith for Dundee in the summer of 1961.

There was no arguing over the pedigree of Gordon Smith before he came to Dens as he already had three Championship medals with Hibernian and one with Hearts as well as having captained his country, but at the age of 37, many fans wondered just how much mileage was left in Smith's legs, particularly as Hearts had given him a free transfer.

Smith's signature in the summer of 1961 however proved a masterstroke and because of his advanced years was described by some, including former Hibs team mate Eddie Turnball as *'the Stanley Matthews of Scottish Football.'*

Raised in Montrose, Smith had played for Dundee junior side Dundee North End before signing for Hibs in 1941. Smith played at Easter Road for eighteen years during which time he collected three league championship winning medals as a member of the Hibs 'Famous Five' forward line and reached the semi-final of the inaugural European Cup.

He earned a total of thirty-two international caps for Scotland, two of which were as captain and his greatest moment for his country was when he led them to a 4-1 victory away to Austria in the return match to the famous 'Battle of Vienna' in which Billy Steel got sent off.

The press dubbed him the 'Gay Gordon' or the 'Gay Cavalier' which had a completely different meaning to today and he was described in the Dundee v Cologne European Cup match programme as *'the greatest soccer pin up north of the border since the war.'*

Smith was freed by Hibs in 1959 when a queue of clubs, including Dundee, chased his signature. He chose to stay in Edinburgh spending two years with Hearts where he picked up his fourth league title in 1960.

His unique achievement of winning the league with three different clubs, none of whom were Rangers or Celtic, was described by Scottish Football historian Bob Crampsey as *'the greatest individual accomplishment in the entire history of Scottish league football.'*

In view of his age, Smith's achievements at Dens are in themselves extraordinary. In total he played eighty-nine times in three seasons, scoring nineteen times. During the Championship season he played thirty-seven games and bettered that a year later with forty-eight appearances including a European Cup semi-final appearance at the age of thirty-nine!

There have been few more graceful players in Scottish Football than Gordon Smith and it was his exemplary attention to fitness that ensured he could play at the top level for twenty-three years. He also paid attention to his diet, being keen to learn about the eating habits of players on the continent. For example, he introduced his team mates to pasta, long before it became common place in footballers' diets.

Having played football in Edinburgh for twenty years, Smith had a grocers business in the capital and lived in North Berwick to the south of the city. He decided to stay there and commute to Dens daily by motor car. Without the luxury of the road bridges over either the Forth or the Tay, the journey entailed a 5.30am start!

Gordon's experience was vital throughout the Championship year and he was one of the players the younger lads looked to during the two month spell in the winter of 1962 when Dundee failed to win a single game, seriously jeopardising their league title hopes.

Smith scored on his league debut for Dundee in a 3-1 win at Brockville as the championship campaign opened and he quickly endeared himself to the Dark Blue faithful in his first league game at Dens by scoring Dundee's second in a 4-1 win over Dundee United which saw him being voted man of the match.

During the European Cup run of 1962/63, Smith's experience would be just as vital, having played in the competition with both Edinburgh sides. In the infamous return game in Cologne in the Preliminary Round, Smith came in for some particularly rough treatment from the Germans and had to be helped from the field by two of his team mates at the end of the game with his legs all black and blue.

During the game itself, the Cologne supporters surrounded the touchline as it became clear that they were going to be knocked out and Gordon was even tripped up by one of their fans when he was running up the wing with the ball.

Conversely in the next round against Sporting Lisbon, Smith's performance was singled out by the Sporting manager Armando Ferreira despite Alan Gilzean notching a hat trick in a 4-1 second leg win.

Smith's last game for Dundee came on January 1st 1964 at home to Aberdeen and at the age of thirty-nine years and nine months, remained the oldest player to have played for Dundee until Bobby Geddes came off the bench in April 2010, ten years his senior.

Smith's precision play was perfect in aiding the development of young forwards Alan Cousin and Alan Gilzean and Gilzean's prowess in the air was the perfect foil for Smith's superb crossing ability.

Gordon Smith was the perfect gentleman both on and off the pitch and he helped raise the profile of Dundee FC as the top journalists starting travelling to Dens just to see Smith before even their league winning credentials were rubber stamped.

Gordon Smith is a Dens Park legend and a hero to all who watched him and there are many that feel the League Flag would not have come to Dens without him.

Honours at Dundee:
Scottish League Champions: 1961/62
European Cup semi final: 1962/63
Appearances, Goals:
League: 70, 10 goals
Scottish Cup: 6, 1 goal
League Cup: 13, 5 goals
Europe: 8, 3 goals
Other: 3
Totals: 100, 16 goals

Billy Steel

Billy Steel was one of Scotland's greatest inside forwards who combined a brilliant footballing brain with a busy work ethic and an explosive shot. He was a genius, a maverick, an individual, a joker, the superstar of his day and was arguably the best player ever to play for Dundee Football Club. Signed for a world record fee that was unsurpassed by a Scottish club for over a decade, he brought with him a national interest in Dundee that had been previously unheard of and brought glory to Dens as The Dee won their first silverware for forty-one years just over twelve months after he arrived.

Born in the Stirlingshire village of Dunipace on May 1st 1923, Billy Steel started his professional career with Leicester City when they nipped in, in front of a host of clubs to sign the sixteen year old but his spell at Filbert Street was short lived when the manager was sacked and no one remembered to renew the young Scot's contract.

After a short spell at Love Street as an amateur with St. Mirren, Billy joined the Buddies' Renfrewshire neighbours Morton but his stint in Greenoock was soon interrupted by the Second World War during which he turned out for the British Army on the Rhine.

Re-establishing footballing connections with other teams on the Continent, the team visited France, Holland, Poland, Switzerland, the Channel Islands and Germany, and Steel played along with such notables as **Leslie Compton**, **Eddie Hapgood**, and **Matt Busby** before being demobbed in December 1946, when he returned to Morton.

In 1947, Billy enhanced his growing reputation when he was selected to play for Great Britain against The Rest of Europe at Hampden Park in Glasgow and he turned in a star performance, scoring Britain's third goal in a 6-1 win.

His place as one of the game's rising stars was now assured and Billy decided to try his luck south of the border once more and Derby County were persuaded to part with a then British record £15,500 for his signature later that year.

By September 1950, 'The Pocket Dynamo' had developed into one of the first football superstars who with seventeen Scottish caps in his locker, was determined to earn enough money form the game to make him financially secure by the time he had retired from playing. His wife however was by then was homesick and Billy moved back to Glasgow with her, only travelling down to Derby on matchdays but it was an arrangement that was never going to work. As he started to attract interest from clubs north of the border, Billy took the unprecedented step of calling his own press conference to announce that he would be leaving Derby, and it looked odds on, that he would be going to boyhood heroes Rangers when he started using training facilities at Ibrox.

What the press didn't know however was that Dundee manager George Anderson had been secretly working on a deal to bring him to Dens and once Billy met the flamboyant Dark Blue boss, he was convinced that Dens Park was the place for him. Steel remembered an act of kindness Anderson had once shown Steel during the War, when he had organised some food and drink for him for the train journey home after playing in a five-a-side competition in the Granite City and so was happy to shake hands on a move with the bowler-hatted gentleman.

The genial Aberdonian was a highly persuasive character and on September 21st 1950, Dundee F.C. called a press conference where a beaming Anderson stunned the assembled media by declaring: *'Gentlemen, I want to introduce you to Billy Steel, ex-Derby County and now of Dundee!'*

The country was shocked as the Club had paid a world record fee of £23,500 for one of the best known players in British football and it was one of the transfer coups of the century.

Two days later, 34,000 fans, around 8000 more than normal turned out for Steel's debut against Aberdeen and while the flaxen-haired forward clearly lacked match practice, his clever positioning and masterly touches were an inspiration. With only nineteen minutes remaining, Steel became an instant hero to his new adoring public when he scored Dundee's opener with a low shot and the extinct volcano known as The Law which overlooks the ground almost erupted with the noise.

'Midget Gem' had been an automatic choice for Scotland since 1947 and further caps against Wales and Northern Ireland that autumn made Billy Dundee's first full internationalist since Colin McNab's Wembley appearance against England in April 1932.

The stocky inside-forward brought power and imagination to the Dundee front-line and by mid-November, Dundee led the Scottish League 'A' Division with only one defeat in ten matches. Dundee continued their challenge for the league title and eventually finished third in April but the real glory was to come six months later when Dundee won their first trophy since they had won the Scottish Cup in 1910 and Billy was at the very heart of it.

'Budgem' as his team mates nicknamed him had outstanding ability which gave him a confidence which was often seen as arrogance and wasn't welcomed by his fellow players.

He had a sharp tongue, which his team mates often found themselves on the wrong end of during the ninety minutes but the impact he made on the park brought them success that had slipped form their grasp in previous years.

The first of those successes came in October 1951 when Dundee beat Rangers 3-2 to lift the Scottish League Cup with Billy setting up skipper Alfie Boyd for the winner. Steel was a genius and he knew it and when Dundee won a free kick with only seconds remaining, after Rangers had just drawn level, Billy told Boyd to get in the box, saying to him, *'I'll place it on your head Alfie'* and he did just that as Boyd leapt high to head home from eight yards out from Billy's high centre.

By the end of the season, Steel had scored six goals on a second road to Hampden but this time Dundee lost out 4-0 to Motherwell in the Scottish Cup Final. Six months later however, Dundee made it a hat-trick of trips to the National Stadium and became the first side to retain the League Cup when Kilmarnock were put to the sword 2-0, with Billy scoring another six on route to the Final.

Steel earned three League caps and thirteen full caps during his time at Dens and during one of those caps became the first Scotland player to be sent off in May 1951 when he took umbrage at the treatment dished out to his good friend George Young of Rangers and sought retribution against one of the offending Austrians in a match which became known as the 'Battle of Vienna.'

His time at Dens lasted four glorious years and his departure from Dundee was in typical Steel fashion when he called another press conference and shocked Scottish Football by announcing he was emigrating to the United States. Steel saw out the rest of his days in America where he managed the Los Angeles Danes before a job in advertising after retiring and where he sadly died aged just fifty-nine in May 1982.

Billy Steel, 'Mr. Perpetual Motion' will never be forgotten at Dens Park where a hospitality lounge and supporters club bear his name and in May 2009, he was inducted into the inaugural Dundee F.C. Hall of Fame, having already been inducted into the S.F.A Hall of Fame three years before.

Steel was a hard little man with bounding vitality who as a perfectionist often did not suffer the short comings of less gifted colleagues but he was adored on the Dens Park terracing and prior to Claudio Caniggia joining the Club fifty years later, no Dundee signing had captured the public imagination and national headlines quite like Billy Steel's record-breaking move to Dens.

Honours at Dundee:	
Scottish League Cup winner: 1951/52, 1952/53	
Scottish Cup runner-up:	1952
Scotland full caps:	13
Scottish League caps:	3
Dundee F.C. Hall of Fame:	2009
Legends Award	
Appearances, Goals:	
League:	94, 27 goals
Scottish Cup:	13, 7 goals
League Cup:	24, 11 goals
Totals:	131, 45 goals

Jim Steele

Jim Steele was a Dundee player for just over five years but he made a lasting impression on the Dark Blue support with his 100 per cent commitment and effort.

Born on March 11th 1950, Steele was signed as a seventeen year old from Tynecastle Boys Club and the trainee mechanical engineer with the National Coal Board made his debut in the first team with a solitary appearance in the 1967/68 season against Stirling Albion at Annfield in front of just six hundred spectators.

It was an uninspiring start to a Dundee career and the wing half saw just five appearances the following season but he soon became a regular in a side which included the likes of Iain Phillip, Jocky Scott and Gordon Wallace.

Even at this early stage in his career, he was considered a hard man and usually came out of a tackle with the ball, but his toughness was allied to skill which led to him being called up for the national side. In a European Championship qualifier against Belgium at Pittodrie in 1971, Jim was a non-playing substitute when a goal from John O'Hare was enough to secure a 1-0 win.

Although unlucky to never get another chance to win a full cap, Jim did receive recognition at Under-23 level when he turned out for Scotland in 1972 against a West German Olympic XI. In January 2001, F.I.F.A. deleted all matches against F.I.F.A. XI's, Olympic XI's or continental representations but most F.A.s including Scotland did not follow this ruling and keep the relevant matches in their records. Although keeping Jim's Scotland appearance on record, there were unfortunately no caps awarded for the match.

The highlight of Jim's career at Dens probably came against another West German side, when he was part of the Dundee team to play against Cologne in the U.E.F.A. Cup second round in 1971.

Having beaten A.B. Copenhagen both home and away (4-2, 1-0) in the first round, Dundee were drawn against their old foes from the ill tempered European Cup tie, nine years before.

The first leg was in West Germany and with the usual talk of revenge which preceded the match, Cologne came out on top 2-1 with Alex Kinninmonth getting the important away goal for Dundee.

This was the first season of away goals counting double in U.E.F.A. competition and Dundee hoped that the 75th minute strike might turn out to be vital.

However, with half an hour to go in the second leg at Dens, the visitors were 2-1 up on the night which gave them a 4-2 lead on aggregate and it looked like The Dees were heading out. Dundee, with the flame haired Steele highly influential, then pounded the German goal and with just five minutes left John Duncan completed a hat-trick to level the scores but The Dee still needed another one with Cologne ahead on away goals.

Almost like the Alamo, Dundee piled on the pressure and when Steele and Duncan had shots cleared off the line, it looked like it wasn't to be but with just sixty seconds left, Bobby Wilson stepped up the crash home the winner.

Dundee went through 5-4 on aggregate and there are many Dundee fans who suggest that this was Dens Park's greatest night. In his book *We Must Be Daft,* author Peter Caproni says, 'The memories of that night will last forever! What a great night! What a great team! The supporters that night seemed to be a twelfth man and I have never heard the fans before or since, urge the team on so much as they did last night.'

In an uncanny twist of fate, another of Dundee's 1962/63 European Cup adversaries were next out of the hat in the third round as Dundee were paired again with semi-final conquerors A.C. Milan. Milan were still one of the top sides in Europe and in the first leg in the San Siro, cruised through the match 3-0. In the last minute Steele had brought out a magnificent save from the Milan goalkeeper which would have given Dundee a vital away goal and they would eventually rue that in the second leg.

Dundee knew that they wouldn't relish coming to Dens and with Jim Steele and his team mates in scintillating form they beat the Italians 2-0. The third goal didn't come however despite bombarding the visitors almost non stop for the entire evening and like 1963, a second leg victory at home could not repair the damage done in Italy in the first leg.

In domestic cup competition, the furthest Steele went with Dundee was the Scottish Cup semi-final against Celtic in 1970 where they lost 2-1 to the holders and was a key part of the side which finished fifth in Division One the following season, Dundee's highest league placing since they won the League Flag.

It was in these high profile games that English clubs first started taking notice of the Edinburgh born midfielder and soon Leeds United and Southampton let it be known that they were interested.

Dundee boss Davie White accepted an £80,000 offer from Saints manager Ted Bates and the player was off to The Dell in January 1972. He was part of the Southampton team which beat Manchester United 1-0 in the 1976 F.A. Cup Final at Wembley and in front of a 100,000 crowd, Steele was voted man of the match.

From six hundred fans at Annfield to 100,000 at Wembley, it really was the stuff of dreams for Jim.

Jim finished his career with a short loan spell at Rangers before a couple of seasons in America with Washington Diplomats, indoor side Pittsburgh Spirit, Memphis Rogues and Chicago Sting.

In 2008, Jim Steele was invited onto the legends table at the Dundee Supporters' Association Player of the Year Dinner and entertained the assembled Dees with stories of his time at Dens. The crowd responded warmly to a bygone hero, who is remembered fondly and who fully deserved his place at the legends' table.

Honours at Dundee:
Scotland Under 23 appearance: 1972
Appearances, Goals:
League: 74 + 1 sub, 5 goals
Scottish Cup: 7, 1 goal
League Cup: 15
Europe: 6
Other: 2
Totals: 105, 6 goals

Ray Stephen

Ray Stephen was a hero to the Dundee support for seven years having signed for the Club in 1979 and gracing a Dark Blue jersey until 1986.

Nicknamed 'Shaky', Ray was a product of the The Dee's youth system and made his debut in August 1980, coming off the bench for the mercurial Jimmy Murphy in a 2-0 home League Cup win over Arbroath.

Ray made his league debut later that season in November when he again came off the bench to replace Murphy and made an immediate impact by scoring the winner in a 2-1 win over Clydebank at Dens.

His scoring league debut meant that he made his first start the following week at home to Motherwell and in total Ray made 226 appearances for Dundee becoming a prolific goal scorer with sixty goals to his credit. He would therefore make more appearances than other striking legends such as Alan Gilzean, Billy Pirie, Charlie Cooke, Tommy Coyne and Claudio Caniggia to name but a few and scored more goals for the Club than the aforementioned Caniggia and Cooke as well as Billy Steel and the same number of goals as Tommy Coyne.

In his first season, Ray helped Dundee secure promotion back to the Premier League, pitching in with eight goals in nineteen appearances, including a crucial winning strike in the penultimate week away to Falkirk.

Ray also earned a place in the starting line up for the 1980 League Cup Final against Dundee United after scoring five goals in seven games since his league debut a little over a month before. He had also featured in the semi-final second leg against Ayr United and in the Final, he was famously brought down in the box by United 'keeper Hamish McAlpine just after 'The Arabs' had opened the scoring only to see Dundee referee Bob Valentine wave away any appeals. Ray was convinced it was a penalty but it wasn't to be and as Dundee went down disappointingly 3-0, Stephen was seen as one of the few Dundee successes on a gut wrenching day.

Upon Dundee's return to the Premier League, Ray became a key player in the side and in 1982 was rewarded for his displays with a Scotland Under-21 cap against Belgium 'across the road' at Tannadice.

Tannadice was a fairly happy hunting ground for 'Shaky' as he was on the winning side away to United on four occasions, most memorably in a 4-3 win in November 1984.

Against the Old Firm, Stephen also had an excellent record, playing in fourteen wins, scoring nine goals. Against Rangers, he played in ten victories, scoring three goals including the third in a superb 3-1 victory at Ibrox in March 1985.

His goal scoring record against Celtic was much better, scoring six times against the Parkhead side and played on the winning side four times. One of those wins, in which he scored, came in a 3-2 win at home in March 1984 and this match came in a third successive game against the Old Firm, with the previous two outings against Rangers in the Scottish Cup.

Ray played the full ninety minutes in all three games which saw a 2-2 draw with The Gers at Dens in the quarter-final before winning the replay 3-2 in Glasgow a week later, three days before another 3-2 win, this time over Celtic.

After that quarter-final win at Ibrox, Dundee faced Aberdeen at Tynecastle and Stephen started on the bench. He came on in the second half to replace Lex Richardson but couldn't prevent Alex Ferguson's Dons from reaching the Final with a 2-0 win.

That semi final would be the furthest Ray would go in the Scottish Cup with The Dee but in the next two seasons, he would score in consecutive 2-1 quarter final replay defeats away the Celtic and Aberdeen after both matches were drawn 1-1 and 2-2 respectively at Dens.

Stephen twice topped the Dundee goal scoring charts when he was top league scorer in 1984/85 and was overall top goal scorer in all competitions the next year with eighteen strikes in thirty-seven appearances.

The following season, 1986/87, Ray pitched in with six goals before he was transferred to Nancy in France in November and the man to take him to France was none other than Arsene Wenger. Then making his way in the game as manager of Nancy, the alert Wenger had been motivated to make the trip to Tayside from north-east France by memories of seeing Stephen play for Dundee in pre-season games in Germany and promptly handed over a fee of £150, 000 for his services.

Stephen was an instant hit in France, scoring on his debut after Nancy had failed to score in thirteen games and today he stands fifth in Nancy's all time goal scoring list; a list headed by Michel Platini and he even played in the French legend's testimonial.

His last game for Dundee though was a memorable one as he played in a 3-0 win a Tannadice but the fans were shocked to learn of his departure in the aftermath of that victory. Ray points out however that the money raised from his sale allowed manager Jocky Scott to shortly afterwards splash out on buying Tommy Coyne and Keith Wright but it is intriguing to think how good Dundee's forward line would have been with all three in the side.

Described by striking partner Eric Sinclair as *'a real powerhouse with a good eye for goal'*, Ray will always be fondly remembered by the Dundee support.

At a supporter's diner in 2004, Ray proclaimed how much he still loved Dundee, how honoured he was to be invited and that the Dundee result was still the first he looked for every week. He also stated how much that 1980 League Cup Final defeat still hurt and that he would love one day to see a rematch in order to get revenge not only for that defeat but also for the penalty that never was.

Honours at Dundee:
Bells' Scottish League Cup runner-up: 1980/81
Scottish League First Division runner-up: 1980/81
Scotland Under 21 cap: 1
Appearances, Goals:
League: 156 + 31 subs, 47 goals
Scottish Cup: 14 + 1 sub, 5 goals
League Cup: 25 + 2 subs, 8 goals
Totals: 226, 60 goals

George Stewart

George Stewart's twelve year career at Dens Park saw him play in a European semi-final, ten domestic semi-final matches and two national cup finals and pick up just a solitary winners' medal as part of the Dundee side which won the Scottish League Cup in 1973.

Born in Edinburgh in 1948, George Stewart joined the Dark Blues from Tynecastle Boys' Club in 1964 and made his debut in the first team three years later in a 0-0 home match against Partick Thistle on February 25th 1967. The big defender came in to the side to replace the out of form Jim Easton and being favourably compared to Ian Ure, Stewart played in eight of the last nine league matches as Dundee clinched a spot in the Inter-Cities Fairs Cup.

Stewart kept his place in the side at the start of the 1967/68 season and when the Fairs Cup campaign began in the Olympic Stadium against D.W.S. Amsterdam, Stewart made the first of twelve appearances in Europe for Dundee. Seven of those appearances came in the 1967/68 season as the Dark Blues reached the semi-final stage where they lost out Leeds United with Stewart playing in both legs and the only match he missed was the 4-1 away win over Royal Leige in the second round.

Fours years later, the Fairs Cup was renamed the U.E.F.A. Cup and Dundee were back in the competition and in the second round they were drawn against old foes Cologne. Having missed both legs of the first round 5-2 aggregate victory over A.B. Copenhagen, Stewart was back in the starting line up in the Müngersdorf Stadium where Dundee lost the first leg in controversial circumstances.

Just after the break Cologne opened the scoring when Rupp's short corner was dummied by Flohe only for Rupp himself to set up Sheermann to score. Two consecutive touches from a corner kick were not in the rule book but the dummy had confused the referee as well as the Dundee defence and the goal stood.

Despite an equaliser from Kinninmonth, Lohr got Cologne's winner seven minutes from time but in the second leg, Dundee got revenge, storming back from 4-2 down on aggregate to win a famous tie 5-4.

The third round paired Dundee again were another old opponent from the 1962 European Cup run in A.C. Milan and Stewart played in both legs where a superb 2-0 win at Dens wasn't enough to overturn the 3-0 defeat in the San Siro in the first leg.

Stewart played in four different European campaigns and scored one of the ten goals he scored for Dundee in the U.E.F.A. Cup at home to Twente Enschede in September 1973.

Domestically Stewart had a good record in cup competitions with The Dee and in 1967 earned a runners-up medal when Dundee lost 5-3 to Celtic in the League Cup Final in one of the best matches ever seen at Hampden.

Six years later, the sides met again in the final of the same tournament and by then Dundee had played Celtic a further ten times in cup competitions losing seven, drawing two and winning just one where they still went out on aggregate in the 1972 League Cup quarter-final. Stewart played in all but one of those matches which included the Scottish Cup semi-final defeats in 1970 and 1973 and with that record in mind, Celtic were overwhelming favourites to win the League Cup again in December 1973.

Against all expectations however, Dundee gained revenge for all those recent losses when Gordon Wallace's superb goal with fifteen minutes left was enough to take the trophy back to the city of 'Jute, Jam and Journalism'. In *The Courier* match report the following Monday, Stewart was given a top score five star rating and it stated that Gemmell, Stewart, Duncan, Ford and Wallace were Dundee's top men.

In was the undoubted highlight of George's career at Dens but he expresses a slight disappointment that having played in so many semi-finals, the League Cup victory was his only winners' medal with Dundee.

Four months after that win, Stewart played again in another semi-final defeat to Celtic in a 1-0 Scottish Cup loss at Hampden and twelve months later endured a fourth semi-final defeat to The Bhoys with an identical score line as the year before.

Season 1975/76 was to be Stewart's last in a Dundee shirt as relegation from the inaugural Premier Division meant that costs had to be cut and George was transferred to Hibs for £37,000.

Stewart was moving to his native Edinburgh having often commuted by train to Dundee during his time at Dens but the enigmatic twenty-eight year old was a big loss to the Dundee defence.

Powerful in the air, with a good touch on the ground, Stewart had been a popular character in both the dressing room and on the terracing and as part of the last Dundee side to win a major trophy, he has been a regular guest at Club functions over the years, always talking with pride of his 292 appearances for The Dee.

Honours at Dundee:
Scottish League Cup winner: 1973/74
Scottish League Cup runner-up: 1967/68
U.E.F.A. / Inter-Cities Fairs Cup semi-final: 1967/68
Appearances, Goals:
League: 199 + 1 sub, 6 goals
Scottish Cup: 19, 1 goal
League Cup: 53, 2 goals
Europe: 12, 1 goal
Other: 8
Totals: 292, 10 goals

Gordon Strachan

The more things change in Scottish football, the more they stay they same and for Dundee F.C., this statement certainly rings true. As Dundee, with their precarious financial situation have had to watch a conveyor belt of nurtured talent leave Dens Park in recent years for a fraction of their worth, it harks back to a time just over thirty years ago when Dundee had to allow their young captain Gordon Strachan to leave, simply to allow the Club to survive.

'There was nothing remotely glamourous about Dundee Football Club behind the scenes, especially when they ran into serious financial difficulties following relegation,' Strachan wrote in his biography *My Life In Football*.

'There were fears we would have to go part-time. It was like the footballing equivalent of 'I'm a Celebrity, Get Me Out of Here'. The players' training kit — including our pants — was only washed once a week on a Friday. After we had trained in it on Tuesday, Wednesday and Thursday, often in terrible weather conditions, you can imagine what kind of state it was in by the end of the week.'

The financial situation for Dundee was dire following relegation from the inaugural Premier Division in 1976 and after failing to achieve promotion at the first attempt, Dundee were forced to sell their undoubted star Gordon Strachan to simply stop the bank closing the doors at Dens.

The then chairman Ian Gellatly went to his manager Tommy Gemmell on Halloween 1977 and told him that the Club had to raise £50, 000 by the end of the week or the bank would foreclose and by the Friday, Strachan was off to Aberdeen for £50, 000 plus Jim Shirra in exchange.

Gordon David Strachan was born in Edinburgh on February 9th 1957 and raised between a rock and a hard place, Strachan's Edinburgh was not the craggy outcrop-cum-tourist trap where the castle stands but more something out of *Trainspotting* on the tough Muirhouse estate. By five he was Hibernian-mad and playing in mass street games and in 1971, when he was a coveted schoolboy international, he was still starring in one such epic at 10.30pm when a Manchester United official arrived at his home. The promise that George Best would be waiting to greet him was meant to be the clincher but showing the principled, stubborn streak that would surface in later years, Strachan sent him away as he had given his word to Dundee.

When Gordon arrived at Dundee from Edinburgh Thistle, there was little doubt about his ability as the wee ginger-haired midfielder was a 'tanner ba' player from the old school and was admired by all for his ball skills.

Despite some question marks over his slight frame, Gordon made his debut for Dundee as a substitute in the first game of the 1973/74 season in a Drybrough Cup tie at Dens against Raith Rovers but teenager found it tough to break into a side that would win the League Cup that campaign and made just one further appearance from the bench a fortnight later.

But the fiery midfielder was fast earning a reputation as a brilliant player in the second team, twice winning the Scottish Reserve Player of the Year award and being at Dens was not just a football education for the flame-haired youngster but it was also an education in life.

Progress was made the following season with a couple of first team starts, and as one paper roared *'Dundee find new Billy Bremner'*, maturity off the pitch was slower in arriving. Caught in the act of quaffing Carlsberg after a Scotland youth match in Copenhagen, he was banned from international duty and another boozy binge, with Jimmy Johnstone, the former Celtic winger, ended when they literally ran into their incandescent Dundee manager in his hotel in Errol!

'I had to look after myself at Dundee', said Strachan in a Celtic online interview in 2009. *'I moved into digs there when I was fifteen, so I had to grow up there quickly. I had to learn to handle the mistakes I made myself.'*

Still staying in Edinburgh, wee Gordon caught the train to Dens on a daily basis and his traveling companions George Stewart and Bobby Ford were known to make the naïve youngster go and get the teas form the buffet car and regularly relieve him of his wages at cards.

~ 153 ~

But he was thriving from the coaching at Dens and told the Celtic Mad website on the eve of his Celtic side's Scottish Cup tie with Dundee in January 2009 that, *'I picked up a lot of good habits there from a coach called Hugh Robertson - he had been a left-winger for Dundee and he was fantastic. So I got good coaching there, too. I watched a lot of good players there - Jocky Scott, Gordon Wallace, John Duncan, Dougie Houston - it was a fantastic place and I picked up a lot of good habits.'*

In August 1975, Strachan outshone Alan Ball in midfield in a pre season friendly against Arsenal at Dens and the England World Cup winner made a point of shaking the hand of the eighteen year old when Gordon was substituted in Dundee 2-1 win. He had now more than staked his claim for a regular berth in the new Premier Division.

Despite his contribution however of six goals in thirty-one starts, Dundee were relegated along with St. Johnstone at the end of the season and he made an even greater contribution the following year featuring in forty-two of Dundee's forty-eight matches, scoring eight goals. It wasn't enough to take Dundee back up however as they finished third in the First Division behind St. Mirren and surprise packets Clydebank.

To everyone it was obvious that the 5ft 6in midfielder was Dundee's key man and at the start of the 1977/78, season, the Dens starlet was appointed Club captain, becoming the youngest player to hold that honour in The Dee's history. His sparkling form had earned Gordon a place on the bench for the Scotland Under-21s against Switzerland but the skilful Strachan was becoming the target for some rough treatment, forcing manager Tommy Gemmell to complain that his youngster was *'being kicked out the First Division'*.

On October 29th, Strachan starred in the 1-1 draw with Hearts at Dens but within days he was away to Aberdeen after the bank's demands and his departure for a relatively small fee would later be the cause for bitter regret.

It was no surprise to anyone who saw him playing at Dens that he would go on to play in two World Cups, win fifty international caps, the European Cup Winners' Cup and Super Cup, two Premier Division titles, three Scottish Cups, one English League title and an F.A. Cup. He would be named Scottish Football Writers' Player of the Year in 1980 and the English P.F.A. Player of the Year twelve years later in a playing career that would last until he was forty.

Strachan was linked with the vacant Dundee managerial job in the summer of 1988 as player/manager but he later took on that role at Coventry eight years later which started off a successful managerial career. Strachan led Southampton to the F.A. Cup Final in the same year Dundee played Rangers at Hampden in the Scottish equivalent and led Celtic to three S.P.L. titles, two League Cups and one Scottish Cup as well as winning the S.P.F.A Manager of the Year, three out of his four years at Parkhead.

'I loved my time at Dundee. I spent about five years laughing. Maybe I enjoyed myself too much there but it was fantastic', Gordon recalls and the Dundee fans also loved watching him turning out in the famous dark blue shirt. They knew they were watching a prodigious talent who was going to make it big in the game, and like so many others in Dundee's history and it is just a regret that he didn't do it with Dundee, through no fault of his own.

Appearances, Goals:
League: 56 + 13 subs, 13 goals
Scottish Cup: 7, 1 goal
League Cup: 11 + 2 subs, 1 goal
Other: 1 + 1 sub
Totals: 91, 15 goals

Alex Stuart

Alex Stuart won a Scottish League Championship medal with Dundee at the tender age of twenty-one and had the honour of captaining Dundee in the 1967 League Cup Final. An accomplished defender, Stuart was famed for his powerful shooting and in his nine seasons in the first team, he scored a very credible thirty-one goals making him the highest scoring defender in the Club's history to date.

Stuart joined Dundee from Aberdeen East End in 1958 and had to wait two years for his debut when he replaced the injured Bobby Cox in the staring line up in a derby against Dundee United at Tannadice on September 17th 1960.

The following season, Dundee reached their zenith when they won the Scottish League championship and Stuart played his part, coming in to cover for the injured Bobby Wishart and got revenge for the 3-1 derby defeat on his debut when his first match of the season was a glorious 4-1 win over United.

Winning the league flag meant European Cup football for Dundee and while Stuart was still very much a squad player, he still managed to make two of his eleven appearances of the season in both legs of the semi-final against A.C. Milan after Bobby Cox injured his cartilage at Fir Park, two days before the flight to Italy.

The following season saw Alex establish himself in the side and play fifty times as Dundee reached the Scottish Cup Final in April 1964. On route to the final, Stuart played in all six games and scored in the 6-3 win over Forres Mechanics in the Highlands in the first round. He took his place at Hampden in front of a crowd of 120, 982 but had to be content with a runners-up medal as Rangers ran out 3-1 winners.

That season saw Dundee score an incredible 156 goals, a club record and Alex chipped in with his first five goals for The Dee. His first strike came in a 6-1 rout of St. Johnstone in Perth in November while scored a double against Partick Thistle in a 5-2 win at Dens the week before the Dark Blues' date with destiny at the National Stadium.

By now a firm favourite with the fans, Stuart became famed for his thundering left-footed free kicks and long range strikes and added another five goals to his tally in season 1966/67. He also scored twice on Dundee's eleven game summer tour of North America at the end of that campaign; the first in a 12-1 win over Buffalo in the opening game.

The tour had been a great success and included wins over English champions Manchester United and cup winners Chelsea and so Thee Dee went into the new season in high spirits with Stuart was appointed as captain. Dundee started the season well by winning their League Cup section and in the two legged quarter-final against East Fife, Stuart scored Dundee's fourth in the second leg at home to round off a 5-0 aggregate win.

A 3-1 semi-final victory over Tayside neighbours St. Johnstone at Tannadice meant Alex had the honour of leading Dundee out in a major cup final at Hampden but he was denied the chance to lift the League Cup when defending champions Celtic retained the trophy by defeating The Dee 5-3 in an enthralling match.

By then Dundee were already in the second round of the Inter-Cities Fairs Cup - the forerunner to the U.E.F.A. Cup - after beating D.W.S. Amsterdam 4-2 on aggregate in the first round and just four days after the Cup Final defeat they now met Royal Leige at Dens for the first leg of round two. After the shock loss of an early goal, the Dark Blues were able to recover and two Alex Stuart 'specials' and a header by Sammy Wilson, gave Dundee a deserved 3-1 win.

A third round bye put Dundee into the quarter-finals and two 1-0 wins over F.C. Zurich sent Dundee into their second European semi-final in five years. Stuart however missed the tie against the Swiss side after having a cartilage operation in February and he failed to recover in time for the semi-final against Leeds United to deny him the chance to play in his second European semi.

It was the beginning of the end for Stuart's Dundee career as he made only nine starts the following year despite scoring in the first two games of the season. He failed to fully recover from the cartilage operation and in April, he was released aged just twenty-eight, alongside championship skipper Bobby Cox, making his last appearance for Dundee on January 4th 1969 against St. Johnstone at Muirton Park.

Stuart moved to city rivals Dundee United but left within the year to become player/manager at Montrose and spent six years at Links Park. He then moved to Premier Division side Ayr United in 1975 and kept the part-time side in the top flight for two season before having a final managerial spell with St. Johnstone at the end of the seventies.

Alec Stuart enjoyed a memorable eleven years at Dens Park when Dundee were at the height of their glory and was the only member of the league winning squad to play in both the Scottish and League Cup Finals. He was the last of the Championship side to leave Dens Park and his departure marked the end of a golden age for Dundee F.C.

Honours at Dundee:
Scottish League Champions: 1961/62
European Cup semi-final: 1962/63
Scottish Cup runner-up: 1964
Scottish League Cup runner-up: 1967/68
Appearances, Goals:
League: 166, 21 goals
Scottish Cup: 13, 3 goals
League Cup: 36, 4 goals
Europe: 8, 2 goals
Other: 12, 1 goal
Totals: 235, 31 goals

Alec Troup

Alec Troup is an all-time Dundee great who played over 300 games for Dundee during two spells after signing from his hometown team Forfar Athletic in 1915. Known to many fans as 'Wee Troupie' due to his small stature, Alec Troup was a wonderfully tricky left winger whose sparkling play, gentlemanly demeanour, good humour and extremely likeable personality undoubtedly brightened up many a troubled heart during the dark days of the First World War and the years that followed. He became a real hero of the people at a time when such role models were in great demand to rouse the population's spirits as well as being an extremely talented player.

Alexander Troup was born in Forfar in Angus on May 12th 1895 and joined local side Forfar Athletic in 1914, having previously played for Junior side Forfar North End. When the Station Park side went into abeyance for the War the following year, Angus neighbours Dundee F.C, were quick to pounce and persuaded the diminutive winger to sign for the Dens Park side, taking Forfar's closure as a chance to pay no fee, despite them asking for one in 1919.

Troup was persuaded to sign for the Dark Blues by a Dundee director while he was working up a ladder repairing a roof for an undertaker and when he came down from the ladder to sign a contract for The Dee, he did so by signing it on top of a new coffin. It was a macabre start to his Dundee career but his Dark Blue debut was anything but when he turned in a scintillating performance on the first day of the 1915/16 season in a 2-0 home win over Ayr United in front of 5000 at Dens. Troup set up the first goal for centre-forward Davie Brown before adding a second himself which *The Courier* described as *'an outstandingly brilliant goal'*.

It was a great start for 'Eckie' whom the Dundee support immediately took to their hearts and *The Courier* stated in their match report that, *'Troup was the star, of course.'*

Over the next two seasons, Troup played forty-one times for The Dee before he volunteered for military service and was called up to join the Royal Engineers. His last game before leaving for basic training at Largs on the Ayrshire coast was against Hearts at Tynecastle on December 16th 1917 but he turned out again for The Dee when they played nearby Ayr United in February before being sent to the Western Front.

Troup also turned out for the Somerset Park side as a guest while training at Largs and played alongside Alex Shankly, elder brother of Dundee's 1962 League winning manager Bob. When he was sent to northern France to fight in the trenches, he played in inter-regiment matches for the '13th Reinforcement Company, Royal Engineers' and he was lucky enough to escape the 'war to end all wars' with his life and returned to his native Forfar in the spring of 1919.

Dundee F.C., like Forfar, had themselves gone into abeyance after being asked to withdraw from the league to save on travelling at the end of the season that Troup had 'joined up' and when they returned for the 1919/20 season, they were delighted to have 'Wee Troupie' back in their ranks.

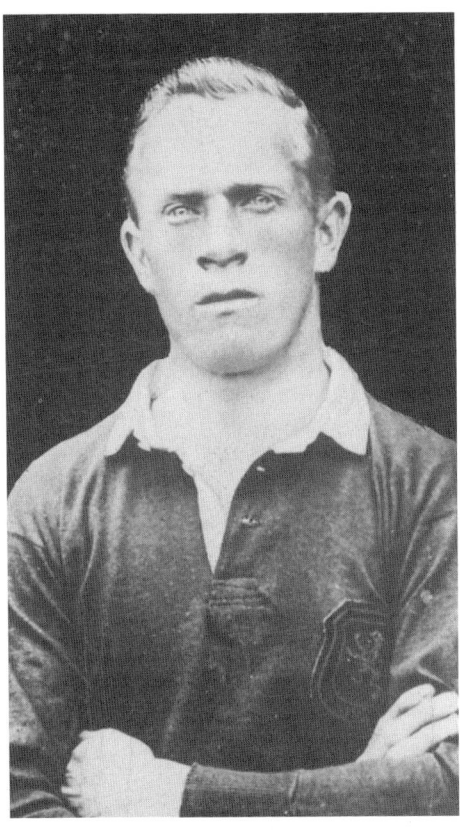

The first game at Dens Park was the public trial match on August 13th when Troup played for the Reds against the Blues alongside another two Forfarians, George Henderson and Dyken Nicoll and in Dundee's first real game back away to Motherwell three days later, he took up his familiar position out on the Dundee left wing.

At Dundee's first home league game the following week, Troup was among the ex-serviceman who were given a special cheer by the Dens Park crowd. Dundee had opened a special enclosure at the match for returning soldiers who were maimed or injured and were now allowed into games for free for life. Troup was distressed at the number of men wearing the 'hospital blue' uniform in the new enclosure and he vowed he would make the most of his career, realising how lucky he was to be playing.

For the next four years, Troup was Dundee's star turn and did much to alleviate the post war gloom. He turned in some brilliant performances despite playing with the handicap of a loose collarbone and often, without apparent cause the shoulder would come out and the winger had to pull up. On then, came the trainer and with one thump, the shoulder would be back in place and 'Wee Troupie' would carry on as if nothing had happened.

Troup was an original touchline terror and would certainly have made more than the four Scottish international and two Scottish League appearances he managed while at Dens had it not been for Rangers' 'wee blue devil' Alan Morton.

By early January 1923, Dundee lay two points behind league leaders Rangers but astonishingly Troup was allowed to join Everton for £4000. Rumours were abound that Dundee had to sell their best player to help pay for the newly opened grandstand, designed by renowned football architect Archibald Leitch but in Troup's absence Dundee could manage only nine points from their last eleven games as they finished a disappointing seventh.

At Everton, Troup was just as popular with the Goodison support as he had been at Dens and he was credited for being a major contributory factor to Dixie Deans sixty goals record for the Toffees.

After seven successful years on Merseyside, where Troup picked up a league championship winning medal in 1928, he returned to Dundee and a terrific crowd of 31, 000 -11, 000 more than the last home game - turned up to watch his second debut in a Scottish Cup fourth round tie with Hearts.

Despite being past his best, Troup still became a key man for the next three years until he retired form the game at the age of thirty-eight. In the next two seasons, Troup missed just two matches in each campaign, despite being into his mid thirties and in his final year, managed another thirty-two appearances.

His last match for Dundee came at Dens on April 22nd 1933 against Celtic, who had won the Scottish Cup the week before and he played his part in a terrific 3-0 win.

Upon retiring, he worked in his gentleman's outfitter shop in Castle Street in Forfar which he had opened upon returning from Everton and he remained a popular local hero until he died in his hometown in December 1952.

Troup was only the second man from Forfar to turn out for Scotland, gaining a fifth cap while at Goodison and in Douglas Lamming's *Who's Who of Scottish Football* he is described as *'a diminutive wingman possessing dazzling ball control, resolution, and a mastery of the measured dipping centre.'* There is no doubt the Dundee forwards appreciated these 'dipping centres' and there is no doubt either that the Dundee support loved his 'dazzling ball control and resolution'.

Honours at Dundee:
Scotland full caps: 4
Scottish League caps: 2
Appearances, Goals:
League: 282, 42 goals
Scottish Cup:23, 5 goals
Totals: 305, 47 goals

Ian Ure

'I will never forget the events on April 28th 1962', said Ian Ure on the fortieth anniversary of Dundee becoming Scottish League Champions, *'and these memories will remain with me for the rest of my life. The pre match trepidation, the after match euphoria, the bus trip back to Dundee from Perth, the team's ecstatic reception on the balcony of Dundee Town Hall by the fans, the celebration dinner and the somewhat hazy, alcohol fuelled recollection of the following few days made it a fantastic, unforgettable weekend.'* However it could have been so different for the bedrock of Dundee title winning defence had he followed his first love of rugby and gave in to the early doubts he harboured about his footballing ability.

John Francombe Ian Ure was born in Ayr on December 7th 1939 and at school, he had excelled at most sports representing them at rugby, cricket and boxing. Ian attended the staunch rugby playing school of Ayr Academy who tried to rear him as a stand-off and he played for the First XV aged just sixteen. Most of his opponents were bigger than him, which helped Ian build his mighty frame but he didn't ignore football, playing for Ayr Albion on a Saturday afternoon after playing with the oval ball in the morning.

It was at Albion that Ure was spotted by Dundee's Ayrshire scout Jimmy Ross who invited Ian to go to Dens Park for a week's trial in 1958 after he had represented Scotland

Schoolboys against England and Wales. After failing to impress boss Willie Thornton, the youngster was told to return home to Ayr but Dundee coach Sammy Kean persuaded Thornton to give the blond 6ft 1in defender another two weeks trial. Still Thornton was unimpressed but Kean persisted in his judgement and persuaded his manager to sign the youngster and with a £100 signing on fee in his pocket, Ure went on to become one of the greatest players to play for the Dark Blues.

After just four months in the reserves, Ian made his debut in the first team in a 3-2 home win over Falkirk. Having signed for The Dee as a left-half, Ian found himself at centre-half almost by accident when he came in to replace regular pivot Billy Smith and soon his performances made the Dundee support forget about the departure of Jimmy Gabriel to Everton.

After spending a few years as understudy to Doug Cowie, Ure had to wait until Bob Shankly took over the Dens Park hot seat before he became a regular in the side and in season 1960/61 made forty-one appearances, establishing the formidable half-back line alongside Bobby Seith and Bobby Wishart.

Season 1961/62 saw Dundee become Scottish League Champions and Ian was an ever present making the number five jersey his own for both club and country. He made the first of eleven international appearances for Scotland, eight of which he won at Dens, in November 1961 against Wales and just three days later was part of the Dundee side which recorded the Club's greatest ever league result, with a 5-1 victory at Ibrox over Rangers.

It was a result which highlighted how serious Dundee's championship challenge was and the following April Dundee won the League Flag after they defeated St. Johnstone 3-0 at Muirton Park, finishing above the Ibrox side by three points.

The next season saw Dundee explode onto the European scene with an 8-1 hammering of West German champions Cologne. The shockwaves that Ure and his team mates were sending throughout the continent continued as Sporting Lisbon and Anderlecht were put to the sword before Dundee crashed out to Italian giants A.C. Milan 5-2 on aggregate at the semi final stage.

Ure's performances in the Champion Clubs' Cup were immense, particularly in the away leg in Cologne when Dundee were under pressure both on and off the park and were put under the most intense intimidation. Down to ten men with keeper Bert Slater stretchered off and 3-0 down at half-time, Dundee were in severe danger of going out in what would have been one of the most extraordinary turnarounds in two legged football, but Ure was one of the few to keep his head and put in a heroic performance to see Dundee through.

In December 1962, his performances both home and abroad saw Ure presented with the Scottish Footballer of the Year Award which was chosen by Rex Kingsley of the *Sunday Mail* and became the first and to date only Dundee player to win a national player of the year accolade. Pre-dating, the Players' Player or Football Writers' Awards, the Kingsley award was presented at the end of a calendar year and Ure became the twelfth man to win the title with team mate Gordon Smith being the first with Hibernian in 1951.

A presentation ceremony was held in the Dundee's Caird Hall on February 24th 1963 and in the souvenir programme, Ure's manager Bob Shankly said. *'Ian is not only a highly skilled player- he is a morale builder in any side. His virtues as a team mate are never more noticeable when the battle is at its toughest. His very presence, as he races to cover ever possible leak or nails it forward to stab it to a mate, means much to his colleagues on the field.'*

Six weeks later, Ian was part of the Scotland side which defeated England at Wembley for the first time since 1949 with a 2-1 win and B.B.C. commentator Kenneth Wolstenholme described Ure as *'the greatest centre half in the world today'* in his coverage of the game.

With early sixties seeing a steady flow of Scottish talent heading south where the big bucks was, it was always going to be difficult to keep a hold of Ure after he had performed so well in such high profile games. Ian wanted to test himself at a higher level and put in a transfer request in the summer of 1963 and after threatening to 'sign on the dole' if he didn't get a move, he eventually moved to Arsenal having impressed against them in two friendlies in 1962.

Ure moved to Highbury for £62, 500, a world record fee for a centre half and after six years in London moved for another world record fee for a centre-half when Matt Busby paid £80, 000 to take him to Old Trafford.

After a short spell with St. Mirren, Ure succeeded Alex Ferguson as manager of East Stirlingshire but his time at Dens remained the highlight of his career. Ure made 146 appearances for The Dee but curiously never scored, considering his height might have posed a threat at set pieces. He was however the heartbeat of Dundee's title winning defence and was a fearsome battler who dominated aerial duels and passed the ball better than most centre halves of his day.

'It was a great experience in my time to have been associated with Dundee Football Club and I think back fondly of my time there,' says Ure. *'I am eternally grateful to have been part of the setup at Dens Park which came together to win the Championship and reach the European Cup semi-final the following year.'*

The Dundee support are also eternally grateful to have had Ian Ure wear the dark blue of Dundee with such distinction.

Honours at Dundee:	
Scottish League Champions:	1961/62
European Cup semi-final:	1962/63
Scotland full caps:	8
Scottish League caps:	4
Scotland Player of the Year:	1962
Appearances:	
League:	107
Scottish Cup:	6
League Cup:	20
Europe:	8
Other:	5
Total:	146

Gordon Wallace

Slade topped the charts when Dundee won the Scottish League Cup in 1973 but it wasn't Noddy Holder hollering *'It's Chriiiiistmassss!'* which lifted the gloom amongst a national energy crisis, miners' strike and horrific weather but a 5ft 9in Dundonian who went by the nickname of 'Stubby'.

Ask any Dundee supporter who Gordon Wallace is and they will tell you that he is the man who scored the winning goal the last time Dundee won a major trophy. He did so on December 15th 1973 when in the seventy-fifth minute when he chested down a Bobby Wilson free kick with his back to goal, turned on a sixpence in one swift move and fired the ball past the despairing dive of Celtic's Ally Hunter to score one of the best goals ever seen in a Hampden final and become an instant a Dundee hero.

In was a magical moment for George Gordon Wallace; born and bred in the city who had grown up watching The Dee and his hero Billy Steel play at Dens Park. He started his own football career playing for Rockwell School, Lawside Rangers and Junior club Dundee North End and it was while at North End that he was given the dream chance to play for the Club he supported when Bob Shankly signed him on provisional forms with the Dark Blues.

He was devastated to learn however that he was not to be offered a professional contract in April 1961 and so returned to the Juniors with Alyth United before former Dens Parker Norrie Christie signed him for Montrose.

The goals soon rained in for the Links Park side and after seventy-five goals in four years, promotion chasing Raith Rovers took note and signed the twenty-three year old Wallace in December 1966.

Gordon enjoyed a very successful spell with the Kirkcaldy club and in season 1967/68 almost single-handedly saved Rovers from relegation with his thirty goals and as a result became the first non Old Firm player to be named as the Scottish Football Writers' Player of the Year.

In September 1969 Dundee boss John Prentice brought Stubby back to Dens for a fee of £14,000 which need never have been spent if Wallace had not been released eight years before but it was a fee that would be quickly repaid as he went on to score 119 goals for the Club, including that League Cup winner, making him sixth on Dundee's all time leading goal scoring list.

Soon after signing, "Gor-don, Gor-don" was the chant on the terracing as Wallace formed a fine scoring partnership with Jocky Scott. Wallace had a lightening quick football brain and was the catalyst of much of the good football enjoyed by the Dark Blue support in the early seventies and he finished Dundee's top goal scorer in three separate occasions. No mean feat in a team which included both Jocky Scott and John Duncan who also shared that honour in the same period.

The winning goal in the League Cup Final wasn't the only memorable goal in Gordon's time at Dens and almost as famous was his winning goal in the dramatic 5-4 aggregate win in the U.E.F.A. Cup against Cologne in 1972 when Dundee came back from 4-2 down with just twenty minutes to go.

Gordon also scored in the previous round against A.B. Copenhagen and scored a brace in the match before the first leg in a famous 6-4 win over Dundee United at Dens. In total Wallace scored seven goals against United and was on the winning side in a further four derbies and when he became manager in 1989, he masterminded another two victories over 'The Arabs', including a famous 4-3 at Dens in August.

Other memorable goals included a thunderous free kick against Morton in 1970 and a cracker against Rangers at Ibrox in a 3-2 win in 1971 but his biggest disappointment at Dundee was the four Scottish Cup semi-final defeats to Celtic which denied Gordon a chance to win an F.A. medal to add to his League Cup one.

Wallace played for Dundee in the inaugural Premier Division season of 1975/76 but it was to be his last as a player for Dundee as the season ended in relegation to the First Division on goal difference, despite his fourteen goals and he was amongst eight players released at the end of the season.

It was far from the end of his association with Dundee when he returned as manager in February 1989 in the wake of Dave Smith's resignation and became one of three members of the 1973 League Cup winning team to manage The Dee. Finishing his playing career with Seattle Sounders in the N.A.S.L. and then Dundee United, Wallace became a coach at Tannadice after a stint as in charge of Raith and it was from United that he joined up with his former club to take over the hot seat.

The undoubted highlight of his time in charge was the 1990 B&Q Scottish League Centenary Cup triumph over Ayr United at Fir Park, when a Billy Dodds hat-trick gave Dundee a 3-2 win after extra time. The competition was a one off tournament for clubs outside the Premier Division to celebrate the centenary of the Scottish Football League and the glass trophy still remains in the Club's boardroom today. Such was the success of the competition that the League decided it should become an annual competition called the League Challenge Cup which Dundee won for the first time as the Alba Cup in November 2009 when Gordon was again in the dug out on the coaching staff.

In September 1991, Gordon left Dundee to become assistant manger to old friend Jocky Scott at Dunfermline but in 2004 returned to Dens for a third time to take up the post of Youth and First Team Advisor, a role he still holds today.

Dundee assistant manager Billy Dodds was one of Wallace's most successful signings when he was in charge while current boss Gordon Chisholm was Wallace's captain when they won the Centenary Cup and he now works in Chisholm and Dodds' backroom team. Gordon was also responsible for bringing back Jim Duffy into the playing side in early 1990 and then subsequently worked on Duffy's coaching staff when he returned to Dundee in 2004 and so his legacy at Dens is widespread.

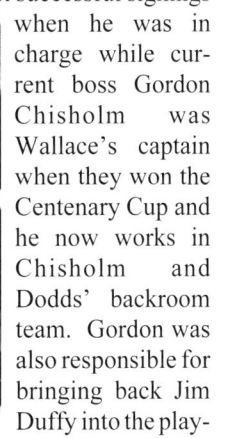

The former striker is always to be seen on match days at Dens and though many fans were not even born in December 1973, they know the name of Gordon Wallace and know that he is a legendary Dundee hero and he was rightly inducted in the 2010 Dundee F.C. Hall of Fame.

Honours at Dundee:
Dundee F.C. Hall of Fame: 2010
Legends Award
(As Player)
Scottish League Cup winner: 1973/74

(As Manager)
B&Q Scottish League Centenary Cup winner: 1990
Appearances, Goals:
League: 189 + 7 subs, 90 goals
Scottish Cup: 20 + 1 sub, 7 goals
League Cup: 38 + 1 sub, 19 goals
Europe: 7, 2 goals
Other: 5, 1 goal
Totals: 268, 119 goals

Managerial Record with Dundee: (1989 – 1991)

	P	W	D	L	F	A	Pts
League:	93	39	22	32	132	123	100
Scottish Cup:	5	2	1	2	4	4	
League Cup:	4	1	1	2	9	8	
S.F.L. Challenge Cup:	4	4	0	0	11	5	
Total:	106	46	24	36	156	140	

William Wallace

Wallace is a name which is famous in the city of Dundee with a few candidates laying claim to legendary status. There is William Wallace, braveheart and hero in the Scottish Wars of Independence who was educated in the city at the predecessor to the modern day High School of Dundee; there is Gordon Wallace who served both of the city's football clubs, most notably Dundee F.C. when he scored the winning goal the last time Dundee won a major trophy and there is another William Wallace, Dundee's longest serving manager for twenty years who was in charge of the Dens Park club when they won their first major trophy, the Scottish Cup in 1910.

When Wallace took over team affairs in 1899, he took over at a turbulent time as Dundee were just recovering from the brink of liquidation. Just twelve months previously the board had voted to put Dundee into voluntary liquidation but following a packed public meeting at Gilfillian Hall, a new Dundee F.C. committee was elected and on that committee was local man and Dundee F.C. faithful William Wallace.

To resurrect the fortunes of Dundee F.C., the committee made two momentous decisions that would help secure the future of the northern most club in the Scottish League. The first decision was to move the club from the current ground at the docks at Carolina Port which was poorly serviced by public transport and which the Harbour Trustees were looking to acquire for expansion. They decided to move it to a new site at the north of the city which was bordered by Provost Road and Dens Road to be called Dens Park.

The second decision, which was just as important at the time, was to put committee member and General Secretary William Wallace in charge of team affairs and make him Dundee's first manager in its sixteen year history.

Wallace took over a team which had finished bottom of the Scottish League Division One and the Club had to apply for re-election along with the two sides directly above them. Fortunately for The Dee they were re-elected to the League along with Clyde but Partick Thistle, who had finished just above Dundee were not so lucky and were replaced by Kilmarnock.

It meant that Dundee could kick off in their new ground still in the Scottish League and Wallace was in charge at the official opening of Dens on August 19th 1899 when Dundee drew 1-1 with St. Bernards.

The move to Dens Park and the appointment of Wallace proved to be the turning point in Dundee's fortunes and with the astute Wallace in charge, sixth place was attained. Despite finishing seventh the following year, only five out of nineteen home games had been lost since the advent of the new regime and this ensured a healthy home support which served to further strengthen the Club's financial footing.

In addition to his part-time managerial post, Wallace was also club secretary and since the turn of the century, he had been ably assisted by another Dundee legend, 'Plum' Longair. The stalwart defender, who continued playing until 1902, was now trainer and another local man, Peter Allan, would play an equally important role.

Renowned as a top local scout, Allan had sent many talented Scots to leading English sides and in a shrewd move by Wallace, he was coaxed to Dens and soon there was a steady influx of stars into the Club, many from south of the border.

The managerial team was now in place to bring Dundee unprecedented success and within the next seven years Dundee finished runners-up in the Scottish League Championship three times.

The Dark Blues were pipped to the post by Hibernian in 1902/03 and then by Celtic in both 1906/07 and 1908/09 where they lost the League by just one point but despite no trophies, Dundee were now a major force in the country.

Dundee enjoyed success in the still prestigious local cup competitions where the crowds were often bigger than matches in the league and they won local bragging rights by winning the Forfarshire Cup four times, the Dewar Shield three times and the Dundee and District Charity Shield once.

Wallace was also in charge for the first ever Dundee derby when they took on the newly formed Dundee Hibernian (who would become Dundee United in 1923) in the Forfarshire Cup first round in February 1910 and two goals from Sandy Hall was enough to give Dundee a historic 2-1 win.

Just two months after that derby win however, Dundee finally got their hands on a major prize when they brought home the Scottish Cup for the first time in the Club's history.

Committee president Baille Robertson stated that *'It is the height of the Club's ambition to win the Scottish Cup'* and in April 1910, William Wallace delivered the world's oldest football trophy to Dens after a successful ten game marathon to lift the Cup.

Dundee took two matches to dispense with non-league Beith in the first round before wins over Falkirk and Motherwell sent Dundee into the semi-final. To reach the Final, Dundee needed three matches to overcome Hibernian with two 0-0 draws at Easter Road and Dens before an epic third tie at neutral Parkhead saw Dundee sneak through 1-0 with a winner from John Hunter.

To lift the Cup, Dundee would again need three matches to defeat Clyde after the first two matches ended all square. Dundee were strong favourites win the trophy at the 75, 000 capacity Ibrox Stadium but with four minutes left Clyde were 2-0 ahead and their red and white ribbons had already been put on the cup.

John Hunter however refused to give up and chased a long hopeful ball down the middle and as the Clyde keeper Watson attempted to clear, the ball flew off the inrushing Dundee centre and into the net.

Wallace then threw caution to the wind and with just thirty seconds remaining Dundee were awarded a corner. Dundee packed the Clyde box and when Bellamy sent over the perfect cross, Langlands crashed the ball high into the net to incredibly take the tie to a replay.

Wallace made one change for the replay with Bert Neal being preferred to Jimmy Lawson at right-back but with the match finishing 0-0, it was back to Ibrox four days later for a second replay.

Clyde again shocked The Dee when they took the lead in three minutes but Dundee drew level in fifteen minutes through Jimmy Bellamy. Ten minutes after half time John Hunter put Dundee ahead and when the score remained 2-1 to Dundee, Wallace had led the Dark Blues to Scottish Cup success.

The team didn't arrive back to Dundee until 11pm that evening but were greeted by a crowd of 20, 000 at the train station to thunderous applause. The team tried to make their way up to Dens by horse drawn cart but half way up Victoria Road, too many of the enthusiastic crowd had climbed on the cart and when the axel collapsed, Wallace and the players had to make the rest of the journey on foot.

It was a night to remember for all concerned and watched by a total crowd of 214, 000 in the Final, it was a real money spinner for the Club. The victory brought William Wallace his finest hour in charge of Dundee and it would take another forty-one years before Dundee could replicate his trophy success. His change of tactics in the first game when 2-0 down were a master stroke and he remains the only Dundee manager to have lifted the Scottish Cup.

Wallace continued as Dundee manager for the next eight season but when the Club went into abeyance for the War at the end of the 1917/18 season after winning the Scottish League Eastern Division and a host of league cup competitions, he did not return as boss when the The Dee returned for season 1919/20 as he decided to resign his post in the early part of 1919.

Wallace took charge of Dundee for a remarkable 684 games and as well as stabilising things in a period of uncertainty, he turned Dundee into a formidable side as he became Dundee's longest serving manager in the Club's history.

His twenty years in charge from 1899 to 1919 brought an incredible fifteen trophies including a major success that is still celebrated at Dundee today and Wallace rightly deserves his place among the legends of the Club.

Honours at Dundee:
Scottish Cup winners: 1910
Scottish League Championship runners-up: 1902/03, 1906/07, 1908/09
Scottish League Eastern Division winners: 1917/18
Forfarshire Cup winner: 1900/01, 1902/03, 1904/05, 1908/09, 1911/12, 1912/13
Dewar Shield: 1900/01, 1902/03, 1904/05
Dundee and District Charity Shield: 1899/1900
Penman Cup winners: 1917/18
Loftus Cup winners: 1917/18
Eastern Cup joint winners (with Dundee Hibs): 1917/18

Managerial Record with Dundee: (1899 – 1919)

	P	W	D	L	F	A	Pts
League:	574	251	130	193	933	761	632
Scottish Cup:	55	22	19	14	86	50	
Other:	55	30	14	11	137	59	
Total:	684	303	163	218	1156	870	

Morten Wieghorst

A player from a Scottish First Division side winning an international tournament with a top five F.I.F.A ranked side may seem unlikely but Dundee F.C.'s Morten Wieghorst did exactly that in 1995 when Denmark won the King Fahd Cup. Known as the King Fahd Cup before F.I.F.A. took over and renamed the tournament the Confederations Cup in 1997, it was played between the continental champions and in the summer of 1995 it was won by the reigning European champions Denmark with Morten Wieghorst featuring in the as a first half substitute in the 2-0 final win over Argentina.

Wieghort had made his debut for the Danish national team in August 1994, when he came on as a half-time substitute and scored the winning goal in a 2–1 friendly win against Finland. Four months later he was called up to go to Saudi Arabia for the King Fahd Cup and came off the bench in the first group game against the hosts to score the deciding goal in a 2-0 win after playing a one-two with Rangers' Brian Laudrup.

Wieghorst was born in Glostrup in Denmark on February 25th 1971 and he started his professional career with Lyngby Boldklub, with whom he won the 1990 Danish Cup and 1992 Superliga titles. Not long after that league title success, Morten was on his way to Scotland when the Dundee chairman Ron Dixon financed the Club record fee of £225,000 himself and the 6ft 3in midfielder was an instant hit when he scored a fabulous goal on his debut in Perth.

In the Premier Division match against St. Johnstone on December 2nd 1992, Dundee lost an early goal and then goalkeeper Paul Mathers was sent off but after Steve Pittman equalised, the lanky Wieghorst announced his entrance to the Scottish game when he ghosted past three players on the edge of the box before sending a low shot past the Saints keeper. It was a wonderful goal but with diminutive striker Duncan Campbell between the sticks, Dundee went 4-2 behind before a late fight back saw the Tayside derby thriller finish 4-4, giving Morten a debut to remember.

Wieghorst quickly became hugely influential in the Dundee midfield with his craft, guile and surging runs and was a key man as Dundee retained their Premier League status in their first season back in the top flight. In their second season however, a combination of a bad start, a mistimed managerial change and the sale of key players contributed to Dundee finishing bottom, despite some impressive performances from the popular Danish under 21 internationalist.

Dundee were installed as favourites to secure an immediate return to the Premier League and come November they were top of the league and in the B&Q Challenge Cup Final where Morten played in the 3-2 extra-time defeat to Airdrie.

The following month Dundee endured a dip in form and it was no coincidence that it came when Morten was away playing in the Confederations Cup. Missing four matches in Dundee's promotion push, vital points were dropped with a 2-2 draw in Perth and a 1-0 loss at home to bogey team Airdrie and these were to prove costly. Dundee missed out on the title by just one point and the play-offs on goal difference and on the last day of the season at Stranraer, Dundee needed a 7-0 win to at least reach the play-off with Aberdeen but could only manage five with Morten scoring twice and then hitting the post late on.

Another season in the First Division was a blow but at the start of the new campaign Dundee started off well in the Coca-Cola League Cup with a 6-0 win over East Stirlingshire in which Wieghorst netted the first.

In the next round, he was on the score sheet again as Dundee dispatched Premier Division Kilmarnock 3-1 at Dens and in the quarter-final Dundee were to draw another top tier side at home when Hearts came out the hat after Dundee and it was a game in which Wieghorst was to be the hero and fondly remembered.

In an incredible night Dundee were ahead 2-0 and 3-2 before Hearts hit back to take the tie into extra-time and in the 94th minute Wieghorst brilliantly shimmied past a couple of defenders before firing a dipping, swerving shot into the roof of the Hearts net.

Hearts however equalised again and the tie went to penalties, and when Hearts goalkeeper Henry Smith missed from twelve yards, Morten stepped up to strike the decisive kick to send Dundee through 5-4 on penalties.

The Dane had only played after passing a late fitness test but it would be his finest performance in a dark blue shirt in one of the most enthralling games ever seen at Dens. It was another memorable goal from Wieghorst and his manger Jim Duffy paid tribute to his man of the match performance when he told the press *'Morten was superb and his goal was nothing short of magnificent.'*

Wieghorst was again superb in the semi-final when a 2-1 win over Airdrie at McDiarmid Park sent Dundee to their first major cup final in fifteen years and in the week before the Final against Aberdeen, Dundee were due to play Dundee United in a league match at Tannadice.

United had been relegated at the end of the previous campaign and were Dundee's main rivals for promotion but by half-time were in dreamland with a 2-0 lead. Weighorst was again pulling the strings and had been involved in both goals and three minutes into the second half was on the score sheet himself when he headed home a corner to make in 3-0. United however fought back to make it 3-2 but a nervy Dundee held on for a win, meaning Morten had scored a winner in a derby to cement his legendary status with Dundee support.

A week later, Morten played his last game for the Club in a disappointing 2-0 defeat in the League Cup Final to the Dons and in the days that followed, he was off to Celtic for club record fee received of £500, 000 plus Barry Smith (valued at £100, 000) as chairman Ron Dixon wanted to recoup his money.

Dixon had returned from his native Canada for the cup final but had demanded that Weighorst be sold to finance some personal business but Jim Duffy persuaded his chairman to allow his star man to play at Hampden before moving to Parkhead.

Weighorst won the Premier Division with Celtic in 1998 and played for Denmark in the World Cup in France the same year but in 2000, he tragically developed a rare illness called Guillain-Barre syndrome which affects the brain nerve endings. He did however bravely battle back to full health to play again with Celtic and Denmark and in 2002 he moved back to his homeland to sign for Brondy and was named Danish Player of the Year in 2003.

In 2005 he joined FC Nordsjælland and took over as manager a year later but Wieghorst stills retains affection for his old club. In May 2010 he offered to recommend players from Denmark to manager Gordon Chisholm, whom he met when his side played Chisholm's Queen of the South in the U.E.F.A. Cup in 2008 and if he manages to find any players even half as good as himself, it will be a major coup for The Dee.

Honours at Dundee:
Coca-Cola League Cup runner-up: 1995/96
B&Q Challenge Cup runner-up: 1994/95
Denmark International caps: 5
Appearances, Goals:
League: 86 + 3 subs, 11 goals
Scottish Cup: 7, 1 goal
League Cup: 8, 3 goals
S.F.L. Challenge Cup: 4 + 1 sub, 2 goals
Totals: 109, 17 goals

Bobby Wilson

The late sixties/early seventies was a great time to be a Dundee supporter with Cup Finals, semi-finals, great European runs and big crowds and at the heart of it all was dependable right-back Bobby Wilson who made 411 appearances for the Club from 1966 to 1976.

With the great Alex Hamilton coming to the end of his career, the Dark Blues were on the look out for someone to take over the number two shirt and in 1966, Dundee manager Bobby Ancell paid Cowdenbeath £5000 for young full back Bobby Wilson who would go on to play for The Dees for eleven seasons to become one of the Club's longest serving players.

Very much in the wing back mould, Bobby made his debut for Dundee on March 9th 1966 in a 2-1 home win over Hamilton at home and he would play in all but one of the remaining games of the season.

In his first full season, Bobby shared the right-back berth with Alex Hamilton but by the end of the season was well established in the team so that the 1967/68 season would see Bobby play in every match expect the very important last one.

It was a season in which Bobby would score the first of his sixteen goals for the Club against Stirling Albion at Dens and it was a season in which Dundee enjoyed success in a number of cup competitions.

In the Scottish League Cup, Dundee enjoyed an unbeaten record in the sectional ties, winning five and drawing one before defeating East Fife in a two legged quarter-final. In the semi-final at Tannadice, Dundee met Tayside neighbours St. Johnstone and after winning 3-1, Dundee reached their first League Cup Final in fifteen years.

Bobby Wilson lined up for Dundee in the Final against Celtic at Hampden in October and in one of the best Finals ever played at Hampden, there was disappointment for Bobby as Celtic won 5-3 in a very exciting, open match.

In another exciting final, Dundee lifted the Forfarshire Cup with a 4-3 win over Dundee United at Dens with a hat-trick from namesake Sammy Wilson and in the Scottish Cup. bowed out to Rangers after a replay at Ibrox but their best performances were reserved for Europe in the Inter-Cities Fairs Cup.

Dundee had qualified for the Fairs Cup the previous season despite finishing sixth as the rules of the competition dictated that only one side from a city could qualify. With Rangers finishing second in the League, they were entered into the Fairs Cup for the 1967/68 season but unfortunately for Clyde, they were denied a place despite finishing third as Rangers were already representing Glasgow. Dundee however would make the most of their unexpected opportunity as they went all the way to the semis where they would lose out to eventual winners Leeds.

Bobby's European debut came in the First Round tie with D.W.S. Amsterdam and after losing 2-1 in the Dutch capital, progressed to the next round with a 3-0 win at Dens.

Round two paired Dundee with Belgian side Royal Leige and after a comfortable 7-2 aggregate win, Dundee were through to the quarter-finals after receiving a bye in the Third Round, where they met F.C. Zurich who were dispatched with two 1-0 wins.

The semi-final draw paired Dundee with Don Revie's mighty Leeds United who had already knocked out Scotland's other two participants Hibernian and Rangers and were strong favourites to make it a hat-trick of Scottish successes.

Over 24, 000 at Dens saw Bobby equalise Billy Bremner's opener but injury prevented the Kirkcaldy born player playing in the second leg at Elland Road. In the only match he missed all season, Bobby could only watch on in anguish as Leeds would progress to the Final with a 1-0 win when they would lift the trophy after defeating Ferencvaros 1-0 on aggregate.

Bobby would also play a part in the famous U.E.F.A. Cup matches against Cologne and A.C. Milan in 1971 and in the match against Cologne crashed home the winner in the second leg at Dens to complete a remarkable comeback from 4-2 down to go through 5-4 on aggregate.

As well as scoring those celebrated European goals, Bobby would play in four different European campaigns with Dundee. In total he would make seventeen appearances in continental competition and as well as having the honour of scoring in a European semi, he also holds the Club record for the most appearances in Europe.

Bobby's highlight in a Dundee shirt undoubtedly came in the 1973 League Cup Final when The Dee gained revenge for the defeat in the 1967 Final as they lifted the trophy by beating Celtic 1-0. Bobby played a key role Dundee's victory as with only fourteen minutes remaining he was fouled on the halfway line by Paul Wilson and when he took the free kick himself, he sent it swerving just inside the Celtic box, where it was controlled by Gordon Wallace, who then struck the winning goal.

In the Scottish Cup, Bobby's progress was repeatedly halted by Celtic as he lost to the Parkhead side on four separate occasions, two of which were semi-finals and he was part of the Dundee side that lost in the three match League Cup quarter-final epic in 1972.

International honours also came Bobby's way while at Dens when he gained one Scottish League cap when he lined up against the Irish League in Belfast in 1967 in a match in which the Scots won 2-1.

Considering all these high profile matches that Bobby played in against Celtic, it was perhaps apt that when the Club awarded him with a testimonial after ten years distinguished service that the match should be against a Celtic XI.

Taking place at Dens on Monday 1st December 1975, the Celtic side included a number of Dundee players such as Allan, Phillip, Gemmell (who had won the European Cup with Celtic in 1967) and Strachan (who would go on to manage 'The Bhoys' from 2005 to 2009) and would be played in front of a crowd of 6000 who warmly appreciated Bobby's efforts over the years.

The match came midway through what would end up being Bobby's final season with Dundee as he among was a group of players who were released in May when The Dee were relegated from the inaugural Premier Division and wanted to trim back their staff.

Bobby will admit to shedding a tear when released from Dens and many fans felt he had been released far too early. Bobby would go on to manage Lossiemouth and Keith in the Highland League as well as his home town team Raith Rovers and was at the helm of Ross County for over ten years and oversaw their admission into the Scottish League in 1994.

Comfortably in the top ten of most appearances for the Club, Bobby Wilson retains a place in the hearts of Dundee fans as a member of the last team to bring silverware back to Dens.

Honours at Dundee:
Scottish League Cup winner: 1973/74
Scottish League Cup runner-up:1967/68
U.E.F.A. / Inter-Cities Fairs Cup semi-final: 1967/68
Scottish League Cap: 1
Appearances, Goals:
League: 293 + 3 subs, 8 goals
Scottish Cup:25, 3 goals
League Cup: 66, 3 goal
Europe: 17, 2 goals
Other: 7
Totals: 411, 16 goals

Bobby Wishart

Bobby Wishart is quite simply a legend of Dundee Football club as one of the members of the 1961/62 Scottish League Championship winning side. As one of only fifteen players who picked up a league winning medal, Bobby holds a very special place in Dark Blue history.

A product of the rugby-playing George Heriot's school in Edinburgh, Bobby signed for Aberdeen from Merchiston Thistle in 1952. Initially an inside left, Bobby became a vital part of The Dons side who the Scottish League Championship in 1955 and was part of the team that won the League Cup the following October. The success he enjoyed at Aberdeen was in no small way due to the link up he enjoyed with Paddy Buckley and Benny Yorston as the Dons found a potent blend in the fifties and he was capped at Under-23 level and with the Scottish League while at Pittodrie.

Signed by manager Bob Shankly from Aberdeen for a fee of £3500 in January 1961, Bobby went on to make 108 appearances, scoring fourteen goals for the Club until he left for Airdrie in 1964. At Dundee he moved to a position where his expertise would be invaluable and would become a cultured left half as a member of the quality Dundee half back line of Bobby Seith, Ian Ure and himself.

Along with Bobby Seith and Gordon Smith, Shankly signed Wishart to provide some experience alongside youngsters such as Gilzean, Ure and Penman who had forced their way into the team and the blend was just about perfect as Dundee would go on to win the Scottish League and then reach the European Cup semi final the following year.

Of Bobby's fourteen goals for the Club, the majority of them came remarkably in important and high profile matches and he started this immediately by endearing himself straight away to the Dark Blue faithful by scoring two goals in a 3-0 victory over Dundee United on his debut.

Bobby kicked off the Championship year in style by scoring the Club's first goal of the season in a League Cup tie at home to Airdrieonians on the 'Glorious Twelfth' and also scored the third in the opening League match in a 3-1 win against Falkirk at Brockville.

Wishart also scored in the famous 5-4 win over Raith Rovers in November 1961, when Dundee were 4-2 down with twenty minutes to go when he scored the comeback goal to make it 4-3 and in fact scored seven, half of his Dundee goals, in the title winning year.

His most famous goal for the Club was perhaps in Dundee's first ever European tie in the incredible 8-1 win at Dens against Cologne in the European Cup. Bobby scored the second goal after only eleven minutes which was described by Craig Brown as *'the most incredible goal I have ever seen'*.

From the edge of the box, Bobby miscued the ball, and as it trundled away, a huge divot went in the opposite direction. The German goalkeeper Fritz Ewart dived across his goal to save the divot, while the ball crept into the net at the opposite side to leave Dens Park stunned for a second as they tried to comprehend what they had just witnessed. You can hear a brief silence on Kenneth Wolstenholme's BBC Radio commentary of the match!

Wishart played thirty-seven times in the Championship season, twenty-nine of which were in the league and in the European season, played forty-seven times, scoring three goals.

In the Champions Cup campaign, Bobby was an ever present, playing in both legs of every tie against Cologne, Sporting Lisbon, Anderlecht and A.C. Milan and that 'fluke' against Cologne was his only goal on the run to the semi final.

Playing in the European Cup, gave Bobby a chance to finally play in Europe's premier club competition having been denied his chance to play in the inaugural tournament in 1955 after The Dons had won the league. Instead of sending the reigning Scottish Champions in what was effectively a tournament by invitation, the S.F.A. in their wisdom decided to send Hibernian and while the other competing associations sent their League winners, the Scottish F.A., who just happened to have the Hibs Chairman Harry Swan as their president, sent the Edinburgh side instead.

It is a decision that still rankles in the North-East today but for Bobby Wishart, his experiences with Dundee more than made up for that disappointment.

Bobby's last game for Dundee came in a 2-1 defeat at Ibrox in December 1963 and having failed to make another appearance that season, therefore missing out on playing in the Scottish Cup Final in 1964, he was allowed the leave on a free transfer in August 1964 and join Airdrie.

In the official Dundee F.C. history video released in 2000, Craig Brown points out that Dundee's alarming winter slump in 1962, which almost cost Dundee the league, was by no means a coincidence of the same period that Bobby Wishart was out injured and describes Bobby as *'a brain in midfield and an excellent passer of the ball.'*

While history quite rightly often points to Gordon Smith's fantastic achievement of winning the Scottish League with three different clubs out with the Old Firm, Bobby Wishart wasn't that far behind by winning two with Aberdeen and Dundee and will remain forever part of the folklore of the legendary side that became Champions of Scotland and Princes of Europe.

Honours at Dundee:
Scottish League Champions: 1961/62
European Cup semi-final: 1962/63
Appearances, Goals,
League: 76, 11 goals
Scottish Cup: 7, 1 goal
League Cup: 12, 1 goal
Europe: 8, 1 goal
Other: 5
Totals: 108, 14 goals

Keith Wright

For Dundee fans everywhere, a mongoose is so much more than a small predatory mammal from Africa, chiefly known for its distinctive long tail. Rather it is a bona fide legend, famed for predatory goal-scoring exploits while wearing a distinctive dark blue shirt, known as Keith Wright. Signed from Raith Rovers in 1986, Wright was part of two successful goal scoring partnerships in his time at Dens but became a legend in his own right when he scored a hat-trick in a memorable derby win over Dundee United in 1989.

Born in Edinburgh on May 17th 1965, Wright started his football career at Starks Park in 1983 where he averaged almost a goal every two games, prompting Dundee manager Jocky Scott to splash out £50, 000 for the twenty-three year old. He quickly linked up with new strike partner Tommy Coyne who was signed within days of Wright and the two went on to form one of the most deadly partnerships in the Club's history.

Coyne had cost Dundee £75, 000 from Dundee United and it proved money well spent for the pair when on December 23rd, the new striking partnership spearheaded Dundee to a 6-3 win over St. Mirren with Wright netting twice on his home debut.

By the end of the season, Wright had netted thirteen goals while Coyne scored fifteen and 'the Cobra' and 'the Mongoose' were born.

Both had scored in the Scottish Cup semi-final with Dundee United at Tynecastle in April 1987 but the 3-2 defeat denied Dundee a place in the Final. In September however, both Coyne and Wright got their revenge in the League Cup quarter-final when the pair were on the score sheet in a 2-1 extra time victory over The Arabs.

With just eight minutes remaining, Coyne took the tie into extra time and in front of a full house of 19, 817, Keith Wright wrote his name into folklore when five minutes into the extra period, he finished off a superb move by Coyne and Graham Harvey to send the Dundee support in raptures.

It was Wright's first derby victory and he would go on to score in three further victories over United in his time at Dens to cement his place as a Dundee legend. Three months after the League Cup win, Wright was again on the score sheet against The Arabs when he scored the third in a 3-1 victory at Tannadice.

However his finest moment in a Dundee shirt came at the start of the 1989/90 season when he scored a hat-trick against The Terrors in a thrilling 4-3 derby win at Dens in August. The visitors had led 2-0 after only twenty-four minutes but by half time Keith Wright had levelled the scores. Mixu Paatalainen made it 3-2 only for Wright to equalise on the hour before Joe McBride curled home a free kick winner with seventeen minutes remaining.

Wright was the hero of the hour and he became the first Dundee player to score a hat-trick against United in the league for the first time since World War Two. The big striker had always proved to be a thorn in the flesh to Dundee's local rivals and he confessed to the press afterwards that, *'I like nothing better than to put one over the lads down the road.'*

Fortunately for Dundee he would do it again in the final derby of the season when he equalised for The Dee in bizarre fashion after Paddy Connelly had put United ahead. Suddenly a squall whipped up as United keeper Alan Main tried to take a goal kick and with the ball struggling to reach the half way line, Maurice Malpas sliced the ball into the air, which caught by the wind and hurled back towards the United box. Keith Wright was on his toes and nipped in ahead of Main to head the ball into the empty night as B.B.C. commentator Archie Macpherson stated *'goal scored by hurricane.'* In truth it had been scored by the 'Mongoose' before Rab Shannon curled in a free kick to give Dundee a priceless 2-1 win.

Six points out of eight against United that season was not enough to save Dundee from relegation but Wright showed Dundee incredible loyalty by deciding to turn down all offers and stick around to try and get Dundee back into the Premier Division at the first time of asking. By then, Tommy Coyne was long gone, having left for Celtic in February 1989 and by the end of the season, Wright finished as Dundee's top goal scorer for the first time.

The next season, Wright struck up another productive partnership with Billy Dodds and although their combined total of twenty-five goals had failed to prevent Dundee from going down, hopes were high that they could shoot their way out of the First Division at the first attempt.

By November, Dundee had reached the final of the B&Q Scottish League Centenary Cup, a new competition for clubs outside the Premier League to celebrate a 100 years of the Scottish League and they had reached the Final thanks to two goals from Wright in the semi-final at Kilmarnock.

On November 11th 1990, Wright was part of the side to win the glassware trophy thanks to a 3-2 extra time win over Ayr United at Fir Park and Wright would again be involved in the Scottish League centenary celebrations when he was chosen to play for the Scottish League against the Scottish international side at Hampden.

It was a tremendous honour for Keith to be called up as the only First Division representative and a tremendous honour for Dundee to have a player called up for international duty in a period in which Dundee had only had one called up for the full national side in the last fifteen years.

The Centenary Cup win was Wright's second winner's medal as a Dundee player, having been part of the side to win the Tennents' Sixes in 1988 but when he failed to win a third at the end of the season with a First Division medal, it was only a matter of time before the predators came looking for his signature.
Wright was by far and away the best striker outside of the Premier Division and he had finished again as Dundee top scorer in the league with eighteen goals so when boyhood heroes Hibernian came in with an offer of £500,000, it was no surprise that he was off to Easter Road.

It was a fee which had matched the Club record received for Tommy Coyne two years previously but for Hibs it was money also well spent as within a year he scored their second goal in the 2-0 Skol League Cup victory over Dunfermline at Hampden to give Hibs their first major trophy in nineteen years.

Keith spent six years at Easter Road where he scored fifty-nine goals in 197 appearances and went on to win a full Scotland cap against Northern Ireland in 1992. He was released by Jim Duffy in 1997 before returning to first club Raith Rovers and then Fife neighbours Cowdenbeath where he spent two years as manager, the first of which as player / manager before he hung up his boots.

His League Cup Final goal earned Keith legendary status in the east end of Edinburgh but it is not just at Hibs that he has such status. His time at Dens yielded seventy-five goals, four hat-tricks and eight braces as legions of Dundee fans also 'Wrightly' remember the 'Mongoose' as a true Dark Blue legend.

Honours at Dundee:
B&Q Scottish League Centenary Cup winner: 1990
Tennents' Sixes winner: 1988
Scottish League appearances: 1
Appearances, Goals:
League: 160 + 7 subs, 62 goals
Scottish Cup: 15 + 1 sub, 4 goals
League Cup: 10, 6 goals
Centenary Cup: 4, 3 goals
Totals: 197, 75 goals

Dundee F.C. International Legends

(A complete listing of Dundee F.C. International and principal representative players)

Full Scotland Internationals

Name	No	(Opposition and year)
Alex Hamilton*	24	Cz, U, W, E 1962, W, NI, E, A, N, Ei 1963, NI, W, E, N, WG 1964, NI, W, E, Fin(2), Pol, Sp 1965, Pol, NI, 1966
Doug Cowie	20	E, Sw 1953, NI, W, F, N, A, U 1954, W, NI, A, H 1955, W, A 1956, NI, W 1957, H, Pol, Y, Par 1958
Billy Steel	13	W, NI, E, A (2), D, F, B 1951, W 1952, W, E, NI, Sw 1953
Lee Wilkie	11	SA, HK^ 2002, Ice (2), Ca, Por, Lth, A 2003. Far, Hol (2) 2004
Ian Ure	8	W, Cz 1962, W, NI, E, A, N, Sp 1963
Gavin Rae	8	Pol 2001, La 2002, G 2003, N, Far, G, Lth, Hol 2004
Colin McNab	6	E, W, A, It, Sw 1931, E 1932
Alan Gilzean	5	N, W, E, WG 1964, NI 1965
Sandy MacFarlane	5	W 1904, W 1906, W 1908, I 1909, W 1911
Sandy Keillor	4	I 1894, W 1895, W 1896, W 1897
Bill Brown	4	F 1958, E, W, NI 1959
Bobby Robinson	4	WG 1974, Sw, NI, R 1975
Alec Troup	4	E 1920, W, I 1921, I 1922
Thomson Allan	2	WG, N 1974
Fred Barrett	2	I 1894, W 1895
Charlie Cooke	2	W, It 1965
Jimmy Robertson	2	A, It 1931
Jocky Scott	2	D, USSR 1971
George Chaplain	1	W 1908
Robert Connor	1	Hol 1986
Jack Fraser	1	NI 1907
Jock Gilmour	1	W 1931
R.C. Hamilton	1	W 1911
John Hunter	1	W 1909
Bob Kelso	1	I 1898
Tom Kelso	1	W 1914
William Longair	1	I 1894
George McLean	1	Hol 1969
Billy Muir	1	I 1907
Andy Penman	1	Hol 1966
Hugh Robertson	1	Cz 1962
Peter Robertson	1	I 1903
Billy Sawyers	1	W 1895
Jimmy Sharp	1	W 1904
David Thomson	1	W 1920
Willie Thomson	1	W 1896

Non-Scottish Internationals

Name	Country	No
Brent Sancho	Trinidad & Tobago	18
Kelvin Jack	Trindad & Tobago	17
Giorgi Nemsadze	Georgia	17
Jonay Hernandez	Venezula	16
Zurab Zhizanishvili	Georgia	15
Mikael Antoine-Curier	Guadeloupe	11
Sam Irving	Northern Ireland	10
Billy Campbell	Northern Ireland	6
Morten Weighorst	Denmark	5
Darius Adamczuk	Poland	4
Sammy Wilson	Northern Ireland	4
Dusan Vrto	Slovakia	2
Fan Zhiyi	China	2
Petr Czachowski	Poland	1
Temuri Ketsbia	Georgia	1
Chris Pozniak	Canada	1
Mark Robertson	Australia	1

Scotland Under 21 Internationals

Name	No	(Opposition and year)
Jim Hamilton	11	SM, Br 1995, Fin, SM, H, Sp, Fr 1996. A, La, Est, Sw 1997
Derek Soutar	11	D, NI, Ice (2), B, Ei, Li, A, G 2003, G, Lth 2004
Iain Anderson	10	Bel, La, D, Fin, Ei, NI 1998, G, Ei, NI, CzRep 1999
Neil McCann	10	A, Egy, Por, Bel 1994, Fin, Gr, SM 1995, Gr, Fin, SM 1996
Rab Shannon	7	WG, Ei 1986, E, B (2) 1987, E (2) 1988
Tosh McKinlay	6	EG 1983, WG, Ice, Sp 1984, Sp, Ice 1985
Gavin Rae	6	Ei, NI, CzRep, 1999, Bos (2), Est 2000
Lee Wilkie	6	Fr, Hol, NI, W 2000, La, Cr 2001
Bobby Geddes	5	Sw, D 1981, E (2) 1982, E 1988
Kevin Bain	4	Por (2), It, Mal 1993
Andy Dow	4	Ice, Mal, Por, It 1993
Kevin McDonald	4	CzRep, Lth, Hol, Fin 2008
Iain Ferguson	3	EG 1982, B, EG 1983
Mark Fotheringham	3	R, D, Ei 2004
Steve Campbell	2	Y 1988, Fr 1989
Paul Dixon	2	CzRep, Hol 2008
Leigh Griffiths	2	Az (2) 2010
Jamie Langfield	2	W 2000, Cr 2001
Ian Redford	2	USA Full International XI^, N 1979
Andrew Shinnie	2	Al, Az 2009
Max Christie	1	Y 1992
Jim Duffy	1	Ei 1986
Gordon McLeod	1	Fr 1990
Ray Stephen	1	B 1982

Scotland Under 23 Internationals

Name	No	(Opposition and year)
Andy Penman	4	B 1960, W 1962, W 1964, E 1965
Alan Cousin	3	Hol 1958, B, E 1960
Alan Gilzean	3	E 1961, E, W 1962
Ally Donaldson	2	E, W 1965
Hugh Robertson	2	E, W 1962
Charlie Cooke	1	E 1965
Jimmy Gabriel	1	W 1960
Mike Hewitt	1	WG Olympic XI^ 1972
Steve Murray	1	E 1968
Iain Phillip	1	WG Olympic XI^ 1972
Bobby Robinson	1	W 1974
Dave Sneddon	1	W 1959
Jim Steele	1	WG Olympic XI^ 1972
Ian Ure	1	E 1961

Scotland B and Future Internationals

Name	No	(Opposition and year)
Bill Brown	1	E (B) 1956
Doug Cowie	1	E (B) 1954
Robert Douglas	1	W (B) 1998
Mark Fotheringham	1	A (Fut) 2005
Gavin Rae	1	G (Fut) 2003
Derek Soutar	1	G (Fut) 2005
Lee Wilkie	1	G (Fut) 2004

Abbreviations

A = Austria
Al = Albania
Az = Azerbaijan
B = Belgium
Bel = Belarus
Bos = Bosnia
Br = Brazil
Cr = Croatia
Cz = Czechoslovakia
CzRep = Czech Rep.
Ca = Canada
D = Denmark
E = England
EG = East Germany
Egy = Egypt
Ei = Rep. of Ireland
EL = English League
Est = Estonia
F = France
Far = Faroe Islands
Fin = Finland
G = Germany
Gr = Greece
H = Hungary
HK = Hong Kong
Hol = Holland
I = Ireland
Ice = Iceland
IL = Irish League
It = Italy
ItL = Italian League
La = Latvia
LoI = Lge. of Ireland
Lth = Lithuania
Mal = Malta
N = Norway
NI = North. Ireland
Par = Paraguay
Pol = Poland
Por = Portugal
R = Romania
SA = South Africa
SFA = Full Scotland side
SL = Southern League
SM = San Marino
Sp = Spain
Sw = Switzerland
U = Uruguay
USA = United States of America
USSR = Soviet Union
W = Wales
WG = West Germany
Y = Yugoslavia

* Alex Hamilton also made an appearance for the Rest of Europe v Scandinavia in 1964 and played in two Scottish Trial Internationals.   ^ No cap awarded

~ 175 ~

Scottish League Internationals

Name	No	(Opposition and year)
Bill Brown	8	EL, IL, LoI 1957, EL, LoI 1958, EL, IL, LoI 1959
Alex Hamilton	8	EL, ItL 1962, ItL, LoI 1963, IL, EL 1964, EL 1965, IL 1966
Colin McNab	4	IL 1928, EL 1929, EL, IL 1930
Andy Penman	4	IL, LoI 1961, EL, IL 1966
Ian Ure	4	ItL, LoI 1962 LoI, ItL 1963
Doug Cowie	3	EL 1953, IL 1954, LoI 1957
Alan Gilzean	3	LoI 1961, LoI 1962, EL 1964
Sandy MacFarlane	3	EL 1904, IL 1910, EL 1911
Billy Steel	3	EL 1951, EL 1952, LoI 1953
Willie Cook	2	IL 1927, IL 1928
Charlie Cooke	2	EL 1965, IL 1966
Alan Cousin	2	IL, LoI 1959
Ally Donaldson	2	IL 1966, IL 1970
Jimmy Lawson	2	IL 1910, IL 1913
Billy Muir	2	EL 1903, EL 1907
Alec Troup	2	IL 1921, IL 1922
Alfie Boyd	1	EL 1949
Findlay Brown	1	IL 1923
John Chaplain	1	IL 1910
Archie Coats	1	IL 1937
Bobby Cox	1	SFA 1961^
Herbert Dainty	1	SL 1910
John Duncan	1	EL 1973
Jimmy Dundas	1	IL 1896
Gerry Follon	1	IL 1947
Tommy Gallagher	1	EL 1949
Jock Gilmour	1	IL 1931
Dave Halliday	1	EL 1924

(Contd.)

Name	No	(Opposition and year)
Fred McDiarmid	1	IL 1902
Danny Malloy	1	EL 1955
Lew Morgan	1	IL 1934
Iain Phillip	1	EL 1972
Willie Rankine	1	IL 1927
Peter Robertson	1	IL 1902
Bobby Seith	1	SFA 1962^
Eric Sinclair	1	LoI 1980
Tom Smith	1	IL 1937
Jock Thomson	1	IL 1930
Bobby Wilson	1	IL 1968
Keith Wright	1	SFA 1990^

Yore Publications was formed by Dave Twydell in 1991, and during these near twenty years, a large number and variety of football books have been published.

We specialise in Football League club histories (arguably the leading publisher in this field), currently over 30 titles, plus several updated reprints and books relating to Scottish clubs. These have included 'Motherwell legends', Partick Legends' and substantial written and statistical histories of both clubs. We have also produced around twenty players' Who's Who books.

With a keen interest in non-League football, the 'Gone But Not Forgotten' series of books, two per year, is also approaching its twentieth year. Each addition covers, in reasonable detail, around six English clubs that have folded or grounds that are no more.

For a full and detailed list of all our publications, see our website:
www.yore.demon.co.uk or write to:
Yore Publications, 12 The Furrows, Harefield, Middx. UB9 6AT